WHAT NUMBER IS GOD?

SUNY Series in Western Esoteric Traditions
David Appelbaum, Editor

WHAT NUMBER IS GOD?

Metaphors, Metaphysics, Metamathematics, and the Nature of Things

by

SARAH VOSS

State University
of New York
Press

✓ 110
 V92w

Published by
State University of New York Press, Albany

© 1995 State University of New York

Production by Susan Geraghty
Marketing by Dana Yanulavich

Printed in the United States of America

For information, address State University of New York Press, State University Plaza, Albany, N.Y., 12246

10 9 8 7 6 5 4 3 2 1

Library of Congress Cataloging-in-Publication Data

Voss, Sarah, 1945–
    What number is God? : metaphors, metaphysics, metamathematics, and the nature of things/by Sarah Voss.
        p.   cm.—(SUNY series in Western esoteric traditions)
    Includes bibliographical references and index.
    ISBN 0-7914-2417-0.—ISBN 0-7914-2418-9 (pbk.)
    1. Metaphysics. 2. Mathematics—Philosophy. I. Title.
II. Series.
BD111.V67   1995
110—dc20   94-18260
                                                                    CIP

The essence of mathematics is its freedom.
Georg Cantor

CONTENTS

List of Figures   *ix*
Foreword   *xi*
Acknowledgments   *xvii*

Chapter 1   Meta-View   1

    Bridges   1
    Metamathematics   3
    Metaphysics   7
    Metaphor   26
    Bridgework   32

Chapter 2   Image-ination in Mathematics and Religion   41

    Blurred Boundaries   41
    A Continuum   43
    Continuums   48
    Literal vs. Metaphorical   53
    Kaleidoscope   56
    Mathematics and Metaphorical Language 60

Chapter 3   Holy Mathematics   71

    Meta-4's   71
    Number Symbolism   73
    Geometry   85
    Computers and Chaos   94
    Holographs/Holygraphs   102

Chapter 4   God the Definite Integral and Cantorian
Religion   111

    Towards Two Metaphors   111
    The One and The Many   111
    God the Definite Integral   115
    Towards a Structure of Judgement   121
    Meta-Stepping   125
    Towards a Cantorian Religion   127
    A Strange Metaphor   132
    Cantoring   134
    Religion of All Religions   140
    Metaphor Muddles   145

Summation   *147*
Afterword   *157*
Appendix A. Understandings of Sign, Symbol, Metaphor,
and Model in Religion and Mathematics:
Summary of an Empirical Study   *161*
Notes   *173*
Reference List   *203*
Index   *209*

LIST OF FIGURES

1.1. Hofstadter's Semantic Network   22

1.2. A Soapsuds Moebius Strip   38

2.1. Simple Continuum   44

2.2. Continuum of Metaphorical Language   46

2.3. Lufthansa Trademark   49

2.4. A Continuum of Isomorphism   49

2.5. Expanded Continuum of Metaphorical Language   50

2.6. Old Woman/Young Girl Illusion   54

3.1. Letter-Numbers of the Hebrew Alphabet   77

3.2. Turtle Shell from a Modern Math Text   86

3.3. Earliest Known Magic Square   86

3.4. Geometric Numbers   87

4.1. Deriving the First Fundamental Law of Calculus   118

4.2. The Cantor Dust   137

4.3. Constructing with Holes   138

4.4. The Koch Snowflake: "A Rough but Vigorous
Model of a Coastline"   139

FOREWORD

Broadly speaking, theology is a part of religion, and religious activity is a part of a larger realm of inquiry known as metaphysics. Standard definitions[1] note that metaphysics is human activity that seeks to explain the nature of being, of knowledge, and of reality, that religion is a specific system of belief and worship built around God (sometimes considered the Ultimate, the Divine, the Real, the Eternal, etc.[2]); and that theology is the study of God and other matters of divinity. These definitions are brief and nontechnical: a more careful exposition will be given of the term "metaphysics" in chapter 1 and of "religion" and "theology" in the Summation. For now, I would emphasize the idea that everything that is theological in some sense is part of religion, although the reverse is not true. Likewise, everything that constitutes religion may be thought of as a part of metaphysical exploration, although again, the reverse does not hold. Pictorially, we might depict this relationship as in the sketch below. The locus of my present investigation falls on the fine line that intersects and joins these three realms. At its most fundamental core, therefore, this study is a study in connection.

Other studies have dealt with the connection between metaphysics, religion, and theology. The metaphysical systems of Kant, Husserl, Whitehead, Cassirer, and Wittgenstein, for instance, have tremendously influenced contemporary theological and religious thought and, hence, have at least implicitly explored the intersection between the three realms. I cite these names from among countless other philosophers because these five, though offering diverse and at times even opposing viewpoints, represent yet another fundamental aspect of my own line of inquiry—all have drawn substantially on mathematics in the development of their theses.[3]

Immanuel Kant's transcendental idealism was based in part on his conception of mathematical propositions as synthetic *a priori*

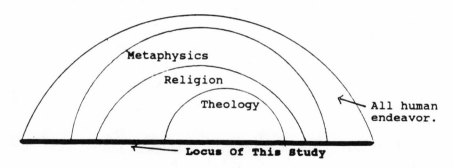

judgements. Edmund Husserl preceded his treatises on phenomenology with an attempt, in his 1891 volume *Philosophy of Arithmetic,* to psychologize numbers, that is, to study the psychological sources from which we derive our number concepts so that we might gain an understanding of the essence of numbers themselves. Process theologian Alfred North Whitehead, like Husserl, was a mathematician as well as a philosopher: his first book, *Treatise on Universal Algebra with Applications* (1898) dealt with ideas in abstract algebra and symbolic logic, and his *Principia Mathematica* (1913) has become one of the most influential books of all time on the logic of mathematics. Epistemologist Ernst Cassirer wrote his dissertation on Descartes's critique of mathematics and physical science (1899) and includes in his third volume of *The Philosophy of Symbolic Forms* (1929) a section on "The Object of Mathematics." Ludwig Wittgenstein's *Remarks on the Foundations of Mathematics* was preceded by more detailed investigations in the philosophy of mathematics in *Philosophical Remarks* and *Philosophical Grammar,* and his famous *Tractatus Logico-Philosophicus* (1922), the only work published in his lifetime, was originally designed as a study of the foundations of mathematics and logic.[4]

While this is certainly nice company to be amongst, I readily admit that it is awesome company and a bit out of my league. In no sense do I claim to make in this study a detailed analysis of the role that mathematics plays in their respective works. What I find significant is the fact that mathematics played a role at all. I suspect that this fact, partially acknowledged by the experts and little understood by many lay persons, deserves greater recognition. I direct my current effort to a generalization of this idea—that mathematics plays a fundamental role in metaphysics, theology, and religion.

What is distinctive about this study is that the factor connecting the three realms is taken to be mathematics. The thesis of *What Number Is God?* is that mathematics has been used throughout human history as a connecting device between metaphysics, theology, and religion. Furthermore, I suggest that the form it takes as such a device is primarily the form of metaphor, that mathematics is currently used metaphorically as a connecting and explanatory device between these three realms (although such use has frequently been overlooked or denied). To make mathematics visible as such a metaphorical tool can be of considerable benefit today in all three fields. It should be noted that this study is targeted towards a general, educated audience, and, specifically, those inquiring individuals who are trying to pull together various different things they know into one coherent whole.

In addition to this main thesis, several subthemes emerge sporadically throughout the work, rather as somewhat unusual musical instruments might offer a recurrent accent in the performance of a symphonic composition. The main subthemes are three in number. First, there is a questioning of the traditional scientific antipathy for contradiction and inconsistency and a suggestion that consistency and coherence may not always be fundamental criteria for testing the validity of a scientific theory. Second, the essence of life is posited as a kaleidoscopic filtering process, a process whereby consciousness self-selects from a nebulous primordial chaos an infinity of possible patterns or designs, each of which might be thought of as a life form. Third, the existence of a dimension of consciousness that transcends time and space is hypothesized, a dimension that humans can access in paranormal ways. None of these three subordinate themes is fully flushed out in the following pages, and some readers may well feel that their inclusion merely obscures my main thesis. Yet while these themes admittedly are highly speculative, I believe that to omit them would strip the work of important accent, thus diminishing its intricacy and intrigue. Their inclusion, on the other hand, provides the reader with additional options and provides mainstream science/religion with the opportunity to reexamine the "traditional" wisdom.

I come to this project as an ordained Unitarian Universalist minister whose earlier career was as a mathematics professor. I spent fifteen years teaching mathematics at the high school, community college, college, and university levels. During the four years immediately before I decided to become a minister, I was the mathematics program director at a small midwestern religious college for women. I came into the ministry convinced of a stronger relationship between mathematics and religion than most people realize. This study represents a substantial portion of my work toward naming and describing that relationship more explicitly. In one sense, I am breaking new ground. In another, I believe I am really just identifying a connection that has always coexisted with human consciousness.

In recent years, the role of metaphor in religion has been widely acknowledged and analyzed. A special camp of thinkers, for example, Arthur Peacocke, Ian Barbour, Sallie McFague, and Janet Soskice, now believes that humankind deals, albeit inadequately and partially, with fundamental existential, epistemological, and ontological issues largely through metaphor.[5] I agree with these critical realists, as they have come to be called, that such endeavors constitute the very heart of a rich religious life.

The role of metaphor in mathematics is less acknowledged. In chapter 1, I will lay the foundation for a metaphysics that goes beyond an analysis of metaphor as it is or is not used within mathematics, suggesting instead that mathematics may itself be used metaphorically. In chapter 2, I will argue that there is considerable ambiguity within both mathematics and religion regarding the use of the term "metaphor" and such related concepts as "sign," "symbol," and "model." I will identify and explore this ambiguity and will bring to the subject two alternative ordering principles, ones that ultimately raise new questions about the relation between the so-called "metaphorical" and the "literal." In chapter 3, I will trace the historical precedent for using mathematics as a metaphorical tool in our theological/religious/metaphysical pursuits, and I will offer illustrations of the contemporary use of mathematics as such a metaphorical tool. In chapter 4, I will offer two specific examples of a new and extended use of mathematics as metaphor for the purpose of providing greater insight into our increasingly pluralistic and oft-times contradictory world. Finally, in the Summation, I will relate my concerns to contemporary religious issues and will explore how the ideas in this study may enhance the liberal religious voice. This study also includes in an appendix the summary of an empirical study I conducted exploring contemporary understandings of the role of metaphor in mathematics and religion.

The subtitle of this work, *Metaphors, Metaphysics, Metamathematics and the Nature of Things,* reflects the general interweaving of the themes I have referred to above. The emphasis on the prefix "meta" is intentional in the sense that the picture-perspective I hope to develop is one that goes *beyond* the physical and *beyond* mathematics. This picture-perspective, as we shall see, is necessarily incomplete. However, despite my subordinate theme of questioning the criteria of consistency, I hope to provide a largely cohesive argument—a consistency about the inconsistency, so to speak. I have no doubt that the reader will help me secure this goal, if not here, then in some future revision. Indeed, I invite such help, for I would like to think that the seeds I am planting in this beginning exploration will be altered and cared for until they emerge into something that, at this point, remains *beyond* my visualization.

ACKNOWLEDGMENTS

Many people have contributed to the completion of this work. I am grateful to Phillip Hefner and Thomas L. Gilbert, of the Chicago Center for Religion and Science, and to John Godbey, of Meadville/Lombard School of Theology. Their input and guidance were invaluable. Langdon Gilkey and Ian Evison were most helpful in the preparation and completion of the empirical study found in the Appendix, and Paul Griffiths made significant contributions to the section on Cantorian religion. Ron Engel's help in the formulation stages of the basic outline was significant. I would also like to acknowledge the general encouragement and support of many other friends and mentors, particularly, Spencer Lavan, Margaret Gooding, Polly Leland-Mayer, Ronald Knapp, Thomas Burdett, Barbara Earl, and Charlotte Justice Saleska. Thanks, also, to Ila Dean Horn for her proofreading and other contributions, to all the people who responded to my survey on the use of metaphor in mathematics and religion, and to the congregation of The Peoples Church, Unitarian Universalist, Cedar Rapids, Iowa, who bore with me through the final stages of completing the manuscript.

I am forever indebted to two other people, without whose constant encouragement, support and help this work would never have materialized. My husband, Dan Sullivan, gave countless hours, not only by way of a listening ear, but also in helping put the completed manuscript into final form. Last, but certainly not least, I want to acknowledge the support of my youngest daughter, who grew with me throughout this project and whose love and affection was of such significance that I would like to dedicate this work to her, Melinda Voss.

In addition, I would like to acknowledge the kind permission of Ethel Longstreet to reprint materials from Samuel Bois, *The Art of Awareness*, 3d ed. (1978). I would also like to acknowledge permission from Shambhala Publishers, to use material from Carlos Suares, *The Cipher of Genesis: The Original Code of Quabala as Applied to the Scriptures*, trans. Vincent Stuart and John M.

Watkins (1970); from the University of Hawaii Press to reprint material from David E. Mungello, *Leibniz and Confucianism: The Search for Accord* (1977); from Brooks/Cole Publishing Company to use material from Karl J. Smith, *The Nature of Mathematics,* 4th ed. (1984); from McGraw-Hill, Inc., to use selections from *Calculus,* 2d ed., by I. Douglas Faires and Barbara T. Faires (1988); and from Rachel Fletcher to reprint excerpts from "Proportion and the Living World," *Parabola,* the Magazine of Myth and Tradition, vol. 13, no. 1, Feb. 1988, 36–51.

Similarly, selections are taken from David M. Burton, *The History of Mathematics:* An Introduction. Copyright 1988 Wm. C. Brown Communications, Inc., Dubuque, Iowa. All Rights Reserved. Reprinted by permission. From *Medieval Number Symbolism,* by Vincent Foster Hopper, © Columbia University Press, New York. Reprinted with permission of the publisher. Reprinted with the permission of Macmillan Publishing Company from *Number: The Language of Science,* Fourth Edition, by Tobias Dantzig. Copyright 1930, 1933, 1939, 1954 by Macmillan Publishing Company, renewed 1958, 1961, 1967 by Anna G. Dantzig, 1982 by Mildred B. Dantzig. Selections from *Complexity: The Emerging Science at the Edge of Order and Chaos,* Copyright 1992 by M. Mitchell Waldrop. Reprinted by permission of Simon & Schuster, Inc. From *Chaos: Making a New Science,* copyright 1987 by James Gleick. Reprinted by permission of the William Morris Agency, Inc. on behalf of the Author. Excerpts and figure from *Gödel, Escher, Bach: An Eternal Braid* by Douglas Hofstadter. Copyright © 1979 by Basic Books, Inc. Reprinted by permission of Basic Books, a division of Harper Collins Publishers, Inc.

I am also grateful to Lufthanza Airlines for their kind permission to use their trademark; to Daniel M. Sullivan for his photograph of "A Soapsuds Moebius Strip;" and to Benoit B. Mandelbrot for my Figures 4.2, 4.3, and 4.4 from his book *Fractal Geometry of Nature,* published by W. H. Freeman and Co. (New York) 1982.

CHAPTER 1

Meta-View

BRIDGES

When I was a child, I lived in an area renowned for its many wooden covered bridges. Sometimes my family would take a Sunday drive just for the pleasure of crossing over one of those bridges. Something was enticing about driving across those creaking boards; just being on that bridge was a little like wandering for a moment into another world. You could not go there just any old way. For example, trucks were not permitted on the bridge—at least not heavy trucks. It always looked different once you had actually crossed over, too. Looking back at a bridge is not at all the same experience as looking toward it.

Those wooden bridges had been carefully constructed so that they could handle a certain load of weight. As I think back on them, I realize that a great deal of mathematics must have been involved in building them. You could not see the mathematics, of course. Yet what you saw there was, in a very tangible way, a reflection of the mathematics involved.

Not long ago I had the opportunity to take my first journey across San Francisco's Golden Gate Bridge. Built of huge steel girders, towering into the skyline, bearing multilanes of bumper-to-bumper traffic, this bridge is a masterpiece of mathematical engineering. You can not travel across it without being sucked up into modern technology. The wonders of our Western world envelop you on this bridge, swaddling you in a physical and emotional setting totally different from that of the wooden bridge. The wooden bridge calls forth a slow, gentle pace—you are tempted to stop the car and walk leisurely, meditatively across. Not so with the Golden Gate. Here, with the rush of traffic, it is undesirable to walk across. If you are on foot, the Golden Gate Bridge is not the bridge for you.

Now, a true footbridge offers a totally different experience. When I was a kid, a creek ran across our property, and the only way to traverse this creek was via a large log that had fallen across it. I was never very surefooted, and so I crossed it only reluctantly and warily. Still, the log bridge had its own enticement. When I was on it, I was unaware of any mathematical genius invoked by it, although I am sure that today I could certainly find mathematical relations that would at least partially describe it. Yet such relationships would be artificial and imposed from without, rather than being an intrinsic part of the design—unless, of course, as astronomer James Jeans once proclaimed, "God truly is a mathematician."[1]

Describing these three bridges may seem like an odd place to begin a study on metaphor, metaphysics, and metamathematics, but I believe there are parallels that make the comparison both appropriate and apt. The landscape you are invited to explore in *What Number Is God?* is mostly the abstract territory of metaphysics. The bridges we will travel are those of something I will call metaphorical language, although, as we will see, that phrase implies neither metaphor nor language *per se*. Furthermore, bound in varying degrees to each of these bridges is a philosophy of mathematics, that is, a metamathematics.

In a sense, this study is itself a bridge, for it offers to take you from wherever you are into the domain of ultimate questions. What is life all about? How did it come about? What will happen to it? Such questions lie beyond the physical, in the territory of the metaphysical. Countless people have explored this territory—many have drawn maps for others to follow. Some have even devoted entire lives to this exploration. Probably every individual examines this landscape at one time or another. This work, too, will touch on these issues, but only peripherally, for the real focus of this study is the bridges themselves. How do we get from here to there? What enables us to cross over that fine line of the concrete and mundane to the abstract and ethereal? What connects the physical to the metaphysical?

Some people would probably say it is religion that connects us. Others might say that it is science. Such answers seem to me to be rather like the vehicles themselves that travel the bridge. The bridge they travel across is, I would suggest, metaphorical language. Tied up in the construction of this metaphorical language is an underlying mathematics. Sometimes, as with the log bridge, the mathematics involved is hidden or only questionably there. In other cases, as with the Golden Gate Bridge, the mathematics is integral to the basic structure of the bridge. However, as with all our normal-world bridges, you might not even see the mathematics unless someone pointed it out to you. It is this attempt to point out the mathematics, to make it visible that serves as the distinguishing feature of this study.

What Number Is God? Metaphors, Metaphysics, Metamathematics, and the Nature of Things is a bridge about bridges—a sort of meta-bridge. To state explicitly the implicit, this study is itself a meta-phor, from the Greek meta, meaning "over," and pherien, meaning "to bear." It is part of a large body of symbolic language that "bears us over," in this case to the realm of metaphysics, using a foundation of metamathematical girders. Let us zero in, now, and take a closer look at metamathematics, metaphysics, and metaphor, in the hope that we may ultimately come to a better understanding of their interaction.

METAMATHEMATICS

The beginnings of metamathematics can be traced to the mathematician David Hilbert (1862–1943), who first used the term in the late 1920s to refer to a formalist foundation of mathematics. His was one of several different attempts within the mathematical world to deal with the disturbing paradoxes or "antinomies," which Bertrand Russell and Alfred North Whitehead had uncovered in the set theory of Georg Cantor. Cantor's ideas had revolutionized mathematical thinking only a few decades earlier. (We will encounter them in more detail in chapter 4). In essence, his set theory offered the notion that the set—an arbitrary collection of distinct objects—could be used as the basic building block of all of mathematics. Many readers may remember the "new math," which captivated our education system in the 1960s and 1970s. This "new" mathematics was an outcome of Cantor's powerful vision of set theory. However, in its more sophisticated forms, set theory led to a series of contradictions that threatened to undermine all of mathematics. Growing out of the desire to avoid such a devastation were three main remedies: the logistic efforts of Russell, the intuitive or constructivist school of the Dutch topologist L. E. J. Brouwer, and the formalist foundation of Hilbert grew out of the desire to avoid such a devastation. Each of these remedies turned out to have its own particular difficulties, but the school of Hilbert primarily concerns us here.

Hilbert's approach was to try to prove *mathematically* the consistency of classical mathematics. Davis and Hersh, in their 1981 study of mathematical development and philosophy, give a succinct account of Hilbert's three-step program as follows.

> 1) Introduce a formal language and formal rules of inference, sufficient so that every "correct proof" of a classical theorem could be represented by a formal derivation, starting from axioms, with each step mechanically checkable. This had already been accomplished in large part by Frege, Russell, and Whitehead.
>
> 2) Develop a theory of combinatorial properties of this formal language, regarded as a finite set of symbols subject to permutation and rearrangements as provided by the rules of inference, now regarded as rules for transforming formulas. This theory was called "meta-mathematics."
>
> 3) Prove by purely finite arguments that a contradiction, for example $1 = 0$, cannot be derived within this system.[2]

The motivation for Hilbert's metamathematical theory was (in his own words):

> to establish once and for all the certitude of mathematical methods. . . . The present state of affairs where we run up against the paradoxes is intolerable. Just think, the definitions and deductive methods which everyone learns, teaches and uses in mathematics, the paragon of truth and certitude, lead to absurdities! If mathematical thinking is defective, where are we to find truth and certitude?[3]

Unfortunately, this quest for absolute conviction, which has so often permeated mathematical thinking, ultimately reduced Hilbert's program to a meaningless game of manipulating formal symbols. The *meaning* of the symbols used in this "game" became what Davis and Hersh term "something extra-mathematical."

The search for certitude and truth, and the conviction that it may be found in mathematics, have a long history. Our earliest records of mathematics date back about 5,000 years. For much of that time, mathematical statements were conceived of as true to the degree that they accurately described or agreed with or predicted the "real" world. Gradually, the statements became more and more isolated from the real world, so that, by Hilbert's time, their truth or falsity could be "deduced" from other statements or postulates that had purely arbitrary starting places. In short, mathematical statements "had an existence and a truth or falsehood of their own, independent of the 'real' world."[4]

Such certitude, and indeed, the whole flavor of Hilbert's formalist foundations, came into serious question when, in 1930, Kurt Gödel published his famous incompleteness theorems. These theorems showed that the quest for absolute truth that Hilbert strove to acquire could be obtained only by sacrificing the consistency of the system of thought. Gödel's theorems brought about (or are bringing about[5]) in the last half-century what has been called a "paradigm shift in mathematics." As John Carpenter puts it, "We have now come to the idea that for mathematical statements, anyway, provability is no longer a necessary criterion for truth."[6]

Hilbert's formal theory of foundations lost much of its impact following Gödel's introduction of his theorems, but the term "metamathematics" hung around. Gödel himself was a metamathematician. He developed an elaborate coding system of numbers (called Gödel-numbering) to represent symbols and sequences of symbols (statements). Then he investigated mathematical reasoning itself by means of this mathematical coding system. Metamathematics, while still referring to a very formal set of symbols with which to study mathematics, began to emphasize its "study" aspect as well as its "formal" aspect. Gradually the term acquired a second, broader meaning as the "philosophy of mathematics."[7]

Perhaps the best-known metamathematician in this more generalized sense of the word is Douglas Hofstadter. In his 1979 Pulitzer Prize winning work, *Gödel, Escher, and Bach*, Hofstadter showed that Gödel's discovery was "in its barest form . . . a translation of an ancient paradox—the Epimenides or liar paradox— into mathematical terms."[8] Gödel's theorem described only deductive systems that had reached a certain level of complexity. Hofstadter speculates that this level of complexity is characterized by the ability of the system to be self-reflexive, that is, to make statements concerning itself. This characteristic of self-reference is one that many people have long associated chiefly with human nature.[9] Although he is cautious in his willingness to generalize implications of Gödel's theorem to areas outside of mathematics,[10] Hofstadter nonetheless creates an intricate "golden braid" between mathematics, art, and music that ultimately serves to delve not only into music and the arts, but also into the very nature of human consciousness itself.

Hofstadter is a computer scientist whose main area of investigation is artificial intelligence. Not surprisingly, he is interested in (and assumes the possibility of) detecting appropriate mathematical guidelines or rules to create intelligence in a machine. His speculations about such rules give us the general flavor of his work and his philosophy, and so I quote from it here at some length.

> Computers by their very nature are the most inflexible, desireless, rule-following of beasts. Fast though they may be, they are nonetheless the epitome of unconsciousness. How, then, can intelligent behavior be programmed? Isn't this the most blatant of contradictions in terms? One of the major theses of this book is that it is not a contradiction at all. One of the major purposes of this book is to urge each reader to confront the apparent contradiction head on, . . . so that in the end the reader might emerge with new insights into the seemingly unbreachable gulf between the formal and the informal, the animate and the inanimate, the flexible and the inflexible.
>
> This is what Artificial Intelligence research is all about. And the strange flavor of AI work is that people try to put together long sets of rules in strict formalisms which tell inflexible machines how to be flexible.
>
> What sort of "rules" could possibly capture all of what we think of as intelligent behavior, however? Certainly there must be rules on all sorts of different levels. There must be many "just plain" rules. There must be "metarules" to modify the "just plain" rules; then "metametarules" to modify the metarules, and so on. The flexibility of intelligence comes from the enormous number of different rules, and levels of rules.[11]

Such is the thought process of a modern day meta-thinker. Is Hofstadter a metamathematician, concerned with the translation of formal systems of mathematics into the informal, animate, flexible realm of human consciousness? Or is he a metaphysician, concerned with the questions of being and knowledge? The answer, I think, is both. This is not to suggest that all metaphysicians are metamathematicians, or vice versa. Yet the borderline between the two zones is fuzzy at best, and here, right on that border, is the place where Hofstadter seems to most like to walk. Perhaps Hofstadter is on a bridge, a bridge built with mathematical care and precision, a bridge that winds around so that it keeps looking back on itself. This is a bridge that connects meta-worlds, a bridge that goes beyond the abstract, speculative world of mathematics and beyond the ordinary, everyday world of the physical to the metaphysical.

METAPHYSICS

"Metaphysics" has varied definitions. Theologian Ian Barbour describes it as "the search for a set of general categories in terms of which diverse types of experience can be interpreted."[12] Philosopher Frank Dilley calls it (following Whitehead) "the philosophical discipline concerned with discovering the ideas which are indispensable to the analysis of everything that happens, the discipline concerned with describing the nature of things."[13] He distinguishes it from science in that it deals with the whole of reality and from religion in that religion deals with human attitudes towards the ultimate. Physicist Paul Davies calls it "theories about theories of physics."[14] Paul Moser defines what he calls "the broad construal of metaphysics" as "the philosophical investigation of what there is or how things are in general." He adds that "the notion of how things are is basically the notion of what items (e.g., objects, features of objects, relations between objects and/or features), if any, exist."[15] For many of us, however, "metaphysics" refers simply to what lies *beyond* or *after* the physical, and it implies the arena of the non-concrete or abstract.

In fact, the term has a fairly concrete origin. It was first used to refer to the portion of Aristotle's collected treatises that followed or came after the section dealing with the physical world. Nicholas Lobkowicz, in an article written for a handbook on metaphysics and ontology, points out that there is nonetheless a congruency between the content of these works and the implications of the title: "Aristotle claims that they contain a 'first philosophy,' 'wisdom,' and 'theology' and deal mainly with realities that are subsi-

stent (or separate from matter) and immobile." He notes an ambiguity in Aristotle's treatment of the topic, however, for Aristotle
"also claims that the subject matter of this part of philosophy is
'being as being' and he indicates that it also deals with the first
premisses [sic] of knowledge."

The inconsistencies in Aristotle's treatises have "puzzled scholars since antiquity." Lobkowicz continues:

> Perhaps the only consistent interpretation was advanced by
> Aquinas. Objects of physics and mathematics are "constituted"
> by acts of abstraction. . . . Metaphysics on the contrary presup-
> poses an act of "separation," i.e., a negative judgement to the
> effect that to be does not necessarily entail being corporeal. Un-
> der this premiss [sic] an observer whose scope of cognition is
> limited to what his senses offer tries to isolate those features of
> physical realities that can be attributed to immaterial realities,
> and by inference construes whatever is to be said about the lat-
> ter. . . . Accordingly, metaphysics deals with whatever throws
> light on what is common to bodies and spirits as well as on their
> interrelation.[16]

Thus the metaphysics of Aristotle and Aquinas, while delving
into the realm beyond the physical, do not quite leave it altogether.
A connection is to be found in metaphysics between the routine,
sense-enriched realm of our normal everyday experience and the
realm that has come to be called "nonmaterial entities."[17] Over
the years, this conception of metaphysics as that which is beyond,
yet still connected to, the physical world has worn many different
frames, frames that alter our entire sense of the conception. In a
vein somewhat similar to the path of mathematics, metaphysics
gradually became more and more closely linked to logic and purely
conceptual issues. In the seventeenth and eighteenth centuries,
metaphysics "began to fall apart into a discipline discussing the
most general concepts and 'natural theology.' . . . [L]ogic and
mathematics became a pattern of thought to which both the method and the content of metaphysics had to adjust."[18]

Some philosophers, including Lobkowicz, see a modern trend
away from this highly *abstract,* speculative framing of metaphysics
toward "aspects reminiscent of what thinkers such as Aristotle and
Aquinas intended."[19] Put another way, it may well be that we are
currently undergoing a "paradigm shift" in our understanding of

what we mean by the very notion of abstraction. Epistemologist J. Samuel Bois is certainly representative of those who believe in such a contemporary trend, although according to his vision, it is more of a move to something *beyond* early Greek and Aristotelian thinking than *back* to it.

Bois has outlined a theory of knowledge based on a metaphysics of human evolution. In particular, he sees the history of Western civilization as undergoing a series of conceptual revolutions, what he calls radical and irreversible changes in some fundamental element of human life. The first of these conceptual revolutions occurred from 650 to 350 B.C.—the age of the Greek philosophers we have just been discussing. While Bois allows that these Greek philosophers did not agree in their various theories, he suggests that they "all held the revolutionary idea that there was such a thing as *the nature of things,* and that whatever existed remained identical with its natural self: a man was a man, and he could not originate from a dragon's tooth, nor could he be transformed into a snake." Aristotle, according to Bois, played the role in this conceptual revolution of "a codifier, or system-builder, who made explicit the methods of thinking that were characteristic of the age."[20]

The second conceptual revolution occurred roughly from the 1500s to the 1700s—the late Renaissance era. Again, theories differed among the great thinkers of this age. But the similarity that Bois believes bound them together and that made it a revolution in conceptual "thinking, feeling, planning, and deciding"[21] was the *birth of the scientific method.* This birth Bois sees as a move from deductive to inductive reasoning. Francis Bacon, like Aristotle before him, was the primary codifier of the revolution, the one who "formulated the methods of thinking characteristic of the period."[22]

The third conceptual revolution, says Bois, is happening right now. The similarity that the geniuses of this period all display again represents a change in our methods of thinking. But it is a change that has yet to be completely identified because "the system has not yet been fully worked out." However, Bois does identify the present counterpart to Aristotle and Bacon as Alfred Korzybski. Korzybski, with his 1933 publication of *Science and Sanity,* founded the field of general semantics, and he

took upon himself the task of explicitly formulating and arrang-
ing into a system the methods of thinking that make our epoch
different from the previous ones. He did not limit himself to
logic, deductive or inductive. He thought in terms of *psycho-
logics,* of a science of thinking, not as an activity that stands by
itself, but as a science of our evaluating processes—of how we
react to persons, events, and symbols according to what they
mean to us at the moment of impact.[23]

Thus, Bois sets forth a theory about how humankind views
itself, a theory he holds is more consistent with our present stage of
evolution on earth than with the conditions of the ancient Greeks
in the Mediterranean world. His outline of the basic assumptions
of this theory are similarly consistent with presuppositions that I
bring to my own present study, and so I reproduce them here.

> 1. Logic—deductive or inductive, symbolic or classical—is
> superseded by psycho-logics. Mental activity no longer stands by
> itself, and it is not studied by itself. It is only one aspect of a
> greater whole, called semantic transaction, which is our main
> unit of discourse.
> 2. There is no one method of thinking that is common to all,
> and no laws of logic apply to all members of the human race.
> There are semantic states, now more and more frequently called
> *epistemes* by Foucault and others, that vary from culture to cul-
> ture, or that change within a culture in the course of history.
> 3. Through our language—and the culture of it is one
> aspect—we have developed a structured unconscious in us that
> involves a metaphysics—the metaphysics of subject and predi-
> cate, of substances and qualities, of agent and action.
> 4. Our experiences are constructs of our own processes in
> transaction. Our contacts with the world "inside" and "outside"
> ourselves can be seen as so many acts of abstracting, and this
> process of abstracting proceeds at different levels. By being aware
> of the differences between these levels we can solve many para-
> doxes and facilitate agreement.[24]

To these four basic themes I would add one more, that one way
(perhaps, for some, even the *best* way) to understand these first
four is with the aid of mathematics. I do not think that Bois would
be uncomfortable with this assumption. For one thing, Korzybski
himself relied heavily on mathematics in the formulation of his
general semantics. Bois, too, later in his work, implicitly assumes

something of the sort when he notes that "The inventor of symbols and symbol systems is the person who blazes the trail of our advance. The mathematician has been doing it with spectacular success for the natural sciences, and it is the task of the epistemologist to do it for the human sciences."[25]

Bois focuses his metaphysics on the way we use language (in the broad sense of the word) in the process of *abstracting*. I quote here from a variety of places in his *Art of Awareness:*

> To "abstract" means to leave out certain features of a situation, to register only those that are relevant to our needs, our purposes, or our habits. (73)

> We abstract—that is we select from among the characteristics of the total ongoing world of processes—what lies within our capacity to observe with our unaided senses or with instruments. (80)

> There is no real permanency anywhere but in our delusional static picture of what is going on in the world and in us. Our acts of abstracting are passing pointed contacts between two moving "realities," or ongoings, the world and ourselves, and the relation between them is an undetermined variable. (80)

> The first step of abstracting takes us from what is going on to what we take into account. . . . The second step of abstracting takes us from what we are concerned with to what we say about it. (81)

> Our assumptions, our preconceived notions—particularly those that served us well in the past—act as a filter for our abstracting processes. (97)

> We become what we abstract, transform, and assimilate. (100)

> . . . fitting thought elements into the proper structure has become one of the main concerns of the epistemology of our generation. Many new words, or old words used in a new way, replace such simple terms as "idea," "thought," "concept," or "reasoning." We now hear of *Gestalt, configuration, conceptual organization, constructs, patterns, schemas, conceptual coordinates, closed and open systems, maps, structures, multidimensional manifolds, and models.* (201–2)

> Words come out of a speaker's mouth one at a time and enter the listener's ear in the same serial order, but they are really labels that express elements of a structure in the speaker's mind, and

they are intended to create a similar structure in the listener's.
This they often fail to achieve. (202)

Bois's comments strongly suggest his presupposition of some
other realm than the one we perceive with our senses. When we
abstract, we leave out *certain features of a situation,* we select from
among *characteristics of the total ongoing world of processes,* we
filter something, we start from a place of *what* is *going on* and
move elsewhere, we are the connection or *passing pointed contact*
between ourselves and something else. This "something else" I
hypothesize as being a kind of "primordial chaos," about which I
will say more later. Further, to alter one of his statements slightly,
I suggest that whatever we abstract, transform, and assimilate out
of this primordial chaos is what we become, indeed, what we are.

This view is not particularly original (but, then, according to
this view, not much is). It bears, in fact, a certain resemblance to
the seventeenth-century metaphysics of mathematician/philoso-
pher Leibniz. According to Leibniz, the entire created universe
consists of mindlike entities, or Monads, some of which are more
developed than others but all of which perceive the whole of the
universe. How much of the universe is self-consciously or know-
ingly perceived is a matter of degree. A material object, for example, perceives the universe only subconsciously. Humans are more
fully aware; but even though we perceive the whole of the universe,
we still are aware of only a small portion of it. Most of it remains
hidden to our consciousness behind some sort of threshold that it
fails to traverse.

Leibniz's metaphysics, according to H. H. Price, lends itself to
an interpretation that today lies on the fringes of science, in an area
beyond the range of normal experience or scientifically explainable
phenomena—what the *American Heritage Dictionary* defines as
"paranormal." Price, a "philosopher who happens to be interested
in psychical research as well,"[26] has argued that Leibniz was the
first modern philosopher to suggest that there are mental processes
below or beyond consciousness. Price sees Leibniz as the one
among the great classical philosophers "whose ideas are most suggestive for the Psychical Researcher," and he says the following
about Leibniz's doctrine of "omniscience."

It is the idea that each of us, below the level of consciousness, is all the time in touch with a very much wider range of facts and happenings than he is consciously aware of.

If we do consider this suggestion, just to see what its consequences are, we find that it alters the questions we commonly ask about paranormal cognition. We no longer ask "Why does paranormal cognition occasionally occur?" Instead, we ask "Why does it occur so seldom?"[27]

Price suggests that such cognitions are brought into our consciousness with varying degrees of symbolism or, alternatively, of literalness. The theory he puts forth meshes so well with my own personal experience that I feel compelled to share here a couple of personal stories.

Several years ago, some friends and I shared Thanksgiving dinner at one of the buildings that house some of the students from Meadville/Lombard Theological School in Chicago, Illinois. Following our rather traditional feast, we decided to join in a game of Trivial Pursuit, a popular social game that I have never particularly enjoyed, probably because I do not seem to have a brain that recalls details easily. Read that another way, and you might say that I am lousy at the game. I am the sort of player whom nobody who takes the game seriously wants to have on their team. It was to everyone's astonishment, therefore, not the least of all mine, when, to the question as to what was the state flower of Alaska (which had stumped *everyone* on our team) I suddenly and at the very last moment ("Oh, just take a guess!") announced (correctly) "Forget-me-not." That is not the typical answer that one expects to "just guess," and I can only say I wish I had had a camera to record the expressions of amazement that my unthinking, intuitive response evoked on the faces of my comrades.

The second story happened many years ago when I was only a young teenager and was visiting my cousin Sue. I remember the incident after all these years because it elicited the same kind of intense, amazed responses from both my cousin and the woman who ran the day care center where Sue worked part time. Sue had taken me with her to the center. We walked in and, immediately, Sue introduced me to the director. Mrs. X, Sue's director, began to give me a short rundown on some of the children who at that particular moment were off elsewhere doing some other activity. She mentioned that one particularly sweet little girl was ill and was absent that day. Almost instantaneously, and without thinking about what I was saying, I asked the Director if that would be so-and-so. The actual detail of her name now slips my memory, but it was, in fact, the correct name of the one child who was not attending that day. To fully appreciate the extent of the Director's and Sue's astonishment, you will note that I had not visited my cousin at her home since I had been a preschooler, I had never before been to this center, I had never heard Sue mention any of the children by name or personality, and I had virtually walked in the door only a couple of minutes earlier. The name, it seemed, appeared "out of nowhere."

Much as I might like to, I cannot, however, claim special psychic powers in either of these two instances. In the one case I am sure and in the other I suspect that the two names that came to me so unexpectedly did not, in fact, appear "out of nowhere." With Sue and her director, I was even able to explain right then and there how I had come to this information. Essentially it was one of those moments when things "just connected" in an unusually quick but otherwise logically deducible fashion. As I came into the center, I observed (I believe not consciously) a number of open cubicles where it was clear that the children normally hung their wraps, kept their sack lunches, etc. Each cubicle was carefully labeled in big print with the first name of the child who would be using it. Of all these cubicles, only one remained rather conspicuously bare: it was the name printed above this cubicle that I had offered as the name of the missing child. All of this had happened very, very rapidly. In fact, I had not even been aware that my brain had observed and processed all of this information until the circumstances surrounding my naming the child had evoked what must have been the conclusion of this mental reasoning process. (Alas, I confess that, to my knowledge, my brain does not *normally* seem to function so efficiently—so perhaps there is yet some justification for the label "paranormal.")

The other incident leaves me more baffled. How was I, who forget trivial details routinely, able to produce "Forget-me-not" almost as an afterthought? Upon reflection, I suspect that it may have been, quite literally, an *after* thought. Somewhere in the dimmest regions of my consciousness I vaguely recall the possibility that I might have encountered the same question at some earlier playing of the game. I am not sure. But certainly it is possible and perhaps even probable that I might have heard the question previously, stored the answer in some barely accessible region of my subconscious, and retrieved it almost without volition when I least expected it.

Thus I can offer convincing (at least to me) rationales for why both of these events, which on the surface appeared to be highly mysterious and clairvoyant, might be well within the "range of normal experience or scientifically explainable phenomena." So much for paranormal occurrences.

Or is it?

For I confess to having experienced, at various times, a number of other, equally baffling, equally mysterious happenings that, try as I might, I can not "explain" in the least. Of course, that in no way assumes that such an explanation is nonexistent—it could merely reflect on my inadequate ability to produce it. In fact, because a part of me likes tidy little understandings, I conjecture up the hypothesis that the whole universe, that Everything, exists in that primordial chaos I mentioned earlier, and that it is only by virtue of some sort of superimposed ordering structure that filters this chaos into meaningful units that we have the world as we know it. I do not know how such an ordering filter might be superimposed (although I suspect it has something to do with what I call God), but I further hypothesize that all sorts of filters are possible. One such filter is what we know of as the human being. This is a self-reflexive filter. It looks back on itself and calls the process of doing so "abstracting."

This self-reflexive filter has possibilities that we have, to varying degrees, ignored in recent years, namely our "psychic" possibilities. Using Price's line of reasoning, the two names that I brought up "out of nowhere" in my stories would be fairly literal pieces of information that had been relegated to the realm of the subconscious or unconscious. Price posits that not all paranormal cognitions are so literal: often they are partially or completely "symbolic"—"what emerges into the consciousness . . . often does not directly and literally represent the fact which one is paranormally aware of, or 'in touch with', at the unconscious level, but represents it only in an indirect and oblique manner."[28] Thus, an idea from the realm of the unconscious may be disguised, or may even have some other image or concept substituted for it before it can pass the threshold into consciousness. "Symbolization (in this sense of the word) is a means of overcoming, or circumventing, some kind of barrier or censorship which tends to keep the paranormally-acquired information from getting into consciousness at all."[29]

Just exactly what is this "Censor"[30] and why should there be one? Price suggests that, first of all, there may have been a time in human evolution when the paranormal powers were more commonly used, but because they tend to be indiscriminate, they would not have been as valuable to survival as the guides provided by sense organs such as the eyes and ears. Hence, they gave way to the more elaborate nervous system and sense organs. Secondly, he sees in this "Censor" a utilitarian purpose: "I think its function in the end is to preserve the integrity of our personality, because if we were at the mercy of thoughts coming at us from all sides, all the time, so far as I can see the unity of our personality could not be maintained."[31]

Price's theory bears some striking similarities to Bois's comments on abstraction. Both involve an evolutionary aspect. Both postulate the existence of a filter or censor. Both posit a wider realm of some sort accessible to the human consciousness. Both lead into the areas of language and symbolism. I am sure that, with a little reflection, I could find a similar list of differences between the two. What intrigues me, though, is the possibility that both theories (which I have treated with only mediocre justice in my abbreviated rendition here) might be attempts to recognize and articulate the same basic, but "new," way of seeing things.

This new way of seeing, this conceptual revolution, is being addressed, as Bois points out, in many different ways by many different people.[32] Like Bois and Price, these investigators are searching for epistemological clues to our existence, but they do so from perspectives that vary from the highly practical to the highly theoretical. To give some indication of the scope and diversity of the treatments of this theme, I will sketch here three additional arguments that come from the realms of psychology, science, and mathematics.

Psychologist Lawrence Leshan and physicist/scientific philosopher Henry Margenau have set forth a theory in *Einstein's Space and Van Gogh's Sky* that Western culture's rigorous and literal attempts to explain reality fall short primarily because they fail to take into account the realm of nonphysical experience. They suggest that a new organization of reality is already being developed, a way that goes beyond a reductionistic scientific "rationality" governing the entire cosmos. According to the two collaborators, science and social science alike generally regard sensory reality, the "ordinary everyday state of consciousness," as being the *correct* reality. Any others are simply aberrations from it. Not so, say Margenau and Leshan. True enough, we humans are "conditioned to assume that we *know* the one truth and that everything else is, somehow, less real. To question this seems to us to be abandoning all reason and placing ourselves in a chaotic and unpredictable cosmos. . . . Nevertheless, very often, if we scientifically follow the data and their implications, our older theories must be abandoned."[33]

According to the two researchers, the way we perceive and organize our perceptions is a learned way, one affected largely by the language we use and by the questions we pose. Somewhat reminiscent of Bois, they suggest three major historical developments that have altered our perceptions.

> The great discovery of the ancient world (about 600 B.C.) was that there was an intelligible structure to the world. The great discovery of the Renaissance in Europe was that we could use this structure for our purposes, that the more we understood it, the more we could control matter and energy. The great discovery of the present-day revolution is that—within limits—the structure is up to us, and different formulations of it must be used with different types of experience and to attain different goals.[34]

What Margenau and Leshan ultimately posit is a pluralistic *domain theory*, where different domains of experience have different observables, different vocabularies, and different metaphysics. There is the domain of the social scientist, of the scientist, of the parapsychologist, of art, of ethics, of consciousness. Sometimes these domains are compatible, sometimes not. But in any case trouble often arises when the rules of organization of one are applied to another and judgements are made on the assumption that there is only one ultimately *correct* domain. According to this thesis,

> [T]he cosmos is divided into *domains* of experience. In each of these certain observables "appear." Some domains bear a se-

quential relationship to each other, and when this is true, a number of definite statements can be made about their relationships. Domains fall into larger groupings called *realms,* and each realm has a special organization of reality (metaphysical system) which is necessary to make the data from it lawful.[35]

These domains are also referred to as "levels," a terminology that the authors maintain often leads to discussions of reductionism (from one level to another) with associated hierarchies of truth-value.[36] They prefer to use a nonhierarchical notion of "transcendent but compatible elaboration." In this view, which the authors still characterize as scientific, the chief interest is not in some trait, such as size, of a particular domain, but in the "observables called into being as we pass from one domain to another. . . . Strictly speaking, what emerges was already there, invisible and unexpected. We, however, wish to emphasize the uniqueness of the new observables, their creation by a new theoretical approach, the scientist's inability of simply conceiving them from a domain in which they have no meaning."[37]

What becomes important for Margenau and Leshan, then, is that different realities or different states of consciousness are desirable and even necessary for the human well-being. From the social science perspective, there are (they claim) at least four different ways of being-in-the-world—the sensory, clairvoyant, transpsychic, and mythic.[38] *All* of these "are needed if the individual is to avoid becoming stunted in his development."[39] They acknowledge that our everyday, verbal language is generally useful and adequate to describe the data in the sensory realm. They argue, however, that in the realms of inner experience, "we have never developed a language relevant to the data. We constantly use metaphors from the see-touch realm as if the data of our inner experience were the same as that of our eyes and touch organs."[40] Metaphor, they feel, is helpful but lacking, and "one of our tasks in developing a science of the inner life will be the development of an adequate language."[41]

There are difficulties with their argument at this point. For example, in developing a *science* of the *inner life,* they appear to blend the very levels or domains that they seem otherwise to separate carefully as alternative but valid ways of perceiving. Furthermore, they observe that the richest language developed thus far for use in the domain of the inner life is that associated with astrology, yet they promptly dismiss astrology as pseudoscience "because it consistently uses both the mythic mode-of-being and the sensory mode."[42] I see here two main weaknesses. First, they treat astrology in the same pejorative manner in which they later criticize, in a sympathetic critique of psi occurrence (extrasensory perception, psychokinesisz, etc.), "most scientists today" for treating parapsychology[43]. Secondly, while they allow for more than the four possible ways of organizing reality noted above, they do not allow for (or, indeed, even consider the possibility of) legitimate domains that are mixes of these four domains. Astrology was rejected as a pseudoscience *because* it blended two ways of seeing. It is not at all evident to me that such a blurring of the domains is not, in fact, precisely what we routinely do much of the time. Nor is it evident to me that such a blurring is anything other than one more, to use their terminology, "altered state of consciousness."

In spite of these reservations, I read their arguments as generally consistent with, though by no means identical to, the sketches I have given of the epistemological approaches of Bois and Price. Bois and Price are coming from the arenas of general semantics and philosophy, respectively; Margenau and Leshan from physics and psychology. From the fields of neurobiology and population studies comes yet another version of this "new way of thinking," set forth in Robert Ornstein's and Paul Ehrlich's *New World New Mind*.

The basic thesis in this more recent book is that there is a mismatch between the human mind and the world people inhabit. The human mind developed to respond to short-term, localized situations such as dodging a lion before it ate you.

> The human mind evolved to register short-term changes, from moment to moment, day to day, and season to season, and to overlook the "backdrop" against which those took place. That backdrop only changed significantly on a time scale of centuries or longer. Not only did our evolutionary background predispose us to live in a world of caricatures and physically equip us to draw only part of the picture, it also predisposed us to focus on certain parts of the "image" and ignore others.[44]

Like all animals, humans have only a limited ability to sense the environment. "*All* sensory systems filter information from the outside world, their environments—and the human system is no exception."[45]

But now, say the authors, our world has changed. We live in a world of gradual changes—changes in the ozone layer, changes in population patterns, changes in nuclear build-up. The human nervous system is not matched to this world of large gradual changes, and so we fail to respond to the new dangers that threaten to annihilate us as surely as the lion threatened to annihilate our hunter-predecessor. "The pattern of selectivity programmed into human beings by the old world is now fatally obsolete in the new. We need a new basis for making selections."[46] We need, in short, a new mind.

Thus the thesis set forth here is similar to the three I have previously outlined in that it posits the need for a new way of thinking that, incidentally, it later suggests we are already beginning to develop. This new way of thinking is based on the idea that we selectively filter (via our perceptions) a "chaotic and changing"[47] external world into "radical mental filtrations" or "caricatures"[48] that "are useful insofar as they correspond *closely enough* with reality that they help us to survive."[49] Furthermore, it is not just our perceptions that are subject to the simplifying processes of the mind, but our thought processes as well; and the filtering of our thought into categories is "peculiar to individual cultures and can be observed in the structure of different languages."[50] Culture, previous experiences, and present attitudes all "strongly affect what we perceive," and in particular, "whatever gets close to us, in space or time, is immediately overemphasized."[51] Finally, like Bois who sought this change in perception through the art of "scientifically guided self-awareness,"[52] Ornstein and Ehrlich suggest that "what we can do is to begin to call the attention of people to their own caricatures of reality and to the new world itself."[53]

But here, the similarity seems to end, for the new way of seeing that Ornstein and Ehrlich promote is one based fully in behavioral modification, education, practicality, systematic programs of change, and so forth. Their catalogue of possibilities for real change is filled with details, explicit everyday examples, down-to-earth secular activities. Not here will we find any talk of altered states of consciousness or paranormal knowledge. Not here will we find, as we do in Bois, talk of meditation, of holistic communication and empathy, of "sensory deconcentration" as a way "of loosening the concentration involved in whatever we do in earnest."[54] Rather, Ornstein and Ehrlich offer the insight that events such as "dramatic therapeutic techniques, fantastic 'cures,' and dramatic 'states of mind,' are, like vivid emergencies, overemphasized. This leads us to distort our perceptions of some of the most important institutions in our lives, such as medicine, psychotherapy, and religion."[55] To them, meditation, for example, is an archaic exercise "which was meant for a particular community in another era" and is now offered "via mass indoctrination to everyone."[56] Here, in Ornstein and Erhlich's firmly entrenched secular humanism,[57] we find a skepticism and cynicism that almost directly contradicts many tenets of the previous three renditions of the same basic "filter" epistemological viewpoint.

An interesting version which in many ways spans the gap between these two viewpoints is that offered by Douglas Hofstadter in *Gödel, Escher, Bach,* which I turn to now in somewhat more depth than in the previous section of this chapter. "It was only with the advent of computers that people actually tried to create 'thinking' machines, and witnessed bizarre variations on the theme of thought," says Hofstadter. "As a result, we have acquired, in the last twenty years or so, a *new kind of perspective* on what thought is, and what it is not" (emphasis added)."[58]

When we try to understand Hofstadter's understanding of thought, we engage, at least according to his theory, in a kind of "quasi-isomorphism" or partial mapping of two key features characterizing the "brains of people whose style of thinking is similar— in particular, a correspondence of 1) the repertoire of symbols, and 2) the triggering patterns of symbols."[59] He likens this thought process to a *trip* we take through the networklike structure of our brains, a structure that is at least somewhat similar to his own brain. Major *towns* we pass through on this trip are the symbols that we activate. Somewhat facetiously, the author helpfully(?) presents a map of a tiny portion of his own "semantic network" (see figure 1.1)[60] so that we can compare our travels. In a Platonic-like quest for an ideal, he observes that our individual thought-maps are dependent upon "external, predetermined geological facts." "It is necessary to begin with identical external conditions— otherwise nothing will match."[61]

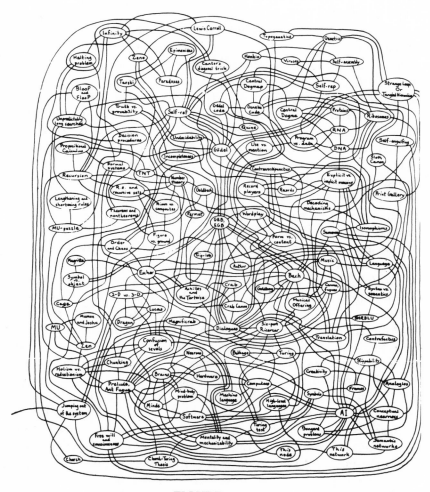

FIGURE 1.1
Hofstadter's Semantic Network

If enough towns or symbols are "visited" in the thought process, we activate a *subsystem*, which is then

> able to act autonomously, making use of some resources in our brains for support. By this, I mean that a subsystem symbolizing a friend can activate many of the symbols in my brain just as I can. For instance, I can fire up my subsystem for a good friend and virtually feel myself in his shoes, running through thoughts

which he might have, activating symbols in sequences which reflect his thinking patterns more accurately than my own. It could be said that my model of this friend, as embodied in a subsystem of my brain, constitutes my own chunked description of his brain.[62]

In an analogy that I cannot begin to do adequate justice to, Hofstadter likens this whole process to one of shared codes that can be used by two or more distinct timesharing programs running on a single computer.

The variations and subtleties that he draws from this theme are as fascinating as they are incredible, and they often touch on philosophical issues. The brain, he argues, functions on different levels much like the different language levels of a computer (e.g., hardwired, machine language, assembly language, compiler language, interpreters).[63] Sometimes levels can be mixed, as when a computer operator forgets which language the computer is using and types something that makes no sense at that level, though it would make perfect sense on another. Some levels (the "higher" ones) are more flexible than others, but, ultimately, they must "bottom out" in "hardware." "This is a kind of primordial self-knowledge which is so obvious that it is hard to see it at all; it is like being conscious that the air is there."[64] Most of the time, we mix levels without difficulty: reading a book, for example, requires us to read meaning into sequences of alphabetic letters and more or less overlook or ignore the hardware marks that make up the sequences. When mixing levels does cause confusion, when we run up against some "defect" of the mind, it is because of the hard-wiring way our brains are organized. Yet somewhat paradoxically, it is this very tendency to go up a level, indeed, to jump out of the system entirely, which, though impossible, nonetheless "lies behind all progress in art, music, and other human endeavors."[65]

A "self-subsystem" (which, like all subsystems, is both a complex of symbols and a symbol in itself) can play the role of "soul."[66] After all, when we are aware of our own thoughts, is that not clear evidence that we are reading our own brains at the symbol level?[67] Are we not, in some Zen-like sense,[68] attempting a sort of self-transcendence? But this raises familiar philosophical questions. Who does the symbol-manipulating? Who is the activating agent? "You cannot quite break out of your own skin and be on the outside of yourself," notes Hofstadter. "A computer program can modify itself, but it cannot violate its own instructions. This is reminiscent of the humorous paradoxical question, 'Can God make a stone so heavy that he can't lift it?' "[69]

Hofstadter's computer/brain analogy is, in many ways, mechanistic. Like Ornstein and Ehrlich, he focuses on physiological limitations and needs: at bottom is the "hardware." Yet his talk of levels is reminiscent of Leshan and Margenau's domains and, even more so, of the emphasis on the levels of abstraction that form the foundation of Bois's transactional theory. Here, too, are implicit and explicit references to the filter theme that runs throughout our earlier discussion: indeed, we find in *Gödel, Escher, Bach* one whole section devoted to the theme of "Finding Order by Choosing the Right Filter."[70] Furthermore, though he cautions against overstressing the role of language in molding thoughts (preferring, instead, to emphasize the role of culture in shaping thoughts),[71] his entire work concentrates on symbols and the extension of formal language systems into the realm of epistemology.

It is here, in his consistent interjection of formal mathematics into all realms of his thesis, that we find what I believe is the truly unique feature of his work. He interweaves this material in two alternating ways. First, he uses direct exposition, proffering a constant mix of formal mathematical theory and epistemological quest. Perhaps the following two short passages will give the flavor of this methodology.

> Stepping out of one purely typographical system into another isomorphic typographical system is not a very exciting thing to do; whereas stepping out of the typographical domain into an isomorphic part of number theory has some kind of unexplored potential. It is as if somebody had known musical scores all his life, but purely visually—and then, all of a sudden someone introduced him to the mapping between sounds and musical scores. What a rich, new world! Then, again, it is as if somebody had been familiar with string figures all his life, but purely as string figures, devoid of meaning—and then, all of a sudden, someone introduced him to the mapping between stories and strings. What a revelation! The discovery of Gödel-numbering has been likened to the discovery, by Descartes, of the isomorphism between curves in a plane and equations in two variables: incredibly simple, once you see it—and opening onto a vast new world.[72]

> We seem to be making a rather abrupt transition from brains and minds to technicalities of mathematics and computer science.

Though the transition is abrupt in some ways, it makes some sense. We just saw how a certain kind of self-awareness seems to be at the crux of consciousness. Now we are going to scrutinize "self-awareness" in more formal settings, such as TNT [Typographical Number Theory]. The gulf between TNT and a mind is wide, but some of the ideas will be most illuminating, and perhaps metaphorically transportable back to our thoughts about consciousness.[73]

One word in the last sentence quoted above gives a clue to the second major way in which Hofstadter weaves metamathematics, the theory of formal mathematical languages, into a metaphysics of knowledge. The word? "Metaphorically." Hofstadter is a master of metaphor. Not only does he fill his expository sections with analogies and likenesses, but he also begins each major chapter with a carefully constructed metaphorical dialogue between Achilles and the Tortoise (of Zeno's vintage) and assorted other characters. The purpose of this technique is, as he states himself:

> to present new concepts twice: almost every new concept is first presented *metaphorically* in a Dialogue, yielding a set of concrete visual images; then these serve, during the reading of the following Chapter, as an intuitive background for a more serious and abstract presentation of the same concept. In many of the Dialogues I appear to be talking about one idea on the surface, but in reality I am talking about some other idea, in a thinly disguised way.[74] (emphasis added)

Hofstadter's fictitious conversations are, in essence, "concrete visual" *bridges* bearing us over into the space of a "more serious and abstract" concept. When we read these dialogues, we may or may not be struck by the mathematics we find in them, for they vary considerably in the degree to which they explicitly express mathematics. But whether or not it squeezes through the filter of our previous experience, the mathematics is undeniably there.

Now, it seems to me that the root common denominator between all five of the metaphysical approaches discussed in this section is that they focus on *how* we see/think, rather than on *what* we see/think. It is as though we are but one step away from the abstract realm of what Plato called a world of Forms, and we decide that we are not really interested in immersing ourselves in this world, after all. What we really want to do is to take a closer look at the steps we are taking to get there. This is an "almost" meta-physics. It is a metaphysics that is not about metaphysics, but about what connects our sense-world to it. It is, in short, a meta-physics about bridges.

Plato knew about this bridge, of course. He called it the World-Soul. Davies points out that the contemporary philosopher Walter Mayerstein "likens Plato's World-Soul to the modern concept of mathematical theory, being the thing that connects our sense experiences with the principles on which the universe is built, and provides us with what we call understanding."[75] While I agree that Mayerstein is "on" to something, I don't think he has it quite right. For while the mathematics is definitely involved in building the bridge, the bridge itself is better called a metaphor.

METAPHOR

The definition I like best of "metaphor" is one given by Sallie McFague in her definitive study on metaphorical theology: "a metaphor is seeing one thing *as* something else."[76] We "see as." We see God as father, and then all our actions are based on this way of seeing or perceiving. We see God as mother, and our actions change according to this way of seeing. The implication that I latch on to here is that metaphor is a way of seeing.

McFague's definition has both a narrow and a broad interpretation. Janet Soskice, for instance, tightens it up considerably when she quite properly (at least according to the dictionary meaning) restricts the setting of metaphor to linguistics: "metaphor is that figure of speech whereby we speak about one thing in terms which are seen to be suggestive of another."[77] Her emphasis here, and throughout her book, is that metaphor is a trope, a figure of speech, that is, a mode of language use and not a physical object, mental act, or process. However, Soskice later systematically loosens this restriction in effect if not in actuality when she claims a meaning for "model" that, so far as I can tell, virtually replicates that of "metaphor" except for this purely linguistic restriction. "Our suggestion," she says "is that model and metaphor are closely linked; when we use a model, we regard one thing or state of affairs in terms of another, and when we use a metaphor, we speak of one thing or state of affairs in language suggestive of another."[78]

Others, less linguistically oriented, are more willing to broaden the basic sense in which they use the term, usually by avoiding or sliding over its purely literary context. Colin Turbayne employs a broad definition as "the presentation of the facts of one category in the idioms appropriate to another."[79] Donald Schon, in *Invention and the Evolution of Ideas,* uses the term in a wide sense that includes what others call model.[80] Robert Romanyshyn says that a "metaphor is a way of seeing something through something else."[81] The emphasis, for Romanyshyn, is on the *through.* "A metaphor . . . is not essentially a way of seeing how one reality is *like* another. It is a way of seeing one reality *through* another. Its resemblance, if we should call it that, is the resemblance which a reflection bears to the reality of which it is a reflection. It is not a real (factual) resemblance but a resemblance where likeness is a difference."[82] Behind this seemingly contradictory statement lies Romanyshyn's thesis that reality itself is "originally metaphorical, and its data are not facts, but metaphors."[83] According to his vision, the human psychological life *forgets* this metaphorical nature of reality.

An example Romanyshyn uses to illustrate his thesis deals with Isaac Newton's discovery that light is composed of a rainbow spectrum of colors. The spectrum of light that Newton saw by dispersing sunlight through a prism (i.e., by "seeing" in a specific way) "explains" the ordinary rainbow in the sense that the

> rainbow is the spectrum in the world. The refraction of the daylight sun, the visible evidence that the spectrum lies *in* nature.
>
> It requires, however, only a brief reflection to realize that this . . . point is not quite acceptable. Although the spectrum may explain the rainbow, the rainbow *is not* the spectrum. Or, to be more precise here, the rainbow *is* the spectrum, provided that this "is" is understood as a metaphor. In other words, the statement is correctly understood when one comprehends that it indicates *a way of seeing,* and not simply something to be seen. "The rainbow is the spectrum" is a prescription about *how* to look . . .
>
> . . . the spectrum is there neither *because* nor *before* Newton looks, but *when* and in relation to *how* he looks. This acknowledgement . . . illustrates the temporality of human experience, a temporality which is marked by the passage to the literal from the metaphorical. A reality which originally appears metaphorically is forgotten and as such becomes a literal, empirical fact. A spectrum which is also a way of seeing becomes only something to be seen.[84]

Romanyshyn insists that this tendency to forget the metaphorical nature of reality and to see the world literally permeates all of our everyday experience. Likewise, he argues that it permeates our scientific experience and that contemporary science is largely unaware of its metaphorical character.[85] His construction of reality, thus, is one in which mind and matter are terms that indicate first and foremost *"ways of seeing,* in relation to which empirical data are established."[86] The human organism is for him a means of envisioning the dualistic interaction between "self-conscious mind" and "liaison-brain." They become literalized realities in themselves to the extent that we forget their original metaphorical nature: "the human person becomes this interacting-dualism, when in fact this dualism is a metaphor of human action, a means of envisioning it, a *vehicle* through which the *tenor* of human embodied life may be seen."[87]

Soskice would strongly object to this (in her eyes) "misuse" of the term metaphor in that it tends to turn it into an act or process.[88] Soskice, as I pointed out, holds to a narrow definition of metaphor as a linguistic term. This is a standard definition and is supported, though perhaps less vigorously, by many of her contemporaries, for example, by Max Black, Monroe Beardsley, Colin Turbayne, Philip Wheelwright, and Paul Ricoeur. Throughout this study I take the broader interpretation, one that sees metaphor as a language term, and language as both verbal and nonverbal communication (e.g., sign language, body language, proxemics).[89] Within this frame of reference, language *includes* linguistics, and, thus, what is applicable to linguistics must be at least partially applicable to the broader interpretation. It is possible, of course, that what holds for the linguistic portion cannot be generalized to all of language. Nonetheless, it seems reasonable to explore an extension of some of the ideas applicable to linguistics to the larger realm, and, indeed, it may be negligent not to do so. It is from this perspective that I draw freely, both in this chapter and the next, from a wide range of writings on the topic of metaphor.

Romanyshyn's comments echo the vehicle/tenor theory of metaphor that I. A. Richards puts forth and that Soskice (generally) seems to uphold. Richards's theory and various alternatives (such as those suggested by Black, Beardsley, Turbayne, Wheelwright, and Ricouer) are basic responses to or tensions against a more traditional concept of metaphor as a simple comparison or as a decorative (and perhaps emotive) substitution.[90] Many (although not all[91]) scholars trace the roots of this comparison theory back to Aristotle and point to a contemporary movement away from this view. McFague is typical when she writes:

> From Aristotle until recently, metaphor has been seen mainly as a poetic device to embellish or decorate. The idea was that in metaphor one used a word or phrase inappropriately but one need not have: whatever was being expressed could be said directly without the metaphor. Increasingly, however, the idea of metaphor as unsubstitutable is winning acceptance.[92]

In other words, the modern theory of "metaphor" is that it offers new information, a "surplus" of meaning as Ricouer put it, a meaning that is unique to the choice of metaphor. What is said with the metaphor can be said in no other way. A metaphor is a way of seeing one thing or reality in terms of another that creates something different in the very act of seeing.

Yet the metaphor is stubbornly paradoxical. Like scatter painting, it creates only by screening out. It omits or "filters" *and* it adds something new.[93] Functionally, it denotes *and* it connotes.[94] Structurally, it resembles *and* it dissembles.[95] Psychologically, it relates *and* it separates. Philosophically, it "is" *and* it "is not."[96]

Such descriptions and conceptions imply that metaphor is the link between two ideas or realities (subjects, meanings, domains, etc.). Until recently, there has been little disagreement over this basic assumption that there are two distinct but connected ideas. What has been contested, debated, examined and reexamined ever since Aristotle first came up with his four classes of metaphor[97] is the way or ways in which these two realities mirror or do not mirror each other, that is, their degree of similarity. Increasingly, there has been a movement toward an understanding that this degree of likeness may vary considerably from metaphor to metaphor. Of even more interest are recent theories that begin to question the basic distinction between the two ideas. Richards's tenor/vehicle relationship, for instance, strongly emphasizes the interactive aspects of the relationship. Soskice goes so far as to suggest that there really are not two *terms* involved at all, but instead a *"unity of subject-matter. . .* which yet draws upon two (*or more*) sets of associations" (emphasis added).[98] Soskice denies that metaphors have two subjects but allows that "each metaphor involves at least two different *networks* of associations."

Speaking from an altogether different arena, Douglas Hofstadter nonetheless catches much of the flavor of these recent theories of metaphor.

> Every mathematician has the sense that there is a kind of metric between ideas in mathematics—that all of mathematics is a network of results between which there are enormously many connections. In that network, some ideas are very closely linked; others require more elaborate pathways to be joined. . . . Other times two ideas are close because they are analogous, or even isomorphic.[99]

In like fashion, one can almost hear Soskice saying that every student of metaphor has the sense that there is a kind of metric between the ideas expressed in a metaphor—that a metaphor gives rise to a network of results between which there are many connections—that in that network, some ideas are closely linked, some being isomorphic, some requiring more elaborate pathways to be joined.

I bring Hofstadter's comments to the forefront here because it seems to me that the vision they depict bears the same relationship to metaphor as does mathematics to the high technology that created the San Francisco bridge. You cannot see the mathematics in the bridge and you cannot see the metric of mathematical ideas in the metaphor. Nonetheless, the one undergirds the other and, I believe, makes it more accessible. Of course, one's theory of metaphor, which is a "way of seeing," is necessarily dependent itself upon a particular way of seeing. In this sense there is a social element to metaphor. There are different attitudes about or levels of seeing metaphor. Different "cultures" see metaphor in different ways. Soskice and Romanyshyn, for instance, view the nature of metaphor from the "cultures" of linguistics and psychology respectively. I, having had considerable exposure to mathematics, tend to see it as the play between a unity and a duality or between the whole and its parts. This is the difference between standing on a bridge, scanning back and forth between two distinct realms, or standing at a great distance, where bridge and realms meld into *one* patterned whole, where the bridge is but the accent between hues of the same color.

Projecting this latter image to my original depiction of a bridge connecting the realms of the physical and the metaphysical, the play between unity and duality becomes the age-old question of whether or not the physical and metaphysical are basically the same thing. The correct response, in my opinion, is "yes." Yes, they are, and, yes, they are not the same thing. In chapter 2, I will explore this dualism from the standpoint of metaphorical language, and in chapter 4, I will develop a more mathematical presentation of it. For now, I wish only to suggest that the is-and-is-not nature of my response ("yes, they are the same, and yes, they are not") parallels the nature of metaphor. That is, my response is essentially metaphorical. It is metaphorical rather than literal.

But here again is one more ambiguity, one more contradiction, one more paradox. For I *mean* my response quite literally. I see the physical and the metaphysical as, *literally,* the same reality, and *also literally,* as not the same reality. This is not a new issue, for the conflict between the literal and the nonliteral comes up over and over again in the theory of metaphor. Usually this conflict is phrased as an opposition between a literal or a metaphorical meaning. Often, if confirmation or persuasion is desired one way or the other, the supporter of the literal interpretation runs off for mathematical reinforcements while the supporter of the metaphorical viewpoint shouts demeaning epithets, frequently of a religious nature, at the departing literalist. Philosopher Ralph Ross argues that it is a basic error to interpret metaphor or any other trope literally. "A metaphor," he says, "is not proof of any assertion. Political campaigns, for example, are replete with arguments like 'Don't elect a new candidate in this time of crisis. You shouldn't change horses in midstream.' Perhaps not, but a crisis isn't a stream and a candidate isn't, actually, a horse." Metaphor, he insists in almost the same breath, "is almost indispensable in writing or talking; it can be minimized only by the use of technical terms, and avoided totally only by the use of mathematics."[100]

A similar distancing between the literal and the metaphorical occurred in the vision of Thomas Hobbes three hundred years ago when he applauded the use of "words proper." Proper use of words led, according to Hobbes, to right reasoning; improper use led to absurdities, one of which he identified as "the use of Metaphors, Tropes, and other Rhetoricall [*sic*] figures. . . . For . . . in reckoning and seeking of truth, such speeches are not to be admitted."[101] Hobbes, significantly, did not practice what he preached. He employed the use of metaphors prolifically and strategically throughout his great political treatise, and he rested his most fundamental arguments on a metaphor of geometry. For "the skill of making, and maintaining Common-wealths, consisteth in certain Rules, as doth Arithmetique and Geometry."[102]

Such a vision dies slowly. Even Ross, who considers mathematics the only way to avoid metaphor totally, finds himself *on the very same page of his book* using mathematics to describe the essence of metaphor itself. "A metaphor," he says "is like a mathematical ratio."[103] Such seemingly incongruous arguments lend credence to Romanyshyn's contention (cited earlier) that contemporary science is *unaware* of its metaphorical character. Increasingly, however, this awareness of the link between mathematics and metaphor is surfacing. McFague, for example, writes that: "Perhaps it is most surprising to those who suppose metaphor belongs only in the arts and religion to discover it at the most basic level in mathematics: the numerical analogue. Seeing the similar number among otherwise disparate entities is a metaphorical act, as in six apples, six moons, six ideas, six generous acts."[104] Similarly, James Gleick notes that biologist Robert May, in making his contributions to the modern mathematical theory of chaos, held that mathematical "equations could *not* represent reality perfectly . . . they were just metaphors."[105] Wayne Booth argues that "even the great would-be literalists like Hobbes and Locke are finally metaphorists and critics of metaphor."[106]

BRIDGEWORK

So where does all this leave us? I am, of course, not sure where it leaves you, but the perspective from my tiny spot on the bridge is a cross between that of a critical realist and an objective idealist. As a critical realist, I affirm the existence of some sort of reality apart from myself and the world as I know it, what I have called the primordial chaos, and I believe that, at best, we can only approximate the experience of this reality. The vehicle for these "partial representations of limited aspects of the world as it interacts with us," to borrow from Barbour,[107] is metaphor (in its broadest sense). As an objective idealist, I am sympathetic to the position that "nothing exists which is not mental either in the sense of being either itself a mind or mode of mind, consciousness, or sentient experience, or in the sense of being what can only exist as an object of mind's awareness."[108] I, however, tend to capitalize Mind and equate it with Spirit (à la Leibniz). The mathematician in me is drawn to the irony, if not the exact sense, in Davis and Hersh's contention that the "typical working mathematician is a Platonist on weekdays and a formalist on Sundays."[109]

I am aware that some of what I have set forth so far seems contradictory, and, hence, lacks the very consistency that I contend in the Foreword that I am seeking. To claim, as I do above, that I am both a realist and an idealist may seem preposterous. To suggest, as I did in the section on *Metaphor,* that the literal and the metaphorical are not in direct opposition and that mind and matter are a dualism of *ways of seeing,* that is, a matter of perspective, borders on relativism to the point of absurdity. To suggest that theories championing esoteric subjects (e.g., meditation, the paranormal) are part of the same metaphysical outlook as those that see such things as scientific exploitations and spiritual degeneration seems to ignore basic differences to the point where the underlying thesis must be seriously questioned.

And what of that underlying theme itself? The thesis of this work, to summarize from the Foreword, is that mathematics has been used throughout history as a metaphorical connecting device between theology, religion, and metaphysics and that an intentional foregrounding of mathematics as such a metaphorical tool will benefit all three fields today. In this chapter I have investigated metaphysical thought relevant to this thesis. Drawing on a variety of viewpoints coming from a variety of subject areas, I have posited that we *know* something only by selectively abstracting, transforming, and assimilating elements of a primordial chaos through the filter of our thoughts, a filter that is shaped by our physical and cultural limitations as well as by the structure of our language. I have further posited that we are what we filter, that we, in fact, are part of the primordial chaos.

Interesting substantiation for this line of thought has come recently from a team of scientific mavericks at Santa Fe who are forging an entire new way of thinking in fields as diverse as eco-

nomics, artificial intelligence, and biology. Economist Brian Arthur, a member of this interdisciplinary "think tank," has contended that there are two types of scientists: "people who like
process and pattern, as opposed to people who are comfortable
with stasis and order."[110] It was his own predisposition toward the
first category that contributed to his "deja vu and excitement"
when he read of recent genetic discoveries suggesting that a cell's
DNA, long recognized as a basic blueprint for the cell, was really
more of a foreman. It was

> a kind of molecular-scale computer that directed how the cell was
> to build itself and repair itself and interact with the outside
> world. . . . Here it was again: patterns. An entire sprawling set of
> self-consistent patterns that formed and evolved and changed in
> response to the outside world. It reminded him of nothing so
> much as a kaleidoscope, where a handful of beads will lock in to
> one pattern and hold it—until a slow turn of the barrel causes
> them to suddenly cascade into a new configuration. A handful of
> pieces and an infinity of possible patterns. Somehow, in a way he
> couldn't quite express, this seemed to be the essence of life."[111]

I am drawn to the metaphysical speculations that seem to be
coming, albeit reluctantly, out of this Santa Fe Institute. Because it
captures much of the flavor of the metaphysical position I have
sketched in this chapter (including the discomfort that comes from
its speculative, absurd nature), I will relate here a fairly lengthy
passage from M. Mitchell Waldrop's rendition of the Santa Fe
experience with what is now emerging as "complexity."

> Like other Santa Fe folk, Arthur is hesitant when it comes to
> speculating about the larger meaning of all this. The results are
> still so—embryonic. And it's entirely too easy to come off sound-
> ing New Age and flaky. But like everyone else, he can't help
> thinking about the larger meaning.
>
>   You can look at the complexity revolution in almost theo-
> logical terms, he says. "The Newtonian clockwork metaphor is
> akin to standard Protestantism. Basically there's order in the
> universe. It's not that we rely on God for order. That's a little too
> Catholic. It's that God has arranged the world so that the order is
> naturally there if we behave ourselves. If we act as individuals in
> our own right, if we pursue our own righteous self-interest and
> work hard, and don't bother other people, then the natural equi-
> librium of the world will assert itself. Then we get the best of all

possible worlds—the one we deserve. That's probably not quite theological, but it's the impression I have of one brand of Christianity.

"The alternative—the complex approach—is total Taoist. In Taoism there is no inherent order. 'The world started with one, and the one became two, and the two became many, and the many led to myriad things.' The universe in Taoism is perceived as vast, amorphous, and ever-changing. You can never nail it down. The elements always stay the same, yet they're always rearranging themselves. So it's like a kaleidoscope: the world is a matter of patterns that change, that partly repeat, but never quite repeat, that are always new and different.

"What is our relation to a world like that? Well, we are made of the same elemental compositions. So we are a part of this thing that is never changing and always changing."[112]

We are part of something never changing and always changing. There is that blatant contradiction, again! The Santa Fe think-tankers seem to have a different view of the acceptability of contradiction. Computer scientist and AI (artificial intelligence) investigator John Holland, for instance, holds that

Consistency be damned: if two of his classifier rules disagreed with one another, let them fight it out on the basis of their performance, their proven contribution to the task at hand—not some preprogrammed choice made by a software designer.

"In contrast to mainstream artificial intelligence, I see competition as much more essential than consistency," he says. Consistency is a chimera, because in a complicated world there is no guarantee that experience will be consistent.[113]

The Santa Fe Institute, itself in existence only since 1986, is at the cutting edge of recent work on artificial life and complex adaptive systems, including economic systems. Much of this recent work centers on a borderline arena between order and chaos known, variously, as complexity, a phase transition, or behavior at the "edge" of chaos. While it has a purely mathematical interpretation, complexity also has analogous counterparts in those nebulous areas between solid matter and fluid matter, between Types I and II and Type III cellular automata classes, between halting and non-halting computation, and (possibly) between a state of existence that is "too static" for life and one that is "too noisy" for life. In their more speculative moments, the Santa Fe mavericks suggest that "maybe life began some four billion years ago as some kind of real phase transition in the primordial soup."[114]

Brian Arthur, as noted earlier, depicts two basic types of scientific personalities. Yet I wonder if there might not be an "in-between" personality as well, one that can, for instance, comfortably call itself both an idealist and a realist. I see myself as one of these in-betweeners. I like a certain amount of equilibrium and order. I also share Arthur's fascination with pattern and process. In many ways, I like contradiction. Thus it is not surprising that the metaphysical view I postulate is a worldview filled with inconsistency and sometimes even absurdity, for such discrepancies seem to be basic characteristics of "complexity."

It would be nice to have a fully developed, systematic epistemology, but I make no claims to having set forth such a philosophy. The metaphysics I suggest is just that—suggestive rather than conclusive. It is sketchy at best, the sort of shadowy impression you might have from the perspective of someone on a bridge looking over into a still-distant territory. "Shadowy" is an appropriate term. "Shadowy" implies a certain flexibility and a certain lack of clarity and precision. "Shadowy" is a subtheme that has emerged in the course of my chapter, a thesis secondary to the main thesis. "Shadowy" is the realm of the contradictory: contradictions and paradoxes lurk in the cave of shadows that we *know* through our filters.

For the most part, contradictions and other inconsistencies are unwelcome creatures in mainline modern-day science. Yet with a curious degree of consistency we find them popping up, even in realms other than pure mathematics, and it is often because of such inconsistencies that new discoveries are made. Recent reports that life not only can exist at above boiling temperatures, but that it may have *originated* at those temperatures, seem to contradict long-held theories regarding the original chemistry of life.[115] The many-worlds interpretation of quantum physics, first developed by American physicists John Wheeler and H. Everett in the 1950s, posits a theory of the object as paradoxically having existence in many different worlds at once.[116] Science abounds with such illustrations. Lewis Thomas captures the discomfort we often face when confronted with the "facts" of modern science when he says that

The twentieth-century world of quantum mechanics is the strangest of all worlds, incomprehensible to most of us and getting stranger all the time. Yet it is indisputably the real world. It seems to change everything we have always taken as reality into unreality, threatening our fixed ideas about time, space, and causality, leaving us in a new kind of uncertainty and bewilderment perhaps never before experienced by our species. A wave is a wave, but it is also a particle, depending on how we choose to observe it.[117]

A wave is a wave, and yet it is not a wave. Again, one runs straight into apparent inconsistency!

Ian Barbour has noted four fundamental criteria for assessing the validity of a scientific theory: agreement with data, coherence, scope, fertility.[118] "Coherence" cannot abide shadows. It will go to great lengths to avoid them. Yet curiously some of science's greatest fertility, its most fruitful produce, has arisen precisely because of such contradictions. Gödel's work with contradictions, for instance, led to Cantor's modern offspring, chaos theory, about which we will see more in chapter 3. The point is, there is a place *in science* for contradictions (and I daresay in religion, too, although the meaning there is less contested). Indeed, science feeds off contradictions.

Through the door of this subtheme of contradictions, I believe, mathematics makes its entrance into the metaphysics I have posited. Mathematics is the one field where contradictions are most easily managed and sometimes even resolved. It is contradictions and paradoxes, what he calls "Strange Loops," that fascinate Hofstadter and that, to a large degree, actually unify his work. Sometimes, he says in his introductory chapter, he uses "the term Tangled Hierarchy to describe a system in which a Strange Loop occurs. As we go on, the theme of Strange Loops will recur again and again. Sometimes it will be hidden, other times it will be out in the open; sometimes it will be right side up, other times it will be upside down or backwards."[119] And why should it be otherwise? As he points out in his chapter on "Minds and Thoughts," our thoughts are tangled hierarchies; in fact, "we all are bundles of contradictions, and we manage to hang together by bringing out only one side of ourselves at a given time.[120]

In this present work, too, the theme of contradictions and paradoxes will come up over and over again, as, indeed, it already has. Metaphor itself implies a paradox. Sometimes these contradictions will be "resolved," but other times they will continue to wave in the shadows, unwieldy, untamable. There they will exasperate the ordinary scientist—and sometimes you and me as well. How, for example, can I ever hope for consistency when I keep promoting such inconsistencies? Yet here is the catch—and for this I must ask you to suspend some of your normal criteria for judgement, especially if you are scientifically inclined. "The scientific

FIGURE 1.2
A Soapsuds Moebius Strip

way of thinking is so familiar to us today that we tend not to realize it is not so obvious that this must be the case," writes physicist Richard Morris in *The Edges of Science*.[121] Morris then goes on to reiterate a theme of his own—that the criteria of testability, or what Barbour might call agreement with data, may no longer always be an appropriate way of thinking.[122] Similarly, perhaps Barbour's criteria of "coherence" also needs to be reexamined. Perhaps science itself calls for such a reexamination. For from the perspective of someone on the bridge, someone peering across into the distant horizon, these shadowy inconsistencies not only are to be expected, they are *entirely appropriate and absolutely essential*. In short, to be consistent, we *must be* inconsistent.

So, from the bridge itself I look in one direction and see the critical realists, and I look in the other direction and see the objective idealists.[123] Alternatively, I imagine myself off the bridge altogether, perhaps flying high above it, getting a meta-view of it and myself on it. What I see resembles what in mathematics is called a Moebius strip,[124] a "two-sided" configuration that only *appears* to have two sides (see figure 1.2).[125] Here, again, is the play between duality and unity that I suggested had something to do with the paradoxical nature of metaphor. It is to this play between duality and unity (or, alternatively, between the one and the many) that I turn next as we examine in more depth the terms "sign," "symbol," "metaphor," and "model" and their use in both theology and mathematics.

CHAPTER 2

Image-ination in Mathematics and Religion

BLURRED BOUNDARIES

Signs, symbols, metaphors, and models share a commonality of belonging to the human image-ination: they all evoke or create an image through which the human mind perceives the basic resemblances between things.[1] A sign carries, among its many dictionary meanings, the notion that it is an "indication, token; a mark or symbol having an accepted and specific meaning." A symbol is "a token, pledge, sign by which one infers a thing." A metaphor has the sense of "an implied comparison" or a "figure of speech in which one thing is applied to another," while a symbol is "something that stands for or represents another thing," and a model is a "preliminary representation of something."[2] Even these partial lexical definitions indicate clearly that the distinctions between these four terms are easily blurred.

In this chapter, I hope to bring some clarity to the meanings of these terms, or, at the least, to make the confusion more understandable. Why, you may wonder, do I find it desirable to devote time and energy to such a project? After all, native speakers of a language *often* have to pick and choose between several closely related terms, and they pretty much do so without difficulty. The subtleties of the distinctions are built into the language culture, and choosing among them is a little like deciding between "rose" or "red." You get a feel for which word best fits the particular situation you are describing, and you go with it.

Blurred distinctions, however, often lead to confusion, ambiguity, and lack of communication with all its incipient problems. Perhaps a personal example will serve to illustrate my point. Several years ago, when I was just beginning to make the transition from mathematics professor to minister, I wrote a paper for one of my professors. In it, I tried to integrate the concepts of mathematics and religion.[3] In particular, I explored the possibility that mathematics is a system of symbols analogous to the system of symbols that some scholars call religion.[4] I made statements such as, "mathematics offers us some of humankind's oldest symbols" and "mathematics abounds in symbols." When I received my paper back, my professor commented tersely that I was comparing oranges with fork lifts. He systematically crossed out each place where I had written "symbol" and replaced it with "sign." A symbol, he held, has a totally different meaning in mathematics than it does in the humanities. From the perspective of those involved in the humanities or in semeiotics, mathematics is composed exclusively of signs. He then suggested (chauvinistically) that if I really wanted "to understand where and how math functions, [I should] trace the grades of Japanese students in U.S. colleges. The more math, the higher their grades—until they get into the humanities where passing is really difficult."

Now, in this man's view, mathematics "relate[s] to nothing in the real world." To my eyes, nature is just mathematics you can touch. Not surprisingly, our different "ways of seeing" crystallized in a clash over terminology. This clash triggered disappointment and misunderstanding on both of our parts. However, it also sent me back to the books to take a closer look at "symbol" and "sign." Our "poor" communication ultimately became the initial motivating factor behind this chapter.

I quickly discovered, however, that it was not an easy task to acquire clarity with regard to the meanings of these terms. My search produced more questions than answers. Soon, I had enlarged the scope of my consideration to include the terms "metaphor" and "model," and I stop now with these four mainly in the interests of practicality. Based on my own experience, I expected to find much ambiguity with regard to the meanings of these four terms among professionals in both mathematics and religion. The results of an empirical study I subsequently designed and conducted[5] strongly confirm this expectation. Individual surveys distinguished between the four terms in fairly cohesive, consistent manners. But when the comments were grouped according to genre (for example, all comments about sign, all about symbol), mixed and even contradictory responses occurred. The following statements illustrate those on the completed surveys:

> Sign and symbol are very similar in meaning.
> I don't have a clear distinction between signs and symbols.
> [A] symbol is a metaphor.
> Signs . . . can have a metaphorical sense.
> I don't see any real distinction between sign and symbol, except that symbol seems to be the more common term.
> Symbols participate in reality.
> A sign not only points to some reality, it is involved in it.
> Symbols . . . indicate meaning by participating in the reality *sign*ified. (emphasis added)
> Metaphor is a symbol.
> A metaphor is a species of symbol.
> A model is a complex of metaphors and symbols.

It appears that even the select group of professionals from mathematics/science and religion/philosophy who participated in this study were confused about the boundaries between sign, symbol, metaphor, and model.

One particularly striking result of the study deals with the relationship between mathematics and "metaphor." Professionals in both fields recognized at least some relevance of the terms "sign," "symbol," and "model" to both mathematics and religion, but *none* of the professionals acknowledged any connection between "metaphor" and mathematics. The study, as a whole, suggests that mathematics is not valued in our culture as a metaphorical language, nor is it seen as contributing much to religion. As the Foreword and chapter 1 of this present work indicate, I disagree that mathematics has little to contribute to religion; and I suspect that the current undervaluing of mathematics as a metaphorical language stems from lack of awareness, rather than hard fact. To investigate this contention, and to minimize unfortunate communication difficulties, we must first investigate more closely the nature of the boundaries between the four related terms involved.

A CONTINUUM

One possible way to clarify the relationships among sign, symbol, metaphor, and model is to locate the four concepts on a simple continuum. Such an organizing device could "place" the various concrete   abstract

FIGURE 2.1
Simple Continuum

terms according to the degree to which their associated images are concrete or abstract.[6] (See figure 2.1) Sallie McFague alludes, perhaps unconsciously, to such a continuum when she writes:

> If our thesis holds that *all* thought is indirect, then all concepts and theories are metaphorical in the sense that they too are constructions; they are indirect attempts to interpret reality, which never can be dealt with directly. Concepts and theories, however, are at the far end *of the continuum* and rarely expose their *metaphorical* roots. (Emphasis added, last two instances)[7]

Her implication is that concepts and theories belong to a continuum of metaphorical language.

If we interpret "language" in its broadest sense, so that it includes, for example, various forms of nonverbal communication, then it is appropriate to stretch the limits of "metaphor" to likewise include nonverbal interactions and exchanges. Such an extension, it should be noted, is directly opposed to the narrow "figure of speech" limitations that Soskice insists any understanding of "metaphor" must observe. However, it is well within the confines of McFague's interpretation, for she observes that "increasingly, over the last two centuries . . . metaphor has been seen not as a trope but as the way language and, more basically, thought works."[8] Accordingly, I label the continuum in figure 2.1 a "Continuum of Metaphorical Language."[9]

Precisely where should we locate "sign," "symbol," "metaphor," and "model" on this continuum? A review of works by scholars who have devoted much attention to these terms turns out to be suggestive but not conclusive. Comments made by such experts tend to be as ambiguous and contradictory as those from my surveys. To illustrate:

1. By signs we understand all marks that indicate the facts of a definite object. (Diethelm, 215)
2. Symbols have one characteristic in common with signs; they point beyond themselves to something else. The red sign at the street corner points to the order to stop the movements of

cars at certain intervals . . . signs do not participate in the reality of that to which they point, while symbols do. (Tillich, 42)

3. Every mental model is, of course, also a sign; and not only is modeling an indispensable characteristic of the human world, but also it permeates the entire organic world, where, indeed, it developed. (Sebeok, 57)

4. All words are symbols, although not all symbols are words. . . . Because symbols are arbitrary . . . we may be tempted to infer that no symbol is a better sign than any other. (Ross, 164–65)

5. [A] sign "is either an *icon,* an *index,* or a *symbol.*" But this plainly cannot be so . . . to allow for recognitions of differences in degree, not signs, but rather *aspects* of signs are being classified . . . [O]ne and the same sign can—and I would insist, must—"function at once as an icon and symbol as well as an index." (Sebeok, 133)

6. In its simplest definition, a symbol is a conventional sign. (Ross, 164)

7. Symbols are the hardware realizations of concepts. (Hofstadter, 350)

8. Metaphor occurs in the already purified universe of the *logos,* while the symbol hesitates on the dividing line between *bios* and *logos.* (Ricouer, 59)

9. Symbolic statements . . . are not so much a way of knowing and speaking as they are sedimentation and solidification of metaphor. (McFague, *Metaphorical Theology,* 16)

10. Man cannot live without symbols. Whatever may distinguish him from the beasts here is one clear mark of difference. He creates symbols, he responds to symbols, he communicates through symbols. (Dillistone, "Function," 104)

11. Metaphors are just the linguistic surface of symbols. (Ricouer, 69)

12. Metaphor is indigenous to all human learning from the simplest to the most complex. In the animal world, and in our own beginnings, all that is known is bodily sensations. But unlike the other animals for whom the meanings of things are largely instinctive and adhere to the things signified, the essence of our uniqueness is that we use our bodily sensations as signs to stand for something else. Signs become symbols: the thing stands for and represents something else. (McFague, *Metaphorical Theology,* 32–33)

13. We are the model makers. . . . [W]hen we invent a human model, we are that which is modeling itself. (Bois, 230)

14. [A] model is a metaphor with staying power. (McFague, *Models of God,* 34)

15. To speak of "models" in connection with a scientific theory already smacks of the metaphorical. (Black, 219)

16. [M]odels . . . are more fully developed than metaphors and yet they are less abstract than concepts. (Barbour, 46)

It should be noted that all of these statements are taken out of context from theories and points of view that are generally consistent within themselves. But of interest here is not the consistency or lack of it in any *one* perspective; of interest, rather, is that, *as a whole,* there is lack of consensus or confusion among the scholars about when and how to use the four words. Statements 3, 4, 5, 6, 11, 12, 14, 15, and 16 all attempt to elucidate the meaning associated with one of the four terms in ways that involve, and sometimes even identify as definitive, another of the terms. Statements 10, 12, 13, and to some degree 3 all reflect on the distinguishing features between humans and other life-forms. What is interesting here is that to one person this distinctive characteristic is best represented by the word "symbol"; to another by "metaphor"; to another by "model," which is, to yet another, "also a sign."

On the other hand, statements 1, 2, 7, 8, 9, 11, and 16 suggest possible placement on our continuum. Signs are basic building blocks—they indicate *the facts of a definite object.* Signs, like the red sign at the street corner, are concrete. Symbols seem to be more concrete than metaphors: they are *hardware* realizations, *less linguistic* and abstract, a *solidification* of metaphor. Models are *more fully developed* than metaphors but *less abstract* than concepts. On this basis, which is largely an intuitive judgement informed by these scholarly statements, we would locate the terms, left to right, concrete to abstract, as in figure 2.2. Such a placement is consistent with an understanding that sees a red light as a sign, a cross as a symbol, "we bear our own crosses" as metaphor, and the parable of Jesus on the cross as a model of God.[10]

```
    sign    symbol    metaphor    model
```

concrete   abstract

FIGURE 2.2
Continuum of Metaphorical Language

This ordering, however, is too restrictive. There is overlap between these terms that the continuum in figure 2.2 does not take into account. Signs and symbols are closely related and often interchanged (e.g., "a symbol is a conventional sign"). Likewise, there tends to be a symbiosis between symbols/metaphors ("metaphors are just the linguistic surface of symbols") and metaphors/models ("a model is a metaphor"). One way to deal with this overlap is to consider sign, symbol, metaphor, and model to be *cluster words,* where each term is really a cluster of related terms. The following clusters, compiled using the survey results, the quotations from scholarly sources cited earlier, and the use of an ordinary dictionary, provide additional clues regarding both distinctions and similarities among the four cluster terms.

sign	*symbol*	*metaphor*	*model*
icon	token	figure	copy
mark	representation	representation	duplicate
emblem	type	comparison	facsimile
code	figure	simile	miniature
pledge		trope	pattern
omen		analogy	design
indication		parable	map
portent			analogy
token			allegory
clue			fable
premonition			archetype
divination			paradigm
			prototype
			ideal
			concept
			theory

The distinctions help us to define the terms. A sign, for example, is a cluster term referring to the representation of something in terms of something else such that it produces a *visual picture* in our minds—a literal sign, such as a stop sign; a code that must be deciphered; a pledge or omen that can be seen, such as rain being considered a sign from the gods; the visible list of thesaurus-like terms (above) that provides us with clues. A symbol, on the other hand, is the representation of something in terms of something else such that it produces a *sensory picture:* a cross is a symbol because it appeals to our senses, causing us to interact emotionally with it. A metaphor might be thought of as the representation of one thing in terms of another that produces a *word picture,* either spoken or written. Model refers to a cluster of methods—mathematical formulas, blueprints, maps, miniature scale model, and so forth—for presenting a *structural picture* of an overall design or plan. All four cluster terms, thus, form a mode of metaphorical language that represents one thing in terms of another, the basic distinctions being that the particular mode is primarily a visual, sensory, word, or structural image. I use these four terms throughout the remainder of this work with this general understanding.

These four interpretations are consistent with a general movement from the visual or concrete to the structural or abstract. Yet, again, we must be troubled by an overlap that blurs even these basic definitions.[11] A metaphor, for instance, may offer *primarily* a word picture, but it very often (at least if it is "alive") also elicits a more emotive sensory response. Such similarities among the cluster words are likewise informative: it becomes immediately easier to see how the four terms could sometimes take on double meanings. The cross, for instance, can be legitimately described as both a sign and a symbol, but somewhat more of a symbol than a sign. One possible way to indicate this tendency on our continuum would be to allow for shading between the four basic cluster words. Like the continuum of the rainbow, each cluster word is a distinct color, but the borders are more "blends" than "demarcations."

CONTINUUMS

Although the "Continuum of Metaphorical Language" gives us one way to understand the differences between common usages of "sign," "symbol," "metaphor," "model," and their related terms, it does so only at the cost of filtering out many other possible relations. Such omission, as we saw in chapter 1, necessarily accompanies any process of abstraction or any use of metaphorical language.[12] Consider, for example, the familiar CBS logo, which is an "eye" with the letters "CBS" imprinted in the "pupil."

This (trade)mark might be best described as a sign (with all its concreteness) *and* a metaphor,[13] for it calls forth the *new* suggestion that CBS has a special vision all its own, that it acts, perhaps, as an extra eye to supplement the human ones, that in some ways it *is* an eye. This (trade)mark has more associations, more interpretations, more levels of understanding to it than, say, the common

FIGURE 2.3
Lufthansa Trademark

stop light or even the similar (trade)mark in figure 2.3. The Lufthansa (trade)mark is an example of an icon, a sign that bears a striking resemblance to that which it represents. The CBS sign (or so its designers would hope) also bears a resemblance. But the likeness is much more subtle, and hence there is correspondingly more room for *dis*similarity.[14]

Something of the same situation can be found in the cluster term "model." Modern scholars tend to agree that several different kinds of models exist. These range from the scale/pictorial, to the analogical/mathematical, to the theoretical/conceptual, or, following Black, to the "root" metaphors of Stephen Pepper.[15] Again, both these situations—the variations in signs and the variations in models—could be labeled as changes in degree of concreteness. Certainly, for instance, the scale or miniature model is more concrete than Pepper's worldviews. Similar cases could be sketched for symbols and metaphors.

However, there is a significant difference between the continuum in these illustrations and the one charted in figure 2.2. In particular, the continuum in figure 2.2 dealt with the degree of concreteness or abstraction of the sign, symbol, metaphor, or model considered as a *unit* in itself. In our latter examples, we are really dealing with a degree of isomorphism or correspondence between the cluster term and the reality it refers to, between referee and referent (see figure 2.4). Thus, we have a second kind of continuum by which to organize these terms—one dependent upon the degree of similarity or identity between a *duality* embodied by the cluster term.

McFague's interpretation of the literalness (or openness) that

---

low resemblance   high isomorphism

FIGURE 2.4
A Continuum of Isomorphism

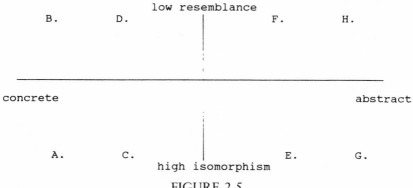

FIGURE 2.5
Expanded Continuum of Metaphorical Language

we attach to metaphors and models fits interestingly into this continuum. For her, literalism leads to irrelevance, to "dead" metaphors and models, and to idolatry. "When a model becomes an idol, the hypothetical character of the model is forgotten and what ought to be seen as *one* way to understand our relationship with God has become identified with *the* way. In fact, as happens when a model becomes an idol, the distance between image and reality collapses. . . ."[16] In other words, referee and referent are taken as identical: the isomorphism between the two is complete.

A technique for combining our two continuums into one more manageable "model" may be taken straight out of Cartesian geometry. We simply intersect the axes as in figure 2.5. Like other models, this expanded continuum adds something new to the way in which we see. By providing a larger scope of placement, each cluster term takes on greater subtleties in meaning, and the appropriateness or inappropriateness of the labels we give these subtleties becomes more apparent.

A few examples will illustrate these effects of an expanded continuum. To look at the extremes, the Lufthansa icon, having both a high degree of concreteness and a high degree of correspondence to its referent, would be placed in the lower left-hand corner of the grid, in region A. The CBS "eye," having a less direct resemblance to its referent, would be closer to region B, and a portent or sign of divination might actually be in region B. The Roman numeral III or the Hindu-Arabic symbol "3" bear a high degree of isomorphism to the sense of "threeness" that they call forth, and hence they would be located around region C. A cross,[17] by contrast, has little such resemblance and would be better placed nearer to region D. What McFague calls an idolatrous metaphor, such as "God *is* father," would be in region E, whereas "God *as* father" would be in region F. The best spot for a scale or miniature model would be in region G, and for Pepper's root-metaphors in region H.

Examining this expanded continuum, we begin to notice that the upper portion of the graph contains a range of meanings in which *each* cluster term is used in ways we commonly think of as "metaphorical"—the metaphorically applied sign, the symbol that conveys meaning far beyond what it actually depicts, "God as father," and so forth. Those senses that fall in the lower portion of the graph are more "literal" ones. Thus, the vertical band in the continuum that we *call* "metaphor" is not necessarily what we commonly *think* of as metaphorical. Furthermore, normal usage of "metaphorical" seems to imply a pluralism of associated meanings.[18] As the resemblance between referee and referent diminishes, the range of meanings and implications we have to choose from widens—the CBS sign, for instance, suggests several different possible interpretations. Likewise, the more isomorphic this relationship is, the more restricted are our choices of interpretation. Total isomorphism implies one choice, for here we find total identity. As we examine this grid, a heretofore hidden aspect of *quantification* associated with common usage of metaphorical language becomes increasingly apparent.

This expanded continuum could itself be numerically expanded. A third continuum (axis) could be added, perpendicular to the first two. Perhaps an added continuum could represent the degree to which each term is emotive or the degree to which each is artificially invented, aspects to which scholars (e.g., Tillich, McFague) have attached much importance in their discussion of symbol/metaphor. Both of these characteristics have thus far been "filtered out" by my two-axis model. If one is willing to set aside the limitations of three-dimensional space and use the language of mathematics, *both* of these axes could be included, forming a four-continuum model. In fact, any number of axes or dimensions could be added to our analysis, and theoretically at least, the distinctions between our key terms could be ever more precisely refined and "located." Presumably, the complex arrangement that would result would stimulate further new insights and questions. My guess (untested) is that it would reveal a more integrated and holistic way of seeing.

A problem with this continuum approach, particularly with a multimodal approach resulting from a multi-axis system, necessarily arises here. Any distribution along a continuum implies that a value, or at least an average value, has been assigned to each of the various characteristics of the terms. In the case of symbols, metaphors, and so forth, the boundaries between even broad cluster values may be so complex as to render such an assignment impossible. A cross, for example, may be a highly abstract symbol in one context and a highly concrete one in another, as in symbolizing the abstract story/myth of the resurrection versus symbolizing some particular, that is, concrete, personal experience that had intense emotional impact. Likewise, the cross might be a highly emotional symbol in one situation, yet carry only minimal emotional impact in another. In either event, the average value assigned to the symbol "cross" for purposes of placement on the axis-system would be difficult to ascertain. In general, the more complex the modal system, the more difficult it would be to determine boundaries of any sort. The resulting integration and holism would then be analogous to the *interpenetration* that occurs when cream is partially stirred into coffee or when different colored threads are interwoven into a tapestry. In other words, the blurring may be so intense that it becomes possible to discern pattern, but no definable boundaries at all.[19]

This problem would become increasingly more noticeable with increased modality. For our present purposes, the two-axis version raises boundary questions sufficient to challenge us for some time. Of particular interest is the relationship between what we call literal or factual and what we call nonliteral or metaphorical. Does literal mean "concrete" in the sense implied (in varying degrees) by the entire left half of the model? Does it mean "isomorphic" in the sense implied by the bottom portion of the graph? Does it embody both senses, thus enveloping virtually everything in the model except those metaphors/models that bear a low resemblance to what they represent, that is, those placed in the upper right hand portion of the grid? If so, then perhaps the model would be better labeled an "Expanded Continuum of *Literal* Language." It is to these questions, to the issue of the literal versus the metaphorical, that I turn next.

LITERAL VERSUS METAPHORICAL

Bois pointed out in his theory of cultural revolutions that there was a time in history, namely, the era of the great Greek thinkers, when humankind began to distinguish between the natures of different things. Others have similarly suggested that the accomplishment of these ancient thinkers was to develop critical consciousness so that, for the first time, it became possible to differentiate between the literal and the nonliteral. According to this view, the world must have appeared much differently to the forerunners of the early Greeks: "The metaphors and figures which primitive men used are not . . . mere embellishments on a literal description of rocks, trees, and battles which otherwise resemble our own, but are indications of a wholly different way of seeing the world; a world in which blood is actually boiled, winds whistled and waves murmured."[20]

An interesting possibility arises when we generalize a view on metaphorical language, put forth by Barfield, Vico, Ferre, and others, that holds that language was never pre-metaphorical. Barfield argues, for example, that, contrary to customary belief, primitive peoples did not coin their language as "plain labels for plain objects."[21] Language, according to Barfield, follows a historical progress that is commonly assumed to originate as a *born literal* reference to material objects or situations, then to expand to a *metaphorical* form with both a primary and secondary meaning (a vehicle with a tenor), and finally to crystallize in an *achieved literalness*. Sometimes, this achieved literalness is such that the language actually refers to immaterial, rather than material, entities.[22] Barfield, however, totally abandons the notion of a *born literal* beginning for words, claiming that it is impossible to believe in a "*first* metaphor in a wholly literal world." "Indeed," he says, "it is impossible to believe because consciousness and symbolization are simultaneous and correlative."[23] A "literal" word or meaning, for Barfield, is roughly equivalent to a vehicle without a tenor or (possibly) a tenor without a vehicle. In any case, literalness "is a quality which some words have achieved in the course of their history; it is not a quality with which the first words were born."[24]

F. W. Dillistone, in a commentary on Barfield's argument, claims that "the whole purpose of Barfield's paper was to urge that *literalness* is a comparatively late development in the history of language. It is the product of the craving for order and permanence which undoubtedly has a legitimate place in society and which has brought immense benefits to mankind."[25] He summarizes Barfield's framework as being a movement, not from the literal to the symbolic back to the literal, but, rather, from the "symbolic to literal, and then back to symbolic."[26] What captures my interest here is the resemblance of this pattern to the wave/particle theory of light that modern physics has charted out. Now it is a wave, now it is a particle. Now it is a figurative format, now it is a literal recounting.

A movement from a metaphorically framed epistemology to one that is literal, then to a metaphorical, then to a literal, ad infinitum, is plausible. Yet it seems likely to me that the real achievement of our current cultural revolution is not that we are moving from one or another of these frameworks (and the chicken/egg question arises again). Rather, the real achievement seems that we are moving to a "meta" position that allows us to recognize the nature of the movement. If I am right, this "meta" position is something new (at least as a whole) to humankind: it is a new sort of consciousness.

I draw here an analogy to a currently popular optical illusion —that of the old woman, young girl (see figure 2.6). Looked at one

FIGURE 2.6
Old Woman/Young Girl Illusion

way, the picture is that of an old woman. Looked at another, it is of a young woman. When you see it as *one* of these two forms, it is impossible to see it as the other. Somewhat similarly, if our vision of the world is metaphorical, it may be impossible to see it as literal and vice versa. However, a third possibility exists. For the picture can be seen, as in fact we *do* see it today, as neither an old woman nor a young woman but as *potentially either* one of them. This potentiality, furthermore, is something we can actually experience in either form at will. Much the same thing applies, I believe, to this world in which we live.[27]

In chapter 1, I outlined a metaphysics in which the human being is a filtering device for a preexistent primordial chaos.[28] The old woman/young woman illusion makes a good, albeit approximate and imperfect, image for this metaphysics. Like the literal and metaphorical *weltanschauungs,* the two women represent different ways of seeing (filtering) from a realm of "no-knowledge." "No-knowledge" I mean in the sense used by R. G. H. Siu to put forth a radical view on the relationship between science and mysticism: according to Siu, there are three modes of knowing—rational, intuitive, and no-knowledge, that is, a mode devoid of time and shape, a mode that transcends events and qualities.[29] The human way of seeing corresponds to a rational mode in that it is concrete, physical, dependent upon empirical data and verification, and so forth. In short, it corresponds to things we often associate with the "literal." The human way is also intuitive, emotional, flexible, abstract, and so forth—what I have here been calling "metaphorical." Just as the two pictures in the illusion, though vastly different, are both women, so too, I want to emphasize, these two modes of filtering are both wholly human.

Paradoxically and significantly, each mode "takes up the whole picture" as well. Nothing is completely omitted in the imaging, although some aspects are "texturized" (hidden? abstracted?) so that they are less overt. By extension, the optical illusion then suggests that the rational and the intuitive, the literal and the metaphorical, are distinct but inseparable human ways of seeing that both do and do not totally reflect the primordial chaos of non-ordered reality. One of the most important implications of such a relationship between the literal and the nonliteral, the rational and the intuitive, is precisely that they *are* in relationship. I understand Dillistone to mean much the same thing when he says (using slightly different language): "The bodily and the mental, the physical and the spiritual, the literal and the symbolical must be held to-gether in vital dialectical relationship. No clear-cut dividing line can ever be drawn between the two."[30]

If the literal and the nonliteral are so completely intertwined, then the line between truth and fiction, fact and nonfact is similarly nebulous. One of the most obvious implications of such a possi-bility is that experimental scientific validation may not be sufficient to establish the truth of hypotheses.[31] Although most scientists reject this position, contemporary writings on the philosophy of science often "adumbrate" it, as sociologist Sal Restivo puts it. "We may be approaching a time when it will not appear incredible to consider the possibility that 'truth value' can be determined by a state of consciousness independent of the direct physical manipula-tion of variables in experiments."[32] Restivo goes on to speculate that truth is thus a manifestation of different ways of attending to things. He speculates further that if "states of consciousness are based on changes in how we attend to things, it may be possible to correlate states of consciousness with criteria for determining "truth value," and furthermore to show that these criteria are inter-related and interdependent."[33] Truth, thus, becomes context-bound.[34] No longer can it be measured or otherwise determined by its degree of resemblance to some singular, external standard.[35]

Leaving now the realm of metaphysics, which we have (again) only barely touched, and retreating to our bridge of metaphor, we suddenly find that the bridge has shifted. Our "Expanded Contin-uum of Metaphorical Language" seems to be bent so that the distance is narrowed between the two ends. The "high literal" end and the "high metaphorical" end appear to be much closer than the continuum warrants. In fact, it is questionable that there is any distance between them at all. Perhaps this new way of seeing, the way that comes from "going back" across a bridge, requires an alternative ordering device to help us understand the boundaries between sign, symbol, metaphor, model, and their related terms.

KALEIDOSCOPE

One such device is the common kaleidoscope. Let us assume, for the moment, that all of our language, in the very broadest sense of the term, forms a sort of kaleidoscopic structure. All our signs, symbols, metaphors, models, and all other language-related notions are gathered together by this structuring device, much as the expanded continuum gathered them together in a different ordering sequence. The kaleidoscope offers a nonlinear, holistic structure that is hierarchy-resistant, flexible, and readily transferable to the sort of metaphysical outlook that I have also been developing. It lacks, however, the strength of precision and clarity offered by the continuum: our sense of the distinctions between the various language forms, for instance, will be less well developed and refined with this new structuring tool.

Given a kaleidoscope of language, however, we see that the differences between the various terms are ones of fine-tuning. Let us allow that there is a realm of language from which we draw in order to express ourselves. Just as the kaleidoscope filters into our eye a certain pattern or design, so, too, do we select from this realm until we settle on some particular word or words or other language communication (e.g., nonverbal signals). Change the filter ever so slightly and a new pattern or design emerges. Give it a swift twirl and the design that appears may be totally unlike its predecessor. Some patterns are tremendously stuffed with "verbiage." At other times, only blank white space appears.

So, too, with the distinctions between our cluster terms. A sign and a symbol, for instance, may share varying degrees of the same pattern. When the patterns are very dissimilar, the two terms represent essentially distinct ideas, and calling them by the same term seems erroneous and misleading. But when the patterns are highly similar, it is natural to call them by the same name. A similar argument holds for the difference between what we call literal and what is nonliteral: the differences between them are ones of gradation. Gradation was present in our continuum as well, of course, but the kaleidoscope offers some new interpretations on the relationship.

For one thing, it is easier to see how a sign and a metaphor (for example) might be highly similar even though they are not linearly contingent to each other—they simply share a great many of the same "design" characteristics or elements. Secondly, literalness (or lack of it) becomes more a matter of personal or collective preference than a measurement of vehicle or a testimony to resemblance. It is as though two people looked at the same design in the kaleidoscope, and one said "Oh, wow, I really like that," while the other said, "No, that's not for me." When fact is considered a matter of taste (cultural, psychological, or whatever) rather than empirical accuracy, new possibilities for communication arise. Thirdly, the kaleidoscope image focuses our attention much more consistently than does the continuum on the role of the filter in differentiating between the various cluster terms. The "design" seen is a function of how it is attended to, of the way in which it is filtered.

The filter interpretation of metaphor has been both enthusiastically supported (e.g., by Black) and heavily criticized (e.g., by Soskice). Since I employ this notion consistently, both in discussing metaphor and in outlining a particular metaphysical view, it warrants closer examination. Soskice's objections are especially provocative and articulate, and I cite them here at length.

> The notion of filtering has particularly come under attack, for while we may use "filtering" to explain how a metaphor works, we are then left to explain how the filtering works. What takes place and what constraints are exercised upon it? Why are some commonplaces selected and not others? How does the screening of interpretation in a metaphor differ from that which presumably takes place in understanding non-metaphorical utterances such as "I love strawberries" (as opposed to "I love my mother")?
>
> Another and more serious criticism of "filtering" is that this term is inconsistent with Black's claim that metaphors do not merely pick out antecedently existing similarities but in some cases actually create them; a filter, at best, brings out what was already there. And, finally, the explanatory notion of "filtering" is in conflict with the explanatory notion of "interaction", and particularly with Black's contention that both subjects of the metaphor are illumined by their interaction, for this double effect is difficult to reconcile with the one-directional connotations of "filtering".[36]

To Soskice's first objection, that explaining metaphor via filtering creates the need to explain filtering itself, I can only agree. She is right, at least on the philosophical level, which is the realm of interest here. Perhaps there will come a day when we *can* explain filtering, but surely it will be at the cost of bringing forth some other equally mystifying term. Soskice herself notes that it is unfair to demand exactly how this filtering takes place without also providing a clear understanding of the type of answer expected. If the answer involves describing a mechanism by which the mind understands language, figurative or otherwise, then, she says, "Black is justified in maintaining silence, for this is not a question which philosophy can answer."[37]

To her second contention, that a filter is uncreative, that it only brings out what is already there, I reply with a clear and unambiguous "yes and no." A kaleidoscope clearly has a limited capacity. After all, only so many designs are possible, so many potential combinations. But bounded does not necessarily mean finite, and when it comes to the creation of something new through some unique metaphorical use, it may well be that the ultimate source of "language" is bounded but not finite.[38] In any case, even a good kaleidoscope, limited as it is, has enough possible variations to convince me that I am seeing something "new." "New," to be trite, is in the eye of the beholder.

Finally, Soskice's objection that filtering is a one-way process and hence noninteractive seems to me to be seriously questionable. Again, considering the kaleidoscope, the design that "shows" inevitably alters the design that does not show. That we cannot see the effect of a metaphor on that from which it is filtered does not imply that no interaction has occurred: it implies, rather, that we may not be able to perceive that the interaction has occurred. Modern science, if it has done nothing else, surely has provided us with countless instances where an interaction occurs beyond our immediate sensory perception. It is not hard to imagine similar interactions that exist beyond our perception even when perception is aided with the best of technology—or with the best of our mind-power.

Filtering might be better considered as "emphasizing." For those who hold, as I do, that human thought and human language are intertwined and co-forming, Bois's conception of abstracting as filtering becomes one of language emphasis. Our capacity to *consciously* know depends upon emphasis upon our perceiving faculties from, following Price, what we *unconsciously* know. Likewise, I would add, our unconscious knowledge is altered, affected, adapted, and so forth, by our conscious emphasis.

Several philosophical questions arise immediately from this way of thinking. To what degree is our thought emphasis a matter of our personal choice or will? Might it be possible to exercise control over this emphasis just as we can control the kaleidoscope? If we do learn new ways to control our filtering and selection processes, are we perhaps inviting new interpretations of things beyond our customary or "normal" perception of reality? If we ourselves are filters (as I suggested in chapter 1) and do develop new ways to influence our filtering processes, are we not in some way going beyond our current human capacities? Might we be evolving into a new mode of existence, one that is in some way meta-human? Could this be a Whiteheadian unending process of becoming? Or are we ever moving toward some ultimate absolute destiny?

These are only a few of the questions invited by my metaphorical kaleidoscope.[39] Such questions have long formed the domain of our most fundamental religious endeavor. I do not pretend to have conclusive answers for these questions. What I have, perhaps, is a slightly new starting point—a perspective that allows us to struggle with such questions with the benefit of modern mathematics. From this perspective we may well begin, if not to formulate satisfactory "answers," then at least to dialogue with one another in a new way that may better prepare us to deal with the challenges and demands of modern society.

MATHEMATICS AND METAPHORICAL LANGUAGE

Thus far in this chapter on "Image-ination in Mathematics and Religion" I have used a variety of images to talk about imagistic language. But I have addressed the topic of religion only indirectly and the topic of mathematics hardly at all. I have (I hope) firmed up the foundation I began to lay in the first chapter by setting forth a holistic structure of metaphorical language and by showing how closely it is interwoven with a metaphysics of knowledge. In so doing, I have touched upon many viewpoints of the major contemporary theologians who have dedicated much of their scholarly work to a study of metaphor in *religion*. I have, on the whole, chosen not to reexamine the many specific metaphors that are already so well addressed in these scholarly writings, and I do not intend to do so here. Instead, I will investigate metaphors that are not so well addressed in the religious literature, namely those that have to do with *mathematics*. In fact, the rest of this work will be devoted in one way or another to a discussion of specific instances of mathematics used metaphorically to explore religious and/or metaphysical ideas. However, before beginning that more detailed investigation, it seems appropriate to look more closely at contemporary understanding of the relationship between mathematics and metaphor among scholars both in mathematics and in religion. It is to this task that I turn in this concluding section of chapter 2.

As I mentioned earlier in this chapter, professionals in both fields do not seem to associate the term "metaphor" with mathematics. A general perusal of mathematical textbooks confirms a similar avoidance of the term. Since mathematical texts (and their interpretations) greatly influence the attitudes of our populace towards mathematics, it is noteworthy that the *emphasis* on metaphor in these texts is virtually nonexistent. Signs, symbols, and models, however, form standard stock in the mathematical vocabulary. Signs and symbols generally refer to various concrete marks signifying specific mathematical ideas. "Symbol" is the more common term, as in calling zero a "place-holder symbol" or as in this statement taken from a basic mathematics text for college students: "Arithmetic with the Babylonian numerals is quite simple, since there are only two symbols."[40] "Sign" often appears attached to a numerical symbol as a means of distinguishing positive from negative or as an indicator of a process such as multiplication or subtraction. In recent years, the word "model" has taken on great significance in mathematics and often receives special textbook attempts to define it. Typical of the explanatory remarks are the following.

> Galileo became a scientist and mathematician, and went on to contribute to virtually the entire range of natural science. His most important theoretical work consisted of expressing natural relationships as relationships between numbers; we would now call such relationships *functions* or *mathematical models*.[41]

> A *mathematical model* is an equation or set of equations in which variables represent real-world quantities—for instance, distance and time intervals in the equation $d(n) = k(2n - 1)$. A mathematical model is often an *idealization* of the real-world situation it supposedly describes; for instance, Galileo's mathematical model assumes a perfectly smooth inclined plane, no friction, and no air resistance.[42]

What stands out in these examples is the emphasis on the literal in the usages. They express or help to express relationships in the *real* or *natural* world. They create no new meaning. They are dispensable and non-emotive. Signs, symbols, and even models (when taken as combinations of signs and symbols) appear to be precisely the arbitrary conventions that my early divinity school teacher insisted were not symbols in the religious use of the word.

The assumption that mathematics is the language of the literal, the exact, the precise—anything but the metaphorical—is implicitly set forth not only by many mathematicians, but also by many of the experts on metaphorical language. McFague is representative when she writes that:

> [A]t the highest level of abstraction and generalization one does not escape metaphor (the exceptions are symbolic logic and higher mathematics . . .).

> They [scientists] also disagree on the nature of scientific explanation: whether it is satisfied by mathematical formulas or whether models are necessary for explaining new and unfamiliar material. . . .

> [T]heories need models to put flesh on mathematical skeletons. . . .

> [E]xplanation is complete when a mathematical formula has been attained and laboratory experiments have verified that the new phenomenon falls under a known law. Only positivists consistently hold to this view of explanation; the low-view people obviously go well beyond it in their appreciation for the heuristic functions of models. Nonetheless, their view that models are expendable suggests that the "explanation" that counts is the mathematical one. . . . [43]

Scholars of metaphorical theology often comment about mathematics only incidentally (as McFague does in these examples), as though they were referencing common knowledge. Sometimes, however, they draw a more intentional distinction between metaphorical language and mathematics. Black and Barbour, for instance, categorize mathematical models as of somewhat less interest than theoretical models because, as Black puts it, "the mathematical treatment furnishes no *explanations*."[44] The main focus of mathematical models is on clarifying, making more predictable, more precise, more understandable their real world counterparts. Bois, too, makes a marked distinction between mathematical models and other mental models. For Bois, a mathematical model is a tool to aid our real world technology. For example, when an inventor builds a machine,

> the first design is translated into a mathematical model, which is a set of equations that represents the required performance of the future machine. Instead of building an actual machine and testing it, the designer tries many possible alternatives in the variables of these equations and uses a computer to figure out the answers. As many mental models as necessary are built, tried, and modified instead of going through the labor and cost of building a machine. . . . The purpose of the thinking models we are now describing is different; they are far from having reached the sharp formulations of mathematics. They are intended to deal directly with semantic activities.[45]

Some scholars seem less certain that the two realms are separate. Soskice, for instance, notes that "in almost all areas of abstract thought (mathematics might be an exception *but even that seems doubtful*), the very frames within which we work are given by metaphors that function in structuring not only what sort of answers we get, but what kind of questions we ask" (emphasis added.)[46] Leatherdale observes the close connection between metaphor and analogy[47] and then notes the importance of analogy to mathematics.[48] Booth questions the resistance of mathematicians to the notion that scientific theories are metaphoric paradigms,[49] and Turbayne devotes an entire section (albeit in an appendix) to pointing out the similarities between models as they are used in formal mathematics and as they are used in metaphorical contexts. In particular, he suggests that "the philosophical concepts of model and metaphor can be explicated in terms borrowed from formal model-theory."[50]

It is not unusual to find such investigators making an explicit separation between mathematics and metaphorical language only to implicitly contradict themselves a short while later. Black, as noted above, categorizes mathematical models as something distinct from theoretical models, but shortly thereafter argues that "it makes perfectly good sense to treat something abstract, *even a mathematical calculus,* as a theoretical model of something relatively concrete" (emphasis added).[51] Likewise Ross, as we saw in chapter 1, noted that metaphor can be avoided only by the use of mathematics, and then he promptly used mathematics to define metaphor. Elsewhere he argues (contrary to Tillich and others) that symbols are arbitrary. However, he then uses a specifically mathematical example to demonstrate the impact that arises from the choice of one symbol over another: "it made an enormous difference to the development of mathematics that Roman numerals were replaced by Arabic."[52]

These illustrations suggest, overall, that scholars of language and theology are beginning to reconsider the tendency to view mathematics as an antithesis of metaphor.[53] However, our best acknowledgement of this changing trend comes from within the mathematical world itself. In one of their several volumes, for instance, mathematical philosophers Davis and Hersh have written explicitly about the following topics: "Mathematics and Rhetoric"; "Platonic Mathematics Meets Platonic Philosophy of Religion: An Ethical Metaphor"; "Metathinking as a Way of Life"; and "The Computer Thinks: An Interpretation in the Medieval Mode." This last topic includes specific subtopics on "The Literal Mode" and "The Metaphorical Mode." A careful reading of these pieces leaves little doubt that Davis and Hersh recognize and appreciate the role that metaphor plays in mathematics. ("Metaphor and analogy exist in mathematics and physics as well as in poetry and in religion."[54]) It is not so clear that they see the potential of using mathematics (as Hofstadter does) *as* metaphor, although occasional comments, such as the following, do tend in that direction:

> Little by little over the past century and a half, under the impact of such developments as non-Euclidean geometry and relativity theory, scientists have been replacing the idea of a theory of xyz with the idea of a model of xyz. There is a world of difference philosophically and psychologically between a theory and a model. The word "theory" seems to imply an idea that is *true*. Permanently. The word "model" implies an idea that is *expedient*, but evanescent.[55]

The two philosophers get hung up in the very separation of the true and the expedient, literal and the nonliteral, which my kaleidoscopic image resists. They carry this separation into an analogy of separation between formal abstract thought and meaning, an analogy that, they say, has made mathematics the culprit of dehumanization. "But some of the High Priests of mathematics must weep," they lament, "because it is in the very nature of mathematics that its abstract symbols suffer a loss of meaning even as they gain in generality."[56] Well, yes, that is true. But it is only part of the story—the same part, perhaps, that has led to a suspicion of formalism in religion, what McFague has called the idolization of the model.

The other part of the story can be found in the writings of yet another mathematician—Tobias Dantzig. Dantzig, while admitting to being "out of sympathy" with the extreme formalism of symbolic logic, nonetheless carefully refrains from allowing this "prejudice" to diminish the overall importance of mathematical symbolism. To Dantzig, "the tremendous importance of this symbolism lies not in such sterile attempts to banish intuition from the realm of human thought, but in its unlimited power to *aid intuition* in creating new forms of thought."[57]

Dantzig reverses the often-stated idea that mathematics is a language.[58] Instead, he says that our normal language is mathematics, a "rhetorical algebra *par excellence.*" Words are abstract symbols of a class that also has

> the capacity to *evoke an image,* a concrete picture of some representative element of the class. . . .
>
> And what is true of words generally is particularly true of those words which represent *natural* numbers. Because they have the power to evoke in our mind images of concrete collections, they appear to us so rooted in firm reality as to be endowed with an *absolute* nature. Yet in the sense in which they are used in arithmetic, they are but a particular collection of symbols subject to a system of operational rules.
>
> Once we realize this symbolic nature of the natural numbers, it loses its absolute character. Its intrinsic kinship with the wider domain of which it is the nucleus becomes evident. At the same time the successive extensions of the number concept become steps in an inevitable process of natural evolution, instead of the artificial and arbitrary *legerdemain* which they seem at first.[59]

To Dantzig, mathematics not only contains metaphor, it acts *as* metaphor. Time and again, his choice of vocabulary and expression echo the vocabulary and expression of the contemporary theologians whose primary focus is on the use of metaphorical language in religion. In speaking of the power of the symbolism of algebra, for instance, he notes that "the A of Vieta or our present x has an existence independent of the concrete object which it is assumed to represent. The symbol has a meaning which transcends the object symbolized: that is why *it is not a mere formality.*"[60] The use of such symbolism "makes possible the transformation of literal expressions and the paraphrasing of any statement into a number of equivalent forms. It is this power of transformation that *lifts algebra above the level of a convenient shorthand.*"[61] And most important (he maintains) is the role that algebraic symbolism:

> played in the formation of the generalized number concept.
> As long as one deals with numerical equations such as

$$(I) \quad x + 4 = 6 \qquad\qquad (II) \quad x + 6 = 4$$
$$2x = 8 \qquad\qquad\qquad\qquad 2x = 5$$
$$x^2 = 9 \qquad\qquad\qquad\qquad x^2 = 7$$

> one can content himself (as most medieval algebraists did) with the statement that the first group of equations is possible, while the second is impossible. But when one considers the literal equations of the same types:

$$x + b = a$$
$$bx = a$$
$$x^n = a$$

> the very indeterminateness of the data compels one to give an *indicated* or *symbolic* solution to the problem:

$$x = a - b$$
$$x = a/b$$
$$x = \sqrt[n]{a}$$

> In vain, after this, will one stipulate that the expression $a - b$ has a meaning only if a is greater than b, that a/b is meaningless when a is not a multiple of b, and the $\sqrt[n]{a}$ is not a number unless a is a perfect nth power. The very act of writing down the *meaningless* has given it a meaning . . . sooner or later the very fact that there is nothing on the face of these symbols to indicate whether a legitimate or illegitimate case is before us, will suggest that there is no contradiction involved in operating on these symbolic beings *as if they were bona fide numbers.*[62]

Thus, for Dantzig, algebraic expressions clearly function as Tillich's symbols or McFague's metaphors. They *transcend* the object symbolized. They are not mere formalities or convenient short-hands. They evoke an image. They act *as if* they were something else.

The ultimate attempt to cite differences between scientific and religious metaphorical language often rests on the claim that the second is emotive and the first is not.[63] Perhaps this is true for some mathematicians. But it certainly is not the case for Dantzig, as the following excerpt clearly demonstrates.

> I recall my own emotions: I had just been initiated into the mysteries of the complex number. I remember my bewilderment; here were magnitudes patently impossible and yet susceptible of manipulations which lead to concrete results. It was a feeling of dissatisfaction, of restlessness, a desire to fill these illusory creatures, these empty symbols, with substance. Then I was taught to interpret these beings in a concrete geometrical way. There came an immediate feeling of relief, as if I had solved an enigma, as if a ghost which had been causing me apprehension turned out to be no ghost at all, but a familiar part of my environment.
>
> I have since had many opportunities to realize that my emotions were shared by many other people. Why this feeling of relief? We have found a concrete model for these symbols; we have found that we can attach them to something familiar, to something that is real, or at least seems real. But why consider a point in the plane—or rather the segments measuring the distances of such a point from two arbitrary axes of reference—why consider this more real than the quantity $a + ib$? What reality is there behind a plane, a line, a point? Why, only a year or two before, these too were but phantoms to me . . . were such things the concrete reality that had caused my feeling of relief?
>
> We have attached a phantom to a fiction, which had this advantage over the phantom that it was a *familiar fiction*. But it had not always been familiar; there was a time when this too caused bewilderment and restlessness, until we attached it to a still more primeval illusion, which again had been rendered concrete through centuries of habit.[64]

It is habit that makes Dantzig's symbols "real." It is habit, familiarity, emphasis. For him, the difference between the symbol and what is behind the symbol is, at root, one of emotional investment.[65]

Now, I am not claiming that no difference whatsoever exists between various gradations of metaphor. I am not claiming that mathematics as metaphor is the same as, say, the Bible as metaphor. I am not claiming that all metaphorical language is blurred and that the difference between fact and fiction, between the literal and the metaphorical, is nonexistent. What I am claiming is that these differences are purely a matter of perspective, a matter of tuning into something that is not blurred, as we tune into the old lady or the young woman from something that is neither. What appears to be literal fact to one person is fiction to another. What appears to be religious metaphor to one is abstract mathematics to another. Both are illusions. Both are unreal images. Both are real images. They are filtered choices of the mind, or, perhaps, of Mind.

When we spend incredible time and energy trying to decipher the distinctions between, say, signs, metaphors, symbols, and models; when we argue endlessly about the virtues of a scientific worldview over a religious one or vice versa; when we chop away at the logical inconsistencies of one theory over another, we miss the point. We should be devoting our efforts to figuring out how we go from one to the other, for in doing so we learn flexibility and new strengths. In doing so, we grow. Paradoxically, one way to acquire this understanding of the bridges that transport us from one realm to another, perhaps the way we seem best able to do this figuring out, is by examining the different sands of the realms we are bridging. It is an action requiring balance. We examine the bridge and we examine the sands that hold it up. We examine the design to understand the filter, and we examine the filter to understand the design.

In recent years, we have been seeing mathematics and religion as two separate designs in a world that knows only a static filter. What do we gain by rocking the filter? The answer is simple. We gain a different view. We gain a new image-ination, a new intuition. We gain what Dantzig zeros in on in his closing paragraphs as one of the many bypaths through which we pursue the "Quest of the Absolute." We gain, in short, a mathematical intuition.

> And what is the source of this creative intuition? What is this necessity which organizes and guides human experience and shields it from the terrors of Chaos? Whence came this thrust that raised the frigid, immobile, and barren rocks of logic?
>
> "The billows are whispering their eternal whispers,
> The wind blows on, the clouds are sailing,

The stars keep twinkling indifferent and cold,
And a fool waits for his answer."

And the wise man? The wise man, resuming his business in life, the spinning of the fictions of today, which may be the realities of tomorrow, casts one last glance at the distant peaks, behind which is lost the origin of thought, and repeats the words of the Master:

"THOUGH THE SOURCE BE OBSCURE,
STILL THE STREAM FLOWS ON."[66]

CHAPTER 3

Holy Mathematics

META-4s

Max Black has written that "perhaps every science must start with metaphor and end with algebra; and perhaps without the metaphor there would be no algebra."[1] This chapter is written in the spirit that perhaps every religion must start with metaphor and end with mathematics, and that without the metaphor perhaps there would be no mathematics. Odd as this may sound, the idea has its precedents.

> Number rules the universe.
> Pythagoreans (ca. 530–510 B.C.)

> God ever geometrizes.
> Plato (429–348 B.C.)

> Nature's great book is written in mathematical symbols.
> Galileo (1564–1642)

> The life of God is mathematics. Pure mathematics is religion.
> Novalis (1772–1801)

> God ever arithmetizes.
> Jacobi (1804–1851)

> God made the integers; all the rest is the work of man.
> Kronecker (1823–1891)

> The sine and the cosine are the natural alphabet of all periodic change.
> Eric T. Bell (twentieth century)

These seven quotations, spanning the centuries since 500 B.C., are all metaphorical assertions that God or the natural (divine) universe is fundamentally mathematical. They are representative of the kind of thinking that we will be looking at throughout this chapter, although both the form of mathematics referred to and the metaphorical expression employed will vary.

Sometimes, as in the assertions above, the metaphor itself will be fundamentally nonmathematical, although it will always wear a mathematical overcoat. Mathematics, for example, is a *ruler* or governor of some sort. God is one who does or who creates mathematics—an arithmetizer or a geometer, a maker of integers —a *person,* in other words, or at least an anthropomorphized deity. Nature is a *book* written with a mathematical alphabet or symbols. I will call this first type of mathematical metaphor *familiar* metaphor, because it is very like many other kinds of metaphor that we routinely use, except that it is dressed in mathematics.

At other times, some mathematical process, conjecture, equation, principle—that is, mathematics itself—will be used in a metaphorical way to describe or illuminate our understanding of what is divine, sacred, religious. We saw this version of metaphor in Hofstadter's fictitious dialogues, although the primary function there was epistemological rather than religious exploration. In Hofstadter's dialogues, mathematics (either explicit or implicit) always wore a metaphorical cloak. I will refer to this second type of mathematical metaphor as *strange* metaphor, because the form it takes is inverted from that of familiar metaphor.

A third type of metaphor we will encounter will be a fusion of these two: like the old lady/young woman double-meaning illusion, the metaphor you see depends on how you look at it. I call this *fused* metaphor. Finally, we will occasionally encounter a variation on this theme that is expository primarily rather than metaphorical; the explanation, however, will in some way imply a metaphorical use of mathematics for religious purposes. An example of this fourth combination of mathematics and metaphor may be seen in the following statement made by contemporary Russian mathematician I. R. Shafarevitch on the occasion of his receiving an award from the Academy of Science in Gottingen, West Germany: "It is my hope . . . that mathematics may serve now as a *model* for the solution of the main problem of our epoch; to reveal a supreme religious goal and to fathom the meaning of the spiritual activity of mankind."[2] (emphasis added) This fourth use I term *theoretical* metaphor, although it is admittedly arguable whether or not it is metaphor at all.

While we will encounter here mathematical metaphor in four variations (familiar, strange, fused, and theoretical), the roads on which are built these metaphor-bridges, that is, the basic organizing structure of this chapter, will center around the actual content of mathematics. We will approach the topic of religion and mathematics from four different subject matters. First, we will examine *number symbolism* throughout the ages. Second, we will look at mathematics as *geometry.* Third, we will consider *chaos and computer mathematics.* Fourth, we will view it from a *holographic* perspective, by which I mean to consider mathematics as an interplay between the one and the many.

These classifications are both broad and arbitrary. Sometimes they will be unambiguously distinct. Often, however, they will overlap or even merge, so that this separation into individual categories may appear artificial and forced. Furthermore, I offer these four approaches, and the four forms of metaphor outlined above, as mere starting routes rather than final destinations. They are beginning attempts to reach a new understanding of the relationship between mathematics and religion. Should they (as I hope) stimulate future studies about "holy mathematics," they undoubtedly will be upgraded and refined.

NUMBER SYMBOLISM

Throughout history, number symbolism, also known variously as number mysticism, numerology, and the science of numbers,[3] has linked mathematics firmly to the sacred. Struik traces it back to neolithic man who "was influenced by magic and religion";[4] Bell finds its roots in the astronomy and astrology of the ancient Egyptians and Babylonians;[5] and Hopper cites specific instances in the Sumerian theology of the scholastic period (twenty-fifth to twenty-third century).[6] Both Bell and Hopper provide extensive historical treatments of the subject, and both point out that the tradition is carried on in contemporary times.[7]

Bell, in spite of his protestations to the contrary,[8] presents an essentially patronizing and unsympathetic account of numerology.[9] Hopper, who may well be just as skeptical as Bell,[10] nonetheless offers a detailed analysis without recourse to the tongue-in-cheek ridicule that pervades Bell's work. He allows that scholars have often explained various number symbols with considerable success. He qualifies what he allows, however, that

> the explanations have tended to clarify the text without illuminating the soul of the author or warming the imagination of the reader. The lack of a frame of reference, together with a failure to comprehend the philosophic as well as the symbolic implications of number, has resulted in a general tendency to regard number symbols as a pleasant variety of anagrams. It is the purpose of this study to reveal how deeply rooted in medieval thought was the consciousness of numbers,[11] not as mathematical tools, nor yet as the counters in a game, but as fundamental realities, alive with memories and eloquent with meaning.[12]

Because of this difference in approach, I find Hopper's manuscript generally more useful to my present study. I draw primarily, though not exclusively, from it in this section.

For Hopper, "nothing in the history of number symbolism is so striking as the unanimity of all ages and climates in regard to the meanings of a certain few number symbols."[13] Four, for instance, is universally the number of earth.[14] Among many primitive peoples there were not only 4 directions, but also 4 winds, and occasionally, a 4-eyed, 4-eared God that supervises earthly creation. Because of the "belief that the stars imaged the will of the gods, and that in sacred number groups might be found the impress of the divine hand," humankind found other examples of fourness in the universe—"4 winds, then 4 seasons, then 4 watches of the day and night, then 4 elements and 4 humours and 4 cardinal virtues."[15]

The ancient Egyptians depicted a cosmos with a heavenly roof "supported by 4 pillars, mountains, or women at the cardinal points."[16] In Pythagorean cosmography, the first solid produced is 4, which describes the first principle (fire); "the fourth solid, the only figure whose surfaces are quadrangular, is assigned to the earth, thus adding philosophical support to the traditional belief in the foursquaredness of earth."[17] In the Old Testament, the tetrad is found in the 4 rivers of Genesis 2:10; "in the 4 winds of Ezekiel 37:9 and Daniel 7:2; in the 4 parts of heaven in Job 9:9; in the 4 golden rings of the ark of the covenant and the table; in the 12 oxen, 3 looking in each direction, which support the sea of the temple; and in the constant 4 beasts, birds, or angels in the prophesies."[18]

Four crops up again later in "Philo's revolutionary 'discovery' of Pythagorean elements in the books of Moses,"[19] in the Gnosticism of the early Christian period (Profundity, Idea, Intelligence, and Truth),[20] and in the Biblical exegesis of the early Christian writers. The Neoplatonist (and one-time gnostic Manichean) Augustine, for instance, noted that man is a tetrad since the name *Adam* is composed of the letters that are the 4 winds: thus, "knowledge of divine things is disseminated throughout the world by the 4 gospels, evangelists or beasts [and is] emblemized by the 4 extremities of the cross, the 4-fold division of Christ's clothing, and the 4 virtues, or forms of love."[21] Innocent III (in a fashion typical of his time) builds allegorically on such scriptural exegesis, interpreting the 4 historical rivers of Paradise as rivers of truth that flow "from Christ through the 4 evangelists, or from Moses through the 4 major prophets."[22] Biblical numerical exegesis spilled over into science, too. There were, for instance, 4 mutations of matter, and Grosseteste, in a manner wholly consistent with Pythagorean thought, reasoned that: "'the supreme body' is composed of form, matter, composition, and compound. Form is represented by the number 1, matter by 2, and composition by 3. The compound itself is represented by 4. By invoking the tetraktys ($1 + 2 + 3 + 4 = 10$), it is clear that 'every whole and perfect thing is ten.'"[23]

While incomplete, this summary nonetheless provides a beginning sense of the metaphysical and religious "reality" of number that Hopper hoped to illuminate. It goes without saying that four is an arbitrary choice for illuminating such reality: I could as easily have chosen any of the other nine basic numerals, as well as many of their combinations. What is surprising is the high degree of consistency in the various interpretations of this number science. Less surprising but equally important to observe is that at the heart of all such elaborate numerical manipulations (which serious scholars throughout the ages have undertaken) rests an unchanging "faith in mathematics as the representation of fundamental truth."[24]

In this representation, there is an "implied congruency of physical and spiritual truths."[25] The conception of number was not simply that of a summation of concrete units, but rather that of an abstract, symbolic idea, what the Pythagoreans referred to as "essences" or "principles." Perhaps I would better write "a summation of concrete units *and* an abstract, symbolic idea," for there was in this view "no . . . disparity between the concept of a number's significance as part of the decimal system, or as an astrological index of time, or as representing symbolically a specific physical or spiritual truth."[26] Like the picture of the young lady/old woman, it was all the same basic notion.

The primary importance of the "picture" drawn by number symbolism, however, has always been spiritual. Cumont says of the ancient Babylonians that "a *number* was a very different thing from a *figure*. Just as . . . in Egypt the *name* had a magic power, and ceremonial words formed an irresistible incantation, so here the number possesses an active force, the number is a symbol, and its properties are sacred attributes."[27] Philolaus, writing about 450 B.C., captured the heart of the Pythagorean philosophy (and of number symbolism) when he noted that "All things have a number, and it is this fact which enables them to be known."[28] Plotinus wrote that "Number exists before objects which are described by number. The variety of sense-objects merely recalls to the soul the notion of number."[29] To Philo, number was "the basis of the design of the Creator"; and "the number itself, rather than its concrete representation, is considered the ultimate reality."[30] Augustine "saw in number an image of the absolute" that led him, by investigation of number symbolism, to "discover the mysteries of God which are set down in Scripture."[31] Later, still, Dionysius the Areopagite wrote that "to the best of our ability, we use symbols appropriate to things Divine, and from these again we elevate ourselves, according to our degree, to the simple and unified truth of the spiritual visions."[32] To this, Hopper adds only that "as usual, the symbols chosen were numerical."[33]

Bell, in spite of his skepticism, nonetheless dispels the notion that this faith in mathematical symbols belongs entirely to an earlier day:

> Any numerological theory of the universe seems queer to a mathematical skeptic only when he persists in staring at the modern aspect of the Pythagorean dogma. Transpose the abstruse metaphors of modern mathematical physics into those of the older mysticism, and the illusion of queerness vanishes. Spectacular novelties take on the familiar form immortalized by Pythagoras when he turned numerologist. Number is at the bottom of everything; the Pythagoreans in the sixth century B.C. said that number *is* everything and that everything *is* number—essentially. They meant that *is* in the fullest sense. More than one modern classic of high physical speculation says exactly the same thing, and numerology says Amen.[34]

Thus, Bell admits some validity of a "transposed" numerology, one that is extended to a more fully developed mathematical system. Indeed, my reading of Bell suggests that his main reservation about numerology resides in the Pythagorean notion that *whole* numbers (1, 2, 3, 4, etc.) hold the key to the cosmic system.

The Pythagoreans themselves had enormous difficulty rejecting this idea. Legend has it that the member of the Pythagorean religious sect who discovered the existence of *irrational*[35] numbers was drowned at sea for his unfortunate insight. Furthermore, whole-number symbolism lives on even today in a variety of forms. Carlo Suares, for example, in his Cabalistic "deciphering" of Genesis, notes that the letter-numbers (see figure 3.1)[36] are complete ideograms in themselves. In his 1967 study, he interprets the first nine letters of the Hebrew alphabet as archetypes of the first nine numbers:[37]

א	ב	ג	ד	ה	ו	ז	ח	ט
Aleph	Bayt Vayt	Ghimel	Dallet	Hay	Vav or Waw	Zayn	Hhayt	Tayt
1	2	3	4	5	6	7	8	9

FIGURE 3.1
Letter-Numbers of the Hebrew Alphabet

Aleph, no. 1, is the unthinkable life-death, abstract principle of all that is and all that is not.

Bayt (or Vayt), no. 2, is the archetype of all "dwellings", of all containers: the physical support without which nothing is.

Ghimel, no. 3, is the organic movement of every Bayt animated by Aleph.

Dallet, no. 4, is physical existence, as response to life, of all that, in nature, is organically active with Ghimel. Where the structure is inorganic Dallet is its own resistance to destruction.

Hay, no. 5, is the archetype of universal life. When it is conferred upon Dallet, it allows it to play the game of existence, in partnership with the intermittent life-death process.

Vav (or Waw), no. 6, expresses the fertilizing agent, that which impregnates. It is the direct result of Hay upon Dallet.

Zayn, no. 7, is the achievement of every vital impregnation; this number opens the field of every possible possibility.

Hhayt, no. 8, is the sphere of storage of all undifferentiated energy, or unstructured substance. It expresses the most unevolved state of energy, as opposed to its achieved freedom in Zayn.

Tayt, no. 9, as archetype of the primeval female energy, draws its life from Hhayt and builds it gradually into structures.

Such is the fundamental equation set and developed in Genesis.[38]

I quote such a lengthy section to show that serious attempts to apply whole-number symbolism to religious matters are part of our *current* contemporary scene. There are, for Suares, no occult implications in this schema, for "the Revelation is not a fantastic message from a supernatural world."[39] Rather, it is a method of transcending the inadequacy of our reasoning faculties.

The words which our reason has concocted belong to a world where everything is measurable and contradictory (as are life and death). In fact, contradiction exists in the very thought that has coined these words. The sacred language of the letter-numbers, however, is not a product of this thought. These signs are apertures through which to glimpse the presence of the cosmic forces. What is more, they permit these forces to penetrate into our very being.[40]

A more typical contemporary view, however, is one that goes beyond whole-number symbolism and, in a sense, extends Suares's "apertures" to all of mathematics. This is the view Bell expounds even as he rejects and devalues the Pythagorean whole-number cosmology. What Bell retains, in a manner particularly characteristic of modern science but not always recognized for what it is, is a faith (or at least the possibility of it) in an isomorphic mapping of all reality onto mathematics. Bell points out (à la Korzybski) that the map of something is not the same as the thing mapped.[41] Furthermore (à la McFague), he suggests that the problem with numerology is that the map is identified with the territory.[42] Yet he allows that it is precisely such a mapping that motivates much of contemporary science.

There are, he observes, many possible maps for one and the same territory, each one having a special purpose, for which the others are useless. But what sense is there in trying to unify all these maps into one simple map that is somehow more than a map? "Who," asks Bell, "but a fanatical unitarian would ever dream of plastering all the geology, sociology, topography, and the rest onto one and the same piece of paper?" The answer, according to Bell, is a great many contemporary scientists.

> Here now comes a curious thing. The dream of physical science is just this, to unify electromagnetism, gravitation, radiation, in fact all physical phenomena, by mapping them on one grand, unified theory. At present fashion favors a purely mathematical unification. This is the vision which Pythagoras saw, only he went farther. He would have included humanity and all that human nature means. Then he would have joined some of the moderns by saying the map *is* the cosmos.[43]

What we have here is a kind of reversal. The Pythagoreans limited their mathematics to whole numbers, and they extended their mapping to the cosmos and the spirit. Modern-day science, on the face of it, seems to have reversed this trend, extending the mathematics and limiting the mapping to the purely physical realm. Yet even this reversal is, in my opinion, suspect. Just the titles alone of some fairly recent popular scientific books suggest an underlying spiritual/metaphysical theme: Fritjo Capra's *The Tao of Physics;* Stewart and Golubitsky's *Does God Play Dice?* and its sequel *Fearful Symmetry: Is God a Geometer?;* Paul Davies' *The Mind of God;* Robert Wright's *Three Scientists and Their*

Gods; Davis and Hersh's *Descartes' Dream: The World According to Mathematics;* and John Barrow's *Theories of Everything: The Quest for Ultimate Explanation,* to name a few.

Just exactly how much of the theme of these books is mathematical and scientific and how much is spiritual and metaphysical is open to question. Certainly the two realms are again curiously fused together. Is the map really identical with the territory after all? According to Bell, maybe it is and maybe it is not. "The most comprehensive dream ever dreamed by our race is short," he says. *"The Cosmos is isomorphic with pure mathematics.* Doubt it, if you like, but don't turn your back on it. It may be true. At present we do not know whether it is a great and simple truth or whether it is just nonsense."[44]

The isomorphic mapping that Bell refers to indicates that number symbolism, and possibly all of contemporary mathematics, has a metaphorical character, "idolatrized" or otherwise. Leaving aside for the moment the question of whether or not contemporary mathematics has this same metaphorical nature, let us further examine the metaphorical aspects of whole-number symbolism. Hopper, writing of the medieval mind, might well be speaking for a contemporary Suares or an ancient Pythagoras or any other adherent of whole-number symbolism when he observes that such a mind embodies "a weblike structure of abstract ideas and concrete realities so closely interwoven that no serious gap was felt to exist between them."[45]

A modern mind, says Hopper, dubs this weblike structure a symbol "with some impatience." However, such symbols were really the inevitable results of an association of ideas that were seen as part of "God's own implanting." Furthermore, a "reasonably extended acquaintance with medieval writings is all that is needed to put one in a frame of mind to accept this 'symbolism,' much as one accepts metaphor or simile or any kind of imagery, whether ancient or modern."[46] The function of this symbolism, according to Hopper, was to bring the abstract into the realm of the concrete, thereby rendering it recognizable and meaningful. Yet, paradoxically, a number symbol is the epitome of abstraction: "What, then, is to be said in explanation of the number symbol where the symbol, far from providing a concrete image, is itself very nearly the limit of abstraction? In all seriousness, does the author of the *Vita Nuova* expect to capture the reader's admiration and regard for Beatrice by describing her as a *nine?* The simple answer is 'yes'. . . . "[47]

Hopper traces a path that shows numbers as sometimes being used in this speculative way and sometimes being used as "highly popular aggregates."[48] First-century Christianity, for instance, was "as wholly isolated as possible from the speculative habit of the time,"[49] a trend reversed by later New Testament exegeticists. The Pauline epistles and the synoptic Gospels, while sometimes containing numbers, do so symbolically only "in the most elementary sense."[50] The implication, then, is that numbers can play a dual role, sometimes representing a practical counting arithmetic and sometimes representing a sacred attribute of the cosmos.

In number symbolism, it seems to me that the two roles are most often blended or fused. Augustine, for instance, calculated that because $50 = 7 \times 7$ plus 1 left over, it is said "Endeavoring the [*sic*] keep the unity of the Spirit in the bond of peace" (Eph. 4:3).[51] Similarly, Philo wrote that

> When . . . Moses says "God completed his works on the sixth day," we must understand that he is speaking not of a number of days, but that he takes six as a perfect number. Since it is the first number which is equal in its parts, in the half, and the third and sixth parts, and since it is produced by the multiplication of two unequal factors, two and three. And the numbers two and three exceed the incorporeality which exists in the unity because the number two is an image of matter, being divided into two parts and dissected like matter. And the number three is an image of a solid body, because a solid can be divided according to a three-fold division. . . . And at all events he desires to show that the races of mortal, and also of immortal beings, exist according to their appropriate numbers; measuring mortal beings, as I have said, by the number six, and the blessed and immortal beings by the number seven.[52]

In these examples (and they are only two of many), number is used both as a direct metaphor (e.g., as representations of unity and of perfection) and as a purely calculative (i.e., mathematical) technique. They are, thus, examples of what I have called *fused* metaphor.

This sort of fused metaphor extends into contemporary attempts to "theologize" via generalized (i.e., beyond whole numbers) mathematics. Such an extension seems clear from the following two examples, drawn, respectively, from the arenas of modern religious and mathematical scholarship. First, I quote from John Hick's 1989 work on religious pluralism in a passage where he summarizes Richard Swinburne's probability argument for the existence of God. Swinburne, he says, attempts to demonstrate by an

> application of Bayes's Theorem that the probability of traditional theism in relation to the evidences of the world is greater than one half. Where P = probability, h = the theistic hypothesis offered as an explanation of the world, e = the items of evidence to be mentioned presently and k = background knowledge, which at the crucial point of the argument is described by Swinburne as tautological . . . knowledge, Bayes's Theorem holds that
>
> $$P(h/e.k) = \frac{P(e/h.k) \times P(h/k)}{P(e/k)}$$
>
> That is to say, the probability of theism is its explanatory or predictive power, multiplied by its prior or intrinsic probability and divided by the prior or intrinsic probability of the evidence occurring by itself.[53]

While the details differ, the metaphorical structure of Swinburne's argument is undeniably similar to that of Augustine and Philo above.

My final example comes from a lengthy article (in the 2 March 1992 issue of *The New Yorker*) about two mathematical geniuses, the Chudnovsky brothers. Gregory and David Chudnovsky have developed one of the world's most powerful supercomputers and have devoted their lives to the study of numbers. "To them, numbers are more beautiful, more nearly perfect, possibly more complicated, and arguably more real than anything in the world of physical matter."[54] One number in particular has intrigued them, and they have spent hours and hours of computer time trying, quite literally, to get a better picture of this number. The number is pi, one of the oldest ratios known to the world.

Pi is the ratio of the circumference of a circle to its diameter. It is a constant. That is, it is always the same value, but, contrary to what many people have believed at various times throughout history, pi is not the ratio of two whole numbers. It is one of those irrational numbers that ultimately wreaked havoc with the Pythagorean brotherhood. Not only is it irrational, it is a *transcendental* number, that is, one that cannot be expressed as the root of an algebraic equation with rational integers. Any metaphorical use of pi thus extends beyond whole-number symbolism and enters the realm of modern mathematics.

Pi is approximately 3.14. This is only an approximate value, and the list of digits that follow the decimal point appears to go on forever. Throughout the ages, many people have been intrigued by this list of seemingly endless digits, and some of them have devoted extraordinary time to the effort of determining this list. In the early 1600, Ludolph van Ceulen of the Netherlands spent much of his life computing pi to thirty-five decimal places; the number (which even today is sometimes referred to as the Ludolphine number) was engraved on his tombstomb.[55] In the late 1800s William Shank spent fifteen years calculating pi to 700 decimal places, the last hundred or so of which turned out to be inaccurate.[56] The Chudnovsky brothers are perhaps the latest to join this group of dedicated pi-finders.

In 1991, the Chudnovskys calculated pi (with the help of their computer) to two billion two hundred and sixty million three hundred and twenty-one thousand three hundred and thirty-six (2,260,321,336) digits. Printed in ordinary type, this string of digits would stretch from New York to southern California. Fortunately, the computer prints these digits, not in a line of ordinary type, but in a colorful "picture" typical of the fractal landscapes many modern computer programs now produce. After the first eight million or so digits were printed out, the brothers realized that, apart from the vivid colors, pi looks like the Himalayan mountain range. "Exploring pi is like exploring the universe," according to one of the brothers. Preston, the author of the article, adds that "in a manner of speaking, the mountains of pi looked to him as if they'd been molded by the hand of the Nameless One, *Deus absconditus* (the hidden God). . . ."[57]

The Chudnovskys believe that pi only appears to be random, that order really underlies these mountains of pi, and that, Platonic-like,[58] knowledge of that order is only a matter of finding it. To the brothers, pi is real, a natural object that seems "to exist apart from time or the world," that seems "to transcend the universe," and that might exist even if the universe did not. Says Gregory Chudnovsky: "Everything in mathematics does exist now. It's a matter of *naming* it. The thing doesn't arrive from God in a fixed form; it's a matter of representing it with symbols. You put it through your mind in order to make sense of it."[59] When the two mathematicians put pi through the filter of their minds (and through their kaleidoscopic computer[60]) they concluded, as Preston phrased it, "that the distinction between chance and fixity dissolves in pi. The deep connection between disorder and order, between cacophony and harmony, in the most famous ratio in mathematics fascinated Gregory and David Chudnovsky. They wondered if the digits of pi had a personality."[61]

Thus the Chudnovskys associate a "possible personality" with this transcendental number. They muse that maybe "in the eyes of God pi looks perfect," or as Preston put it, "they wonder whether the digits contain a hidden rule, an as yet unseen architecture, close to the mind of God."[62] Such essentially religious inquiries are, as we have already seen, often attached to or built on numbers, that is, the two subjects are fused together as are the peaks and the valleys of the mountains of pi.

History, somewhat unexpectedly, shows that a connection between what is sacred and the number pi is as old as it is current. In ancient India, for example, where "mathematics served as a bridge between understanding material reality and the spiritual conception,"[63] mathematics often appeared in the context of *mantras,* or spiritual expressions. The following Vedic verse was both a petition to Krishna and, because the Sanskrit letters were also numbers, a code for pi.

> *gopi bhagya madhuvrata*
> *syngis'o dadhi sandhiga*
> *khala jtvita khatava*
> *gala hala rasandhara*

This may be translated as:

> O Lord anointed with the yogurt of the milkmaids' worship (Krishna), O Savior of the fallen, O master of Shiva, please protect me.[64]

Decoded, this verse yields the value of pi/10 to thirty-two decimal places. Although the exact dating of this particular verse is uncertain, the dual role it plays in both religion and mathematics echoes the function of numbers in humankind's earliest civilizations. The Vedic collection *Shulba Sutras* (fifth to eighth century B.C.), for instance, has shown "that the earliest geometrical and

mathematical investigations among the Indians arose from certain
requirements of the religious rituals."[65] Thus, we end this section
back where we started it—with ancient mathematics. However, we
move now from the West to the East and from the strictly numerical to a consideration of geometric aspects of mathematics. It is
here, with Occidental geometry, that we begin our next consideration of mathematics and religion.

GEOMETRY

According to an ancient Chinese legend, about two thousand years
before the birth of Jesus, a man named Wu of Hsia made improve-
ments that stopped the disastrous floodings of the Yellow River. As
a result, Wu became emperor. While he was making these improve-
ments, he discovered a turtle with unusual markings on its shell.
Since common belief then held that God resided in the shell of a
turtle and the horns of the water buffalo, Wu took this encounter
as a sign of blessing and as a source of inspiration. On the basis of
the markings on this turtle shell, he developed a system that incor-
porated the collective knowledge of the time with guidelines for
living a happy prosperous life.

Reference to this legend of the turtle shell has come down to us
today in at least two ways. Takashi Yoshikawa, for instance, uses it
as the basis of a kind of modern horoscope or oracle. Yoshikawa,
who was an "advisor" to John Lennon and Yoko Ono, sets forth
his theory as a method to understand and control the vital "Ki"
energies which he posits are "the breath of life itself."[66] Modern
science, I believe, would disdain this method as a highly occult
superstition. Nonetheless, modern science depicts this same turtle
shell in a perfectly "acceptable" college general mathematics text
(see figure 3.2)[67] where it is used to introduce a discussion of magic
squares and "The Nature of Patterns and Inductive Reasoning."[68]

In both instances, the open and dark circular figures on the
turtle shell (reflecting male and female energies or numbers, respectively[69]) are translated into the numerical square pattern of
figure 3.3.

The unusual and mathematically-intriguing characteristic
about this pattern is that the sum of the numbers in any row,
column, or diagonal is always "magically" fifteen.

It is not the purpose of this study to determine the rightness or

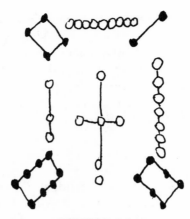

FIGURE 3.2
Turtle Shell from a Modern Math Text

wrongness of either of these two uses of the Turtle Shell Legend. What I wish to emphasize here is that there appear to be two *separate* modern uses, one to develop guidelines for living, the other to develope guidelines for reasoning. Whether or not these are really separate issues today is debatable, but certainly the emphasis each author brings to this pattern of numbers is markedly different; one is scholarly, intellectual, and largely secular in nature, whereas the other is more intuitive, divinatory, and what might be termed religious. In ancient times, these two realms were thoroughly interwoven.

We already saw in the section on number symbolism how intricately mathematics and religion were connected in earlier times. What we only touched upon then was that the method of depicting numbers in this symbolism was often geometric. The geometric designs on the turtle shell are our first clue to the importance of

```
4   9   2

3   5   7

8   1   6
```

FIGURE 3.3
Earliest Known Magic Square

geometry in religious endeavors. Struik, in his article on Stone Age mathematics, noted not only that numbers played a role in ancient religious rituals. He also noted that primitive peoples often displayed a fascination with geometric patterns, developing some that would require modern topological techniques to describe mathematically.[70] In any case, by the time of the Pythagoreans, numbers *were* geometric figures.

Burton suggests that the early Pythagoreans "must have thought of numbers in a strictly visual way, either as pebbles placed in the sand or as dots in certain geometric patterns."[71] Numbers, thus, were triangular, square, pentagonal, and so on. Figure 3.4[72] shows

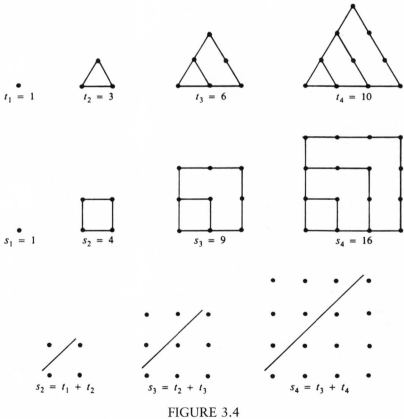

FIGURE 3.4
Geometric Numbers

the first four triangular numbers, the first four square numbers, and a few illustrations of geometric addition.

Christopher Butler, in his study of art and number symbolism, notes that later Greeks extended and elaborated the Pythagorean system. Plato believed that 1 was a point; 2, a line; 3, a triangle (the first plane figure visible to the sense and hence the first *real* number); and 4, the first solid, a pyramid or tetrahedron (composed of 4 triangular surfaces, with 4 apices).[73] Taking the triangle as his basic building block, Plato constructed a cube, the octahedron, the pyramid, and the icosahedron, which he then "assigned" to the four elements—earth, water, fire, and air respectively. A fifth figure, the dodecahedron, cannot be constructed from the basic triangles, and since it approaches a sphere in volume, Plato associated it with the sphere of the heavens.[74]

In the Greek view, God created a cosmological harmony based on fixed and simple numerical ratios, what is known now as the Pythagorean "music of the spheres."[75] Plato developed this harmony into a systematic theory of creation. First, God (actually a Demiurge that was not worshiped) divided "an indeterminate chaos of space into the four elements of fire, air, water and earth, by forming them out of geometrical solids."[76] Then the Demiurge chose specific proportions for the world's body and "disposed the celestial bodies in space."[77] Typical of Plato's thinking is this passage from his *Timaeus:* "So God placed water and air between fire and earth, and made them as far as possible proportional to one another; so that air is to water as water is to earth; and in this way he bound the earth into a visible and tangible whole."[78]

Clearly, it is impossible in this short chapter to fully explore all the dynamics of this relationship. Four factors stand out as worthy of special mention here. First, the motivating factor for Greek geometry was primarily religious and was coupled by an implicit faith in the truthfulness of mathematics. As van der Waerden put it: "Mathematics formed a part of their religion. Their doctrine proclaims that God has ordered the universe by means of numbers. God is unity, the world a plurality, and it consists of contrasting elements. It is harmony which restores unity to the contrasting parts and which molds them into a cosmos. Harmony is divine, it consists of numerical ratios."[79]

Second, this geometric harmony was and is empirically present in the physical world.

[T]hese symmetries can be identified in the natural world with examples from plant, animal, and human life, demonstrating that the triangle, the square, and the pentagon relate the various elements of the living world and bind them together. In this sense, their proportions can be regarded as common denominators or blueprints for living forms and they explain, at least in part, why these forms inspire wonder and delight.[80]

Furthermore, these proportions were considered mirrors of the greater cosmos, that is, they "were supposed to be the very same as those which underlay the structure of the cosmos as a whole."[81]

Third, the geometric aspects of the metaphysics of Pythagoras and Plato have had enormous influence down through the centuries on the religious as well as the secular realms. Butler observes that "the idea of God as a being who in his creation proceeded *more geometrico*" was an idea "of immense importance for Hebrew and Christian theology from the Jew Philo through the Church Fathers to the astronomer Kepler."[82] Burton notes that Pascal, who apparently underwent in 1654 a life-changing mystical experience "in which God came and spoke to him for two hours,"[83] subsequently wrote his *Treatise on Figurative Numbers* in a manner impacted by the Pythagoreans.[84] Leibniz (1646–1716) compared his "Universal Characteristic or calculus of symbols to a Cabala of mystical word or arithmetic of Pythagorean numbers," and he confirmed "the persistence of Pythagoreanism in his mature work and its connection with his religious motives in several passages in the *Theodicy*."[85]

On a less overtly religious vein, Butler notes Pythagorean elements in the works of such recent artists as Yeats and James Joyce, and he points out that Jung's analytical psychology considers objects in dreams as connoting "basic psychic properties of quaternities, trinities, squares, the *homeo quadratus* without blemish, and other symbols, which in various ways are projections of the self."[86] Jung, according to Butler:

> asserts that he has encountered many separate cases of this [the Pythagorean tetraktys], in which "Number symbolism and its venerable history is a field of knowledge utterly beyond the interests of our dreamer's mind." But this knowledge allows the analyst, aware of the numerological tradition, to diagnose images of the circle or globe containing four divisions as signifying the Deity. . . . Yet the patient, unaware of these facts, takes the image

to symbolize himself or something in himself. On this evidence, Jung tells us that it is mere prejudice to believe that the Deity is outside man—the image really signifies the God within. Jung goes on: "I cannot omit calling attention to the interesting fact that whereas the central Christian symbol is a Trinity, the formula of the unconscious mind is a quaternity." . . . The added fourth constituent, he says, is the feminine aspect, earth and woman, the anima, and it provides the final clue to the solution of the patient's problem: avoidance of the suppressed anima, partly but unsuccessfully overlaid by a religious concern. He thus implicitly criticizes the doctrine of the Trinity, as lacking any representation of the "inferior function" of the anima, which it can only do if expanded into a quaternity.[87]

Jung's theory, then, has a definite religious overtone while at the same time it relies heavily on the archetypal mental "figures" of the subconscious. Even today, says Butler, when we use "figure" in the sense of "number" (as in "calculating the sum of these figures"), we are really thinking in Pythagorean terms.[88]

The fourth and final point I wish to make with regard to Greek spatial symbolism is that, as Fletcher put it, "it is generally assumed that Plato was speaking metaphorically when he compared the elementary geometrical figures to the structure of the universe."[89] However, Fletcher goes on to emphasize that these "symmetries" actually occur in the natural, cosmic, and human realms, the implication being that there is a literal as well as a metaphorical aspect in this metaphysics. Butler, too, acknowledges this dual role, but he seems to emphasize the metaphorical aspects over the empirical ones. He notes, for example, that the Pythagoreans devised "an astronomical system which was a working *model*" (Butler's emphasis). This "could have been a basis" for a continuously correctable mathematical explanation of physical processes comparable to our modern science, but it remained, via Plato, "objects of the religious contemplation of Ideal Forms."[90] It seems to me that Butler's criteria for practical empirical investigations are colored by modern-day expectations, and that the Greeks thought themselves to be undertaking an empirical analysis of the physical world while simultaneously expanding their spiritual understanding. Put another way, this is to say, again, that the geometric number symbolism of the Greeks was fused metaphor.

So far in this section I have emphasized a kind of geometry that is closely connected to numbers and to the number symbolism of the previous section. However, most of us do not consciously think of numbers as geometric "figures." Etymologically, "geometry" means "earth measure." For most of us, the word conjures up relationships of visible space (usually Euclidean) that might be measured by numbers, but that are in some way fundamentally different from numbers. Yet if we consider the isomorphism between geometric space and the algebraic Cartesian coordinate system developed by Descartes in the seventeenth century, this difference may be more negligible than we realize.

Descartes performed an amazing service for the mathematical world when he associated each point in a plane with an ordered pair of numbers and thereby allowed us to "map" plane figures onto an algebraic plane.[91] After Descartes, a geometric figure could be completely described by an algebraic equation. A circle, for example, is completely interchangeable with the algebraic equation $a^2 + b^2 = r^2$. It was not long before this idea was extended first to three-dimensional space and then to nth-dimensional space, so that we could completely describe with algebraic numbers shapes we could not even begin to visualize. Initially, conservative mathematical tradition had a great deal of trouble with such thinking. Ivars Peterson points out that "establishment mathematicians refused to admit that higher-dimension geometries were even conceivable, maintaining that such concepts would call into question the very existence and permanence of mathematical truth, as represented by three-dimensional euclidean [*sic*] geometry."[92]

One interesting metaphorical work that came out of this controversy was Edwin Abbot's nineteenth-century narrative *Flatland*. While it was a pointed satire on social issues of Victorian Britain, according to Peterson it was also "one of Abbot's attempts to reconcile scientific and religious ideas and to clarify the relationship between material proof and religious faith."[93] In this book, a Square, confined to two dimensions, is visited by a ghostly three-dimensional Sphere, who tries desperately to convince Square that he is a Solid made up of an infinite number of circles of varying diameters. Square, not unlike the men in Plato's cave of shadows, will not buy any part of the existence of "Spaceland."

"Inexorable mathematical logic forces the next step," says Peterson. "Through mathematical *analogy* [emphasis added], Abbot sought to show that establishing scientific truth requires a leap of faith and that, conversely, miracles can be explained in terms that don't violate physical laws."[94] Such metaphorical use is basically a fused use—these are *people* dressed up as geometric figures (i.e., familiar metaphors) that nonetheless draw on fundamental mathematical concepts (in particular, the existence of higher dimensions) in order to provide some new kind of insight.

It was not just the outcome of Descartes's invention that led to geometric metaphors. Indeed, Turbayne notes that Descartes's own theory (and, later, Newton's, as well) was filled with a "metaphor or heap of metaphors, known as 'the geometric model.'"[95] Descartes was so devoted to the Roman Catholic church that he set aside work that he realized would agree with Galileo's cosmology rather than (in his own words) "publish anything that contains a word that might displease the Church."[96] It is one of the curiosities of history that the work he did publish was banned both by the Church and the universities within fifteen years of his death.[97] In any case, Descartes was deeply religious, and it was a prophetic dream rather than empirical logic that, as Turbayne puts it, "enabled him to envisage the extension of the geometrical model to every subject. All his subsequent work amounted to presenting outlines of, and exercises in the use of, this model."[98] Descartes's method, says Turbayne:

> involves the representation of the facts of all the sciences in idioms appropriate to geometry. Moreover, it involves make-believe throughout; for example, that forces reside in bodies, that the properties of the world are the properties of geometry, and so on. These satisfy the test of metaphor. We see just as clearly that it is an extended metaphor which, because the properties of this metaphor are carefully specified, is a model. Descartes, out of his genius, had invented one of the great metaphors of mankind. It is as though, waking from his dream, he uttered: "Geometry, be my metaphor!"[99]

Turbayne cites three specific properties of this geometrical metaphor: motion, extension, and deduction.[100] Perhaps the greatest significance of these properties is that they combined to extend and reinforce the kind of deductive axiomatic thinking that Euclid set forth in his famous *Elements*. The *Elements* actually contained much subject matter related to number theory and to elementary (geometric) algebra, as well as to the rudiments of the plane and solid geometry that most of us learned in high school. It also has essentially dominated all teaching of geometry for more than two millennia. Bell notes that no other work, except the Bible, has been more widely used, edited, or studied.[101]

The kind of reasoning that Euclidean geometry has always promoted assumes the truth of a limited number of statements and the logical proof of other statements following from these initial few postulates and axioms. Just as the "cross," for some people, calls forth an association with Jesus and Christianity, the very word "geometry," for some people, calls forth an association with axiomatic deductive reasoning. Humankind has long had an ardent faith in the validity of this reasoning. Science historian Joan Richards points out that "Euclidean geometry has stood for a long time as the exemplar of a kind of knowledge which was absolute and true. Particularly in British writings, you could find statements like: It is as certain that God exists as it is that the sum of the angles of a triangle is equal to 180°."[102] Geometry, when used in such statements, is a metaphor for the certainty of God's existence.

Although he spoke from a frame of reference that many modern scholars interpret as basically atheistic, Thomas Hobbes is perhaps the exemplar of one who put his faith in a very similar metaphor, for he uses geometry as the grounding for his monumental seventeenth-century social/political statement *Leviathan*. Geometry, to him, was "the onely [*sic*] Science that it hath pleased God hitherto to bestow on mankind." His reliance on geometry as a metaphor for universal certainty can be seen in the following passage.

> By this imposition of Names, some of larger, some of stricter signification, we turn the reckoning of the consequences of things imagined in the mind, into a reckoning of the consequences of Appellations. For example, a man that hathe no use of Speech at all, (such, as is born and remains perfectly deafe and dumb,) if he set before his eyes a triangle, and by it two right angles . . . he may by meditation compare and find, that the three angles of that triangle, are equall to those two right angles that stand by it. But if another triangle be shewn him different in shape from the former, he cannot know without a new labour, whether the three angles of that also be equall to the same. But he that hath the use of words, when he observes . . . will boldly conclude Universally, that such equality of angles is in all triangles whatsoever; and register his invention in these generall termes, *Every triangle hath its three angles equall to two right angles*. And thus the conse-

quence found in one particular, comes to be registred and re-
membred, as an Universall rule; and discharges our mentall reckoning, of time and place; and delivers us from all labour of the
mind, saving the first; and makes that which was found true
here, and *now,* to be true in *all times* and *places.*[103]

Hobbes's central thought here is that universal certainty is like the
body of learning that we call geometry; if you can understand
geometry, then, at least to some extent, you can begin to understand universal certainty. Although Hobbes probably would have
denied it,[104] this is metaphorical thinking of a kind familiar to all
of us. It is, in short, familiar metaphor.

Poor Hobbes would have been appalled had he lived two centuries later when Janos Bolyai and Nicolai Lobachevsky, in large
part because of the algebraic techniques invented by Descartes,
developed two perfectly valid non-Euclidean geometries. In one of
these geometries, the sum of the angles of a triangle exceeded and
in one the sum was less than two right angles. So much for universal certainty. These discoveries rocked the "absolute" world and
broke it up into an ethical relativism. As Richards notes, the major
epistemological assumption that pervaded all pre-non-Euclidian
thinking was that "all knowledge was unitary. If one found a kind
of certainty in geometry, then one could hope for the same kind of
certainty in physics, in biology, in ethics, or in religion."[105] Non-
Euclidean geometry undermined this exemplar of perfect knowledge and paved the way for the scientific naturalism[106] that was to
dominate the nineteenth and early parts of the twentieth century.

Some would say that the shock effects of non-Euclidean geometry left a major change in the paradigm landscape, and they might
well be correct. But although metaphors are born and die, they
seem, rather like the Eastern concept of reincarnation, to keep
coming back in some transformed version. Today, this same kind of
quest for unitary knowledge is reappearing under the hats of the
physicists and in the guise of TOES—*Theories Of Everything.*[107]
To examine this topic, however, we need to turn to a different kind
of geometry—fractal geometry—and to the computers that made
such a geometry possible.

COMPUTERS AND CHAOS

To the ancient Greeks, "proportion" was the Greek *logos* or "analogy,"[108] which, as we have seen, was closely connected with the

idea of metaphor.[109] But proportion, according to Fletcher, is also "synonymous with the ancient view of symmetry, which recognized a world of mutually related parts and wholes."[110] The classical Greek word for "symmetry" is ΣYM-METPIA, meaning "the same measure" or "due proportion."[111] The basic Greek worldview rested on a confidence that harmonious living could be achieved through symmetry, that symmetry was "a binding rather than a dividing process," and that through symmetry "the unique differences in our world might be preserved, yet also integrated."[112] Symmetry ("same measure") was then and is now closely associated with geometry ("earth measure").

Over the ages, however, this broader Greek interpretation of symmetry has largely disappeared. For most of us, symmetry usually connotes a kind of polarized repetition of parts, a "bilateral arrangement of parts in anatomy or else as it applies to methods of crystal classification where the whole is divided into a number of identical elements, which are then uniformly distributed around a point, a line, or a plane."[113] Yet today, a curious phenomenon seems to be happening, or happening again, as the case may be. In the last half of the twentieth century, mathematicians have been stretching our notions of symmetry (and geometry) much as the Pythagorean discovery of incommensurable ratios (i.e., irrational numbers) stretched Greek cosmology—perhaps with some surprisingly "asymmetric" results.

Symmetry, to contemporary mathematicians, is the form an object retains after it has undergone some sort of transformation. More precisely, symmetry may be defined *as* transformation, transformation that, paradoxically, leaves whatever was transformed relocated but apparently unchanged.[114] Perhaps it should better be called transferred, rather than transformed. In any case, the language that is typically used to describe this transformation is the language of group theory, and group theory, according to Felix Klein, is geometry. Actually, Klein held the reverse, that geometry is group theory, that "geometrical properties are characterized by their invariance under a group of transformations."[115] In this perspective, symmetry echoes the role it played in Greek thought in that it is more fundamental than geometry. As Stewart and Golubitsky put it:

> Until now, we've been viewing symmetry as a kind of accident of geometry. In typical fashion, mathematicians turned everything

upside down, and began to view geometry, or more accurately, geometr*ies,* as a consequence of symmetry. Geometries? Isn't one enough? Certainly not! In Euclid's day there *was* only one geometry—Euclid's, naturally—but by the 1870's geometry had proliferated into an unruly mob: Euclidean geometry and non-Euclidean geometry, projective geometry, affine geometry, conformal geometry, inversive geometry, differential geometry, and the first flushes of topology. A believer in a Geometer God would have had to be a pantheist.[116]

What has most stretched our notions about symmetry, however, is not its inverted relationship to geometry, but rather, the effects of *breaking* the symmetry in a system. When a symmetric system starts to behave less symmetrically, some of the symmetry "gets lost." The actual result of this loss of symmetry is, again paradoxically, the formation of pattern.

> An oddity of the human mind is that it perceives *too much* symmetry as a bland uniformity rather than as a striking pattern; although some symmetry is lost, pattern seems to be gained because of this psychological trick. We are intrigued by the pattern manifested in circular ripples on a pond . . . , but not by the even greater symmetry of the surface of the pond itself. . . . Mathematically, a uniform, featureless plane has a vast amount of symmetry; but nobody ever looks at a wall painted in a single colour and enthuses over its wonderful patterns.[117]

Symmetry-breaking, it turns out, plays a major role in pattern formation. Symmetry-breaking takes several known forms, one of which has become known as "chaos."[118] Chaos, it also turns out, contains an underlying order in its very randomness, in its "elegant geometric forms that create randomness in the same way as a card dealer shuffles a deck of cards or a blender mixes cake batter."[119] While it may seem, as the authors of *Fearful Symmetry* put it, that "there is an unbridgeable gulf between symmetry and chaos . . . one of the most exciting prospects for future discoveries lies in their interaction."[120]

The two authors are very earnest when they emphasize that it is "in their interaction," for it is under the larger mathematical umbrella of dynamic *processes* that they place the theories of symmetry and chaos. Essentially, they bridge this "unbridgeable gulf" by a mathematical process that they somewhat loosely refer to as a Geometer God.[121] There is, here, a parallel to, or at least a compatibility with, the kind of thinking that leads theologians such as Ian Barbour to observe that "process thinkers understand God to be the source of novelty and order."[122] For Barbour and other process theologians, "God elicits the self-creation of individual entities, thereby allowing for freedom and novelty as well as order and structure."[123] It may well be that chaos theory and symmetry-breaking are apt metaphors for this kind of theological position.

Process theology aside, there can be no doubt that chaos theory and symmetry-breaking have promoted a rash of recent theological speculation from the realms of mathematicians, physicists, and other scientists. Stephen Hawking, in his *Brief History of Time* (a book interlaced with just such speculations), probably captured the penultimate aim of these endeavors when he notes that if we can discover a complete theory of why we and the universe exist, then we will "know the mind of God."[124] Chaos theory and symmetry-breaking have, indeed, led to grand and even grandiose attempts to unify the fundamental forces that act on elementary particles.[125] In a way, these efforts to find Grand Unified Theories (GUTS) or Theories of Everything (TOES) replicate the Greek efforts to harmonize through symmetry—to "bind" rather than to "divide." Yet they do so in a manner that focuses, not on the symmetric, but on the *a*symmetric aspects of the universe.

Much of this effort can be understood through the medium of fractal geometry, a new kind of geometry "discovered" only in the last few decades and "named" in 1975 by Benoit Mandelbrot, an IBM researcher in New York.[126] Fractal geometry is geometry that occurs, not in two, three, or even *n* dimensions, but in *fractional* dimensions.[127] It developed, unexpectedly, as a result of attempts in the early 1960s to model weather forecasting with a computer. It is, one might say, totally computer-dependent, for without the graphic- imaging abilities of the computer, we could never have detected the elaborate and sometimes weird patterns that occur over and over at different scales within an otherwise chaotic picture. It is these heretofore hidden repetitive patterns that form the core of fractal geometry and that give rise to the notion that there is an underlying order in chaos.

Fractal geometry, which is really just one of several kinds of symmetry-breaking, is a good place for us to concentrate some of our attention because it has given birth to so many mathematical "nature" metaphors, some of which carry religious overtones and most of which ultimately raise ethical questions of a religious nature. Many of these metaphors are drawn only loosely and, I suspect, somewhat unconsciously. In a recent article in *Discover* magazine, the metaphor between mathematics and nature is drawn as loosely as possible—through side-by-side pictures of "twin" sea shells, one of which is nature's creation and the other of which is programmed from a computer. Just in case the implication, that nature is a mathematician, is not conveyed strongly enough by the images, the message is spelled out in words.

> Nature should also get credit . . . for being a first-class mathematician. The patterns and shapes of living things correspond to some of the most abstract ideas in math. The humble mollusk, for example, without a single course in algebra, can draw the equation $r = ae^{\theta}$.[128]

James Gleick, in his best-selling book on chaos theory, notes the similar viewpoint of Michael Barnsley, whose original work with ferns eventually led to the kind of duplicating process described above. Barnsley contended, says Gleick, that "In some sense . . . nature must be playing its own version of the chaos game."[129]

Over and over in Gleick's unfolding history of chaos we find such striking metaphors, some overt, some merely implied. Mathematical chaos, it would seem, is metaphorically linked to:

> Color: "Redness is not necessarily a particular bandwidth of light, as the Newtonians would have it. It is a territory of a chaotic universe." (166)

> Climate: "No one realized it then, but Lorenz had looked at the same equation in 1964, as a metaphor for a deep question about climate." (168)

> Turbulence in a Fluid: "With his calculator he began to use a combination of analytic algebra and numerical exploration to piece together an understanding of the quadratic map, concentrating on the boundary region between order and chaos. Metaphorically—but *only* metaphorically—he knew that this region was like the mysterious boundary between smooth flow and turbulence in a fluid." (171)

> An Electric Power Grid: "But scientists studying fractal basin boundaries showed that the border between calm and catastrophe could be far more complex than anyone dreamed. 'The

whole electrical power grid of the East Coast is an oscillatory system.' " (235)

Artificial Intelligence: "Many other scientists began to apply the formalisms of chaos to research in artificial intelligence. . . . A physicist thinking of *ideas* as regions with fuzzy boundaries, separate yet overlapping, pulling like magnets and yet letting go, would naturally turn to the image of a phase space with 'basins of attraction.' " (299)

The Heart: "But researchers using the tools of chaos began to discover that traditional cardiology was making the wrong generalizations about irregular heartbeats, inadvertently using superficial classifications to obscure deep causes. They discovered the dynamical heart." (281)

Life: "Life sucks order from a sea of disorder." (299)

Evolution: "Evolution is chaos with feedback." (314)

Gaia: "Whatever their purpose, maps and models must simplify as much as they mimic the world. For Ralph Abraham, the Santa Cruz mathematician, a good model is the 'daisy world' of James E. Lovelock and Lynn Margulis, proponents of the so-called Gaia hypothesis, in which conditions necessary for life are created and maintained by life itself in a self-sustaining process of dynamical feedback." (279)

The Universe: "The new geometry mirrors a universe that is rough, not rounded, scabrous, not smooth." (94)

God's Grapevine: "The Mandelbrot set is the most complex object in mathematics, its admirers like to say. An eternity would not be enough time to see it all, its disks studded with prickly thorns, its spirals and filaments curling outward and around, bearing bulbous molecules that hang, infinitely variegated, like grapes on God's personal vine." (221)

Free Will: "On a philosophical level, it [the phenomenon of chaos] struck me as an operational way to define free will, in a way that allowed you to reconcile free will with determinism." (251)

The Genesis Creation: "We had no concept of the real difference that nonlinearity makes in a model. The idea that an equation could bounce around in an apparently random way—that was pretty exciting. You would say, 'Where is this random motion coming from? I don't see it in the equations.' It seemed like something for nothing, or something out of nothing." (251)

These metaphors, which are essentially familiar metaphors, liken the chaos of fractal geometry not only to areas of interest to scientists, but also to many topics that normally belong to the confines of philosophy and theology.

That this one concept can be used in such a vast array of metaphors is a function of the universality of chaos. Chaotic universality implies scaling, the sense, as one scientist put it, that there are "structures in nonlinear systems that are always the same if you look at them right."[130] Mitchell Feigenbaum, the mathematician who discovered scaling and who believes that "the only things that can ever be universal, in a sense, are scaling things,"[131] also indicates that finding such universality is a matter of the way you are looking.

> There's a fundamental presumption in physics that the way you understand the world is that you keep isolating its ingredients until you understand the stuff you think is truly fundamental. Then you presume that the other things you don't understand are details. The assumption is that there are a small number of principles that you can discern by looking at things in their pure state—this is the true analytic notion—and then somehow you put these together in more complicated ways when you want to solve more dirty problems. If you can. In the end, to understand, you have to change gears.[132]

If the gears you have to handle are, as Feigenbaum implies, holistic ones, the method by which you look may well be metaphorical. The following description of fractal geometry, for example, sounds very much like a McFague version of metaphor. Fractal geometry, says Christopher Scholz, an early pioneer in chaos, is

> a single model that allows us to cope with the range of dimensions of the earth. . . . It gives you mathematical and geometrical tools to describe and make predictions. Once you get over the hump, and you understand the paradigm, you can start actually measuring things and thinking about things in a new way. You see them differently. You have a new vision. It's not the same as the old vision at all—it's much broader."[133]

This new vision, as we have already noted, is indelibly connected with the computer, for without the extraordinary capabilities of this human invention we would never be able to crunch out enough numbers to form even the simplest fractal image. These very same extraordinary capabilities, however, have led to some highly provocative issues regarding the computer's status as an intelligent entity. The brain, says Barrow, performs algorithmic compressions on whatever information is made available to it.[134] The fact that the computer performs such operations, or at least some such operations, with more skill and speed than the human brain can suggests the possibility of computer-life.

"The computer thinks," contend Davis and Hersh, "and by its thoughts we are elevated. By its good deeds we are bettered."[135] While we have clearly anthropomorphised the computer,[136] we are nonetheless reluctant to give it the full status of life. Yet recent developments[137] in the creation of artificial realities, with simulators that create new worlds so real they fool us, begin to blur the distinction between animate and inanimate. A recent article in the New York Times highlights our contemporary dilemma regarding the dividing line between life and nonlife: "A 'creature' consisting of ones and zeros has emerged from its computer womb and caused a scientific sensation: without human guidance it reproduces, undergoes spontaneous genetic changes, passes them on to offspring and evolves new species whose interactions mimic those of real biological evolution and ecology."[138] This "creature" not only gives birth, it mutates and is susceptible to a built-in "reaper"—the equivalent of death.[139]

Living computers, i.e., artificial life-forms, are part of the cutting edge of science which an interdisciplinary team of academic mavericks are currently studying at the Santa Fe Institute.[140] Here, computer experts have developed a "marvelous structure" emerging out of an initial set of totally random rules—the computer equivalent of primordial chaos. Such emergent models, they are finding, have implications for a "thoroughly scientific version of *vitalism:* the ancient idea that life involves some kind of energy, or force, or spirit that transcends mere matter." Carrying this notion just a little further, some of the participants have speculated that "life isn't just *like* a computation, in the sense of being a property of the organization rather than the molecules. Life literally is a computation."[141]

In their exploration of such "complex adaptive systems," participants in this institute are keenly aware of the role of metaphor. "Nonscientists tend to think that science works by deduction," explains economist Brian Arthur. "But actually science works mainly by metaphor. And what's happening is that the kinds of metaphor people have in mind are changing."[142] In particular, the reductionistic logic of the Newtonian worldview is now being supplanted by a notion that amazingly simple systems give rise to enormously complex, self-adaptive, coevolutionary unpredictable consequences. "Instead of relying on the Newtonian metaphor of clockwork predictability, complexity seems to be based on metaphors more closely akin to the growth of a plant from a tiny seed, or the unfolding of a computer program from a few lines of code, or perhaps even the organic, self-organizing flocking of simpleminded birds."[143] Just how far, one wonders, can this metaphor of the computer be extended? "Is the universe a computer?" asks Barrow.[144] Well, maybe. And maybe not. Maybe it is just the latest, most fashionable paradigm in an ever-growing Pepper root-metaphor expansion.[145] Or maybe it is, in fact, a Gaia-like living being, birthing simulated earths complete with dinosaurs and humans. Yet again, maybe it is just the mind of God. A complete consideration of the status of the computer today inevitably brings forth such essentially religious considerations. It flips us back and forth between the world of mathematics and the world of religion, so that, in some ways, the two worlds seem to converge. As Davis and Hersh said in the concluding sentences of a chapter on mathematics and ethics:

> The computer thinks. "I know that my redeemer liveth," said Job, to which the New Job added: His name is King Messiah Ultra Computer. It supercomputes and will transfigure mankind into bits.
> It ultrathinks and *we* shall be saved. We *shall* be saved.
> *O Sancta simplicitas!*[146]

HOLOGRAPHS/HOLYGRAPHS

The subject of order versus chaos is closely connected with questions about the location and revelation of meaning, or so says Douglas Hofstadter when he introduces the following strange metaphor, taken from J. M. Jauch's *Are Quanta Real?*

SALVIATI   Suppose I give you two sequences of numbers, such as
7 8 5 3 9 8 1 6 3 3 9 7 4 4 8 3 0 9 6 6 0 8 4 . . .
and
$1, -1/3, +1/5, -1//7, +1/9, -1/11, +1/13, -1/15. . . .$

If I asked you, Simplicio, what the next number of the first sequence is, what would you say?

SIMPLICIO   I could not tell you. I think it is a random sequence and that there is no law in it.

SALVIATI   And for the second sequence?

SIMPLICIO   That would be easy. It must be $+1/17$.

SALVIATI   Right. But what would you say if I told you that the first sequence is also constructed by a law and this law is in fact identical with the one which you have just discovered for the second sequence?

SIMPLICIO   This does not seem probable to me.

SALVIATI   But it is indeed so, since the first sequence is simply the beginning of the decimal fraction [expansion] of the sum of the second. Its value is $\pi/4$.

SIMPLICIO   You are full of such mathematical tricks, but I do not see what this has to do with abstraction and reality.

SALVIATI   The relationship with abstraction is easy to see. The first sequence looks random unless one has developed through a process of abstraction a kind of filter which sees a simple structure behind the apparent randomness.

It is exactly in this manner that laws of nature are discovered. Nature presents us with a host of phenomena which appear mostly as chaotic randomness until we select some significant events, and abstract from their particular, irrelevant circumstances so that they become idealized. Only then can they exhibit their true structure in full splendor.

SAGREDO   This is a marvelous idea! It suggests that when we try to understand nature, we should look at the phenomena as if they were *messages* to be understood. Except that each message appears to be random until we establish a code to read it. This code takes the form of an abstraction, that is, we choose to ignore certain things as irrelevant and we thus partially select the content of the message by a free choice. These irrelevant signals form the "background noise," which will limit the accuracy of our message.

But since the code is not absolute there may be several messages in the same raw material of the data, so changing the code will result in a message of equally deep significance in something that was merely noise before, and *conversely:* In a new code a former message may be devoid of meaning.

Thus a code presupposes a free choice among different, complementary aspects, each of which has equal claim to *reality,* if I may use this dubious word.

Some of these aspects may be completely unknown to us

now but they may reveal themselves to an observer with a different system of abstractions.

But tell me, Salviati, how can we then still claim that we
discover something out there in the objective real world? Does
this not mean that we are merely creating things according to our
own images and that reality is only within ourselves?

SALVIATI   I don't think that this is necessarily so, but it is a
question which requires deeper reflection.[147]

In this strange metaphor we find what amounts to a series of
braided and even nested metaphors. The two sequences of numbers representing mathematics are likened to order and chaos,
which, with the insight of this new image, suddenly appears as a
unity. The process of understanding this idea is an abstract process,
which is compared to a filtering brain (although the word brain is
not formally used). Out of this metaphorical relationship is created
a new structure or law. Then the whole notion is repeated in a
different frame of reference: nature, rather than mathematics, presents order and chaos as though it were an abstract message that
our filtering brains must decode. Analogically, the message is the
structure is the law is the code. Likewise, order-and-chaos is mathematics is nature. The *process* of interrelating these (and this
should recall the newer interactive interpretations of metaphor as
well as Bois' epistemological metaphysics) is what happens in our
"filters" and is the source of meaning.

Now, there are at least two other frames of reference here, one
spelled out and one only implied. The spelled-out frame deals with
free will and reality. Underlying the *process* outlined above is a
presupposition of a choice between realities, a kind of multi-world
preexistence that brings *noise* into focus through the very process,
oddly enough, that it undergirds. The implied frame of reference,
however, is to Galileo, for the characters who voice this strange
metaphor are borrowed from Galileo, then transported to a modern-
day setting. Galileo, it will be remembered, struggled with precisely the same issues of free will and different choices of reality. Thus,
in a curious sort of way these two frames of reference merge much
as do the two sequences of numbers that, again in a rather odd
tangle of repetition, began the whole strange metaphor. I label it
"strange" because this very sort of tangled loop is a metaphor in
itself for the fundamental theme of Hofstadter's book on metamathematics.[148]

What we find in this analysis is the sense that "there are structures . . . that are always the same if you look at them right," that is, the sense of scaling. The same pattern appears over and over at different levels, just as it does in fractal geometry. This scaling, with its self-similarity, suggests yet another mathematical metaphor—a holographic metaphor. The holograph has been set forth recently as a possible model for the human brain and/or for the world as a whole. Summaries of this metaphor can be found from a number of different sources, including Fritjof Capra, Marilyn Ferguson, F. David Peat, and, more recently and completely, Michael Talbot and Stanislav Grof.[149]

Holography is perhaps most popularly understood today as a technique for producing three-dimensional images with a laser. Walking through a museum that contains holographic art work is a little like walking through a land of fantasy.

> There's something both magical and elusive about holography that you can't really understand until you meet a hologram face to face. When the lighting is right, it creates an unmistakably three-dimensional image in midair. Still, you would never mistake the holographic image for the real object; the colors are not natural, there's a subtle graininess, and the image fades or disappears if you view it from the wrong angle. Even so, your instincts tell you to reach out and touch it; but when you close your hand, it will touch only thin air.[150]

In a sense, a hologram is a picture; but it differs significantly from a picture, say, that an ordinary camera might take. In general, both ordinary photographic and holographic techniques capture light that is reflected in wavefronts from objects about us. These wavefronts are the entire source of all the information that reaches our eyes. Each wavefront has certain properties, namely frequency, amplitude, and phase. To be somewhat oversimplistic, a photograph captures the frequency and amplitude while a hologram captures all three properties. That is, a hologram records and then re-creates the entire wavefront as precisely as possible.

The mathematical roots of this technique can be traced back a couple hundred years ago to the work of a Frenchman, Joseph Fourier who, while studying heat waves, showed that any wave can be written as a unique sum of trigonometric sine waves. This discovery was the key to a "new wave language [that] is the foundation stone of all wave-based sciences including communications theory, modern optics, sound reproduction, oceanography, and quantum theory."[151] In 1947, while trying to improve the electron microscope, Dennis Gabor conceived the idea of recording both amplitude and phase by superimposing two wavefronts of light and tracking the intensity pattern of their interference. The actual construction of a hologram, however, had to await the invention of the laser some twenty years later.

David Bohm, physicist and coworker of Einstein, was probably the first to identify the metaphorical possibilities of holography. Holography has the unusual property that a small portion of it can be used to reconstruct the entire image. Bohm has taken this idea to develop a model of reality that sees each part of energy and matter representing a microcosm that enfolds the whole. As Grof puts it:

> He [Bohm] suggests that the world we perceive through our sense and nervous systems, with or without the help of scientific instruments, represents only a tiny fragment of reality. He calls what we perceive the "unfolded" or "explicate order." These perceptions have emerged as special forms from a much larger matrix. He calls the later the "enfolded" or "implicate order." In other words, that which we perceive as reality is like a projected holographic image. The larger matrix from which that image is projected can be compared to the hologram. However, Bohm's picture of the implicate order (analogous to the hologram) describes a level of reality that is not accessible to our senses or direct scientific scrutiny.[152]

A hologram is based on mathematical principles that are almost eerily reminiscent of Pythagorean number symbolism. In 1966, brain surgeon Karl Pribram proposed that the hologram might be used as a model for how the brain stores memory. As Ferguson recounts it:

> Over the next several years he and other researchers uncovered what appeared to be the brain's calculative strategies for knowing, for sensing. It appears that in order to see, hear, smell, taste, and so on, the brain performs complex calculations on the frequencies of the data it receives. Hardness or redness or the smell of ammonia are only frequencies when the brain encounters them. *These mathematical processes have little common-sense relationship to the real world as we perceive it.* Neuroanatomist Paul Pietsch said, "The abstract principles of the hologram may

explain the brain's most elusive properties." The diffuse hologram makes no more common sense than the brain. The whole
code exists at every point in the medium. "Stored mind is not a
thing. It is abstract relationships. . . . In the sense of ratios, angles, square roots, mind is a mathematic. No wonder it is hard to
fathom."[153]

Mind is a mathematic. That is quite a metaphor, and yet it is
similar to what we have been saying all along. But if the brain
knows by putting together holograms, who or what is doing the
interpreting? As we asked in chapter 1,[154] who does the filtering?
Although we circumvented the question earlier, there are some
possible answers to this question. Be forewarned, though. They are
not particularly satisfying answers to those who despise contradiction and inconsistency. St. Francis of Assisi, for example, said,
"What we are looking for is what is looking." Tobias Dantzig,
whose beautiful comments on number theory ended chapter 2,
wrote that: "We cannot change the rules of the game, we cannot
ascertain whether the game is fair. We can only study the player at
his game; not, however, with the detached attitude of a bystander,
for we are watching our own minds at play."[155] Marilyn Ferguson
and Karl Pribram suggest that "Maybe the *world* is a hologram!"[156]

The essential idea behind such comments is that the part is
related to the whole in ways that allow it to in some way replicate
or embody the whole. Bohm has coined the term "holomovement"
to express the "dynamic phenomenon out of which all forms of the
material universe flow."[157] He regards consciousness itself as an
essential feature of this holomovement, because he "sees mind and
matter as being interdependent and correlated, but not causally
connected. They are mutually enfolding projections of a higher
reality which is neither matter nor consciousness."[158] Grof, in
noting the similarities between Pribram's model of the brain and
Bohm's theory of holomovement, echoes this thought when he
points out that

> The holographic model offers revolutionary possibilities for a
> new understanding of the relationships between the parts and the
> whole. No longer confined to the limited logic of traditional
> thought, the part ceases to be just a fragment of the whole but,
> under certain circumstances, reflects and contains the whole. As
> individual human beings we are not isolated and insignificant

Newtonian entities; rather, as integral fields of the holomovement each of us is also a microcosm that reflects and contains the macrocosm. If this is true, then we each hold the potential for having direct and immediate experiential access to virtually every aspect of the universe, extending our capacities well beyond the reaches of our senses.[159]

This vision developed by supporters of the holgraphic metaphor is surprisingly consistent with ideas of Eastern religion.[160] Ferguson notes that if "the nature of reality is *itself* holographic, and the brain operates holographically, then the world is indeed, as the Eastern religions have said, *maya*:[161] a magic show."[162] Bohm likewise contends that all apparent substance and movement are illusory. By Ferguson's account, Bohm says that:

> Ever since Galileo . . . we have been looking at nature through lenses; our very act of objectifying, as in an electron microscope, alters that which we hope to see. We want to find its edges, to make it sit still for a moment, when its true nature is in another order of reality, another dimension, where there are no *things*. It is as if we are bringing the "observed" into focus, as you would bring a picture into resolution, but the *blur* is a more accurate representation. The blur itself is the basic reality.[163]

In this perspective, the world is not what we usually think it is: it is not stable, tangible, visible, or audible. It is a world in which "scientific findings are always fraught with contradiction."[164] It is a world that shifts, a world open to mystical experience, a world in which, as Pribram put it, "if we get ESP or paranormal phenomena —or nuclear phenomena in physics—it simply means that we are reading out of some other dimension at that time."[165] It is a world described by an ancient Hindu sutra: "In the heaven of Indra there is said to be a network of pearls so arranged that if you look at one you see all the others reflected in it. In the same way, each object in the world is not merely itself but involves every other object, and in fact *is* every other object."[166] It is, to use Ferguson's words, a world that is "dynamic and kaleidoscopic."

And it is here, with this kaleidoscopic world, that I conclude this look at other people's mathematical metaphors and begin to look at some new ones. Should these new ones turn out to exhibit, as I suspect they might, shapes of old familiar patterns, then so be it. For, in the twentieth century we are now finally realizing that:

The Great Architect of the Universe now begins to appear as a pure mathematician.
　　Sir James Jeans

What the mathematicians have called abstraction is reality.
　　Buckminster Fuller

Set theory can be viewed as a form of exact theology.
　　Rudy Rucker

One could perhaps describe the situation by saying that God is a mathematician of a very high order, and he used very advanced mathematics in constructing the universe.
　　Paul Dirac

Science is a differential equation. Religion is a boundary condition.
　　Alan Turing

God is a definite integral.
　　Sarah Voss

CHAPTER 4

God the Definite Integral and Cantorian Religion

TOWARDS TWO METAPHORS

In chapter 3, we examined some of the ways that mathematics has been used metaphorically over the centuries to augment, explain, create, and validate various spiritual and metaphysical insights. In this chapter our attention turns to needs of the present moment, the basic supposition being that we can serve the cause of liberal religion in today's society by intentionally fostering the metaphorical use of mathematics. In particular, I present here two new mathematical metaphors, along with what I hope will be the beginnings of a dialogue about their implications. The first metaphor may be summarized somewhat oversimply as "God is a Definite Integral." The second may be thought of as a religious perspective that bears similarities to Cantorian set theory. In both instances, we might recall the "is" and "is not" character of metaphor, for I intend these examples to be provocative rather than definitive.

THE ONE AND THE MANY

Modern mathematics and physics have presented contemporary society with the necessity of reexamining its ideas about the relation of the whole to its parts. "The tidy old reductionist idea of a universe which is simply the sum of its parts is completely discredited by the new physics," says Paul Davies. "There is a unity to the universe, and one which goes far deeper than a mere expression of uniformity. It is a unity which says that without everything you can have nothing."[1] As we saw in chapter 3, scientists seeking to

111

understand this unity have sometimes noted the similarities of modern physics to Eastern thought, with its emphasis on the holistic aspect of existence and the subtle connection between the whole and its parts.

A contemporary metaphor for this relationship between the whole and its parts has cropped up in the last half century— the metaphor of the holograph. Bohm likens the holograph to the universe while Pribram likens it to the mind. The work of Michael Talbot in *The Holographic Universe* and Stanislav Grof in *The Holotropic Mind* substantially extend and deepen these two analogies in ways that are highly controversial. The point here, however, is not that they are controversial, but that they exist as metaphors drawn first and foremost from the realm of mathematics. Some scholars trace the holographic metaphor back through the Fourier transforms (special mathematical functions) which allowed mathematical expression of wave action, through the integral calculus which undergirded Fourier's work, to the philosophical thought of the seventeenth-century philosopher and mathematician Leibniz who coinvented the calculus.[2] Leibniz hypothesized that the universe consisted of fundamental entities called *monads,* each of which contained a reflection of the entire universe, while simultaneously representing "more distinctly the body which is particularly attached to it and of which it is the entelechy."[3] Each also bore an important duality of what he called particular and universal aspects:

> Insofar as the body is particular, the monad represents the body. But since the body is connected with all other bodies, the monad also represents all other bodies or mirrors the universe. In its role as entelechy or actualizer of this potential body, the monad must be the source for representing these particular and universal aspects and therefore it must itself bear particular and universal relationships to other monads. Leibniz insists that parts do not exist, so the relationship must be an organic hierarchy of monads leading up to the supreme monad, which is sometimes referred to as God.[4]

This sense of duality is pervasive throughout Leibniz's thought. It is not only a duality between the universal and the particular. On the metaphysical level, it is also a duality between "monads and perceptions, of a clear and confused type, respectively." On an abstract phenomenological level, it is a duality between "primitive active and passive forces." On the observable level of phenomenology, it is between "bodies that continue the twofold division into derivative active and passive forces.[5]

Yet transcending the duality is an overriding unity, a unity that harbors back to the thought-systems not only of the ancient Greeks,[6] but also to certain Eastern religious traditions. While scholars disagree about the amount of influence which it had on Leibniz, they generally agree that a notable resemblance exists between the metaphysical system of Leibniz and that of the Chinese. They point, specifically, to

> correspondences between Leibniz' organicism and Neo-Confucian organicism, between Leibniz' concept of the monad and the Neo-Confucian concept of *li* (principle), between Leibniz' binary arithmetic and the hexagrams of the *Book of Changes*,[7] between Leibniz' tendency to reduce physics and ethics to the more common denominator of the monad and the Chinese tendency to merge the natural world with the moral world, between Leibniz' notion of force (*vis viva*) and the Chinese notion of *ch'i* (material force).[8]

Leibniz, particularly in his latter years, frequently drew on Chinese thought to reinforce his own. One such citing of considerable significance to his own philosophy is "his emphasis on passages from neo-Confucian texts that describe the dual aspects of *li* as both universal and particular, of both one and many."[9]

For Leibniz, the one and the many did not imply a separation into atomistic "parts." Rather, "parts" could be referred to figuratively, in the same way we might refer to "souls" as "parts" of the Divinity. The parts are illusions, for, as with the Chinese, "All things are one."[10] As Leibniz put it in the *Monadology,* no. 13, the "particular [trait of what is changing] must comprehend a multiplicity in the unity, that is in the simple. For since all natural change proceeds by degrees, something changes and something remains. Consequently, there must be in the simple substance a plurality of affections and relations, though it has no parts."[11] This idea, which is "Leibniz' interpretation of [the] Chinese notion of a universal-particular relationship,"[12] plays an essential role in the metaphysics of this intellectual genius. The unity or "harmony" of his philosophy, Mungello later notes, "was specifically aimed at countering the chaos of his time."[13]

Leibniz was brilliantly intellectual and his work has sometimes been accused of spiritual shallowness because he relied exclusively upon discursive methods of obtaining knowledge.[14] However, in Mungello's view, spiritual cultivation was synonymous with intellectual cultivation for Leibniz.[15] When he was a young man, Leibniz apparently had a mystical experience that "strengthened his faith and made him capable of a new experience of God and a realization that the world is created by the act of the spirit."[16] Among the various types of mystical experience one can have is thought to be an experience that is primarily analytic in nature, the so-called "contemplative insight," and it is this type of mystical experience that certain scholars attribute to Leibniz. In this view, "Leibniz' mathematics enabled him to replace the identity of a mystical and intuitive nature with a new notion of identity in which systems of relations become representative of one another."[17]

Without doubt, Leibniz relied heavily upon mathematics as a means to discover the wisdom of God.[18] In his presentation of the Universal Characteristic, he

> seeks to construct an "alphabet of human thought" that will function as a type of calculus and likens this language to the arithmetic of Pythagorean numbers or a Cabala of mystic vocables.[19] Leibniz distinguishes between *contingent truths,* which involve truths of fact and whose demonstration requires an infinite analysis capable only by God, and *necessary truths* or truths of reason, whose demonstration involves a finite analysis within the range of human ability. Leibniz implies that this Universal Characteristic will involve truths of a necessary nature, but that careful construction of a system of characters is necessary to make them amenable to calculation. By "signs" Leibniz means the symbols our thoughts use to signify things—for example, words and letters, chemical, astronomical, and algebraic notions. By "characters" Leibniz means signs that are written, drawn, or carved.[20]

That he was skilled at the invention of such "characters" is indicated by the fact that, although both he and Newton are credited with the simultaneous discovery of the integral calculus, it is Leibniz's symbolic notation that you will find in contemporary calculus texts.[21] It is both to Leibniz's calculus and to his *characters* that I turn next as *signs* that *symbol*ize our (or at least my) thoughts regarding the fundamental nature of our universe, thoughts that use mathematics *metaphor*ically as a *model* for identifying the ultimate Absolute, normally referred to simply as God.

GOD THE DEFINITE INTEGRAL

While the holograph has been offered recently as a mathematical model for the universe, for mind, and perhaps even for Universe and/or Mind, I find that the more primitive, simpler notions embodied in its forerunner, the definite integral of calculus, serve me well as a metaphor for much of what I think of as God. There have, over time, been many different images of God and even more different characteristics associated with the concept. God is seen as Father, Mother, Creator, Life-force, Spirit, Christ, Friend, Mind, and so forth. As with all metaphors, all of these fall somewhat short of being fully adequate to the task of describing/defining God. All of them implicitly set forth certain characteristics of God that are peculiar to their own idiosyncrasy. God as Father, for instance, offers a personal, protective image of God, one that our Western society has historically associated with a personal deity who hears our prayers and who looks after the well-being of individuals and of society in general. God as Life-force, on the other hand, offers an abstract, process orientation that often appeals to someone of a more scientific or Eastern outlook. McFague, in her work on models of God, notes that since the root-metaphor of many religions—and certainly of Christianity—is *relationship*, a variety of interpretive models can help to depict this relationship. She notes that the "network or structure of *relationships* involved in these models and the commonplaces associated with them are what is central, not the ontological assertion that God is father or mother."[22]

Relationship is probably the one characteristic that I personally find most appealing to highlight in any metaphor of God. It is, as McFague observed, fundamental to the notion of God in Christianity. It is also fundamental to more oriental philosophies. Capra, for instance, notes that the "most important characteristic of the Eastern world view—one could almost say the essence of it—is the awareness of the unity and mutual interrelation of all things and events, the experience of all phenomena in the world as manifestations of a basic oneness."[23] The relationship between the one and the many (or, more accurately, the One and the many) most captures my imagination and heart when I think of God. And from this orientation I offer the mathematical metaphor of the definite integral of calculus as a relatively simple concept that embodies the complexity, the subtlety, and the mystery of the structure of this relationship.

The definite integral of calculus is usually introduced via the following notation as the limit of a summation process. It has another interpretation involving the process of differentiation, but I am using it primarily in the former sense. In particular, by the definite integral of calculus, I mean

$$_a\int^b f(x)\ dx = \lim_{n \to \infty} \sum_{i=1}^{n} f(x_i^*)\ \Delta\ x_i$$

which is read: The integral from a to b of the function f with respect to the variable x is defined as the limit as n approaches infinity of the sum of function f of x_i^* times Δx_i.

To give the nonmathematician at least some idea of what this notation is all about, I would engage you in the following mental exercise. Picture a sheet of paper. A regular, roughly 8 by 11 sheet is fine—the kind that comes out of a photocopier. Now 8 by 11 means what? It means the lengths of the sides according to some arbitrary measuring scale (we use inches), and it gives us a method of figuring out how much space is used up by that sheet of paper. In mathematics, this idea might be modeled by the equation $A = lw$, in this case $11 \times 8 = 88$ square inches.

Suppose someone rips the paper across the top so that three sides look like a rectangle and one side is irregular. Now it no longer takes up eighty-eight square inches of space, but exactly how much space does it take up? Perhaps 77 inches? Or 80 inches? Or 80.5 inches? It is hard to tell, and if you are typical, you are probably wondering right about now, who the heck cares?

For the moment, pretend you really care. One thing we could do would be to cut it into eleven strips, say, all one inch wide. By measuring the length of each of these strips, say, at its longest length, we could get a rough estimate of how much area each of the strips took up and, by adding all eleven of them together, we would have a fairly good idea of the actual area of the torn sheet of paper. It would not be exact. It would be off a little bit, because each torn strip is not exactly a rectangle and there would be a little "extra" unwanted paper on each strip. It would be pretty close, though. It would certainly be closer than 88 square inches.

If we wanted to get an even closer answer, we could cut thinner strips. That way there would be smaller amounts left over (in mathematics, the "error"). We could, in theory at least, cut thinner and thinner, ever more refined strips so that we could find closer and closer approximations to the exact area. Setting aside all physical problems—such as the fact that we cannot quite cut that small—and assuming that we were going to live forever and would do nothing whatsoever other than engage in this process of summing up the areas of more and more slender strips, we would, according to the First Fundamental Law of Calculus (which is the essence of my argument from calculus about the nature of God), arrive at an *exact* measurement of the area of our torn sheet of paper.

If you have caught the drift of what I am saying, then you are half way through the first year of a beginning calculus course, which is quite an accomplishment for a couple of pages of reading. Of course, a regular calculus course would present the concept much more rigorously and would probably use a series of illustrations and some complicated notation to get across the same idea. Figure 4.1[24] shows part of a typical school-text rendition of this portion of my argument. A calculus text, however, would undoubtedly point out another significant aspect of this process, namely, that it does not make any difference (in theory) how you go about the process.

Many ways of cutting up the strips work. We could have started with six strips instead of with eleven, for example. They could have been different widths, too—one of them 1 inch, another 3/4 inch, another 1/2 inch and so on. By cutting these six strips into ever smaller strips, and summing them up, eventually we would arrive at the same precise answer. We would arrive at an Absolute. The point is that *lots of ways work*. Rephrasing that, we might say that many ways lead to one absolute which in some sense jumps *beyond* or *transcends* the specific. A word of caution is needed, however, for, as anyone who is familiar with the calculus knows, given the particular limitations of our numeration system, *some ways work better than others*. That is, there is a call for judgement here.

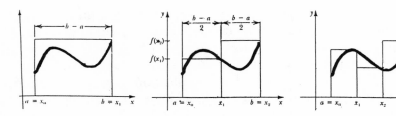

so the sum A_2 of the areas of the rectangles in Figure 4.3 is

$$A_2 = f(x_1)\left(\frac{b-a}{2}\right) + f(x_2)\left(\frac{b-a}{2}\right)$$

$$= [f(x_1) + f(x_2)]\left(\frac{b-a}{2}\right).$$

Dividing the interval $[a, b]$ into three equal subintervals, as shown in Figure 4.4, and letting

$$x_1 = a + (b-a)/3 \quad \text{and} \quad x_2 = a + 2(b-a)/3$$

gives the sum of the areas of the three rectangles in this figure:

$$A_3 = [f(x_1) + f(x_2) + f(x_3)]\left(\frac{b-a}{3}\right).$$

At the nth stage, $[a, b]$ is divided into n equal subintervals (see Figure 4.5) and an approximation to A is

(4.1) $$A_n = [f(x_1) + f(x_2) + \cdots + f(x_n)]\left(\frac{b-a}{n}\right),$$

where

$$x_i = a + \frac{i(b-a)}{n}, \quad \text{for each } i = 1, 2, \ldots, n.$$

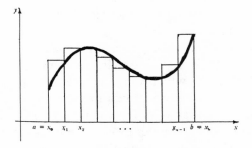

FIGURE 4.1
Deriving the First Fundamental Law of Calculus

This process of finding exact areas of such odd-shaped regions by breaking them up into infinitely smaller sections and then summing the areas of these sections is called "integration." It is symbolized by the definite integral of calculus, given in notation as $_a\int^b f(x)\,dx$. For our purposes, we do not need to delve further into the details of this notation. It is important to note, however, that the never-ending process represented by this symbolism divides a *whole* into discrete *parts* which, at one and the same time both *do and do not* "add up" to the original whole. In one sense, there is *always* a gap between the approximated area and the desired exact area. Yet, paradoxically, this process also provides a way to bridge that gap, so that it does, in fact, give the *exact* measurement of the whole.

In my earlier career as a mathematics teacher, I often had the privilege of watching my students, after struggling with the various symbols and figures involved, absorb the full sense behind this seeming contradiction. There is nothing quite so satisfying as watching the beauty of this seemingly abstract, mysterious process unfold into sudden comprehension and acceptance. My students would then begin to apply this concept of the definite integral to more sophisticated aspects of life, such as anticipating population change or acquiring maximum economic efficiency. I would point out that the paradox or contradiction implicit in the symbolism (which is unresolved only if one assumes that the imagined never-ending sequence of addition steps must actually be carried out) was presented many years ago in Athens in the form of Zeno's paradox about Achilles and the turtle. The "answers" to this paradox involve notions of continuity, limits, and infinite aggravates—all abstractions unknown to the ancient Greeks, but easily handled by the concept of the integral calculus.[25] I would point out that the integral calculus provided necessary tools for humankind to put flying machines into the air and to send rockets to the moon and other such "magical" things. The summation process implied by the definition of the definite integral, I would say, has become an extremely powerful *model* for many processes that have nothing to do with cutting sheets of paper into strips. It is a pattern. It is a pattern symbolized by a bit of fancy mathematical notation.

Today, I would suggest something more controversial by arguing that this same notation can also be thought of as a model for our spiritual relationships to each other and to a transcending One that embodies all of these many individual "others" and yet is always somehow something more than their mere summation. The process of living out our individual lives is a little like existing in a minute rectangular time frame of eighty or so years: each individual aggregate stands, in a sense, alone, separate, as a discrete entity from all else. This is the existential sense in which most people "know" themselves. Yet the model of the definite integral offers an alternative to this "aloneness." We have worked with this model in what the "father" of general semantics Alfred Korzybski calls the only language in existence that is, "in the main, similar in structure to the world around us and to the human nervous system."[26] We can see, because we have worked with it, a continuity and a unifying oneness to all our individual separateness. That continuity and unification is what I refer to as God, and the never-ending process of splitting that God-whole up into discrete separatenesses is analogous for me to the experience of living as individuals in this world of discrete physical objects. When we sum it all up, however, when we take the totality of all our assorted experiences, we are, to borrow from the biblical Paul, "as one body."

The use of the definite integral as a metaphor for God has, like all other metaphors, certain limitations. For one thing, it is very process oriented, and hence it loses the personal aspect that many people seek out in their conceptions of God. For another, technicalities of the mathematics involved in the idea of the *definite* integral (as opposed to, say, the indefinite integral) raise questions regarding the possible finiteness of God, a possibility that runs contrary to the intuition of most people. But as a structural representation for our relationship with a transcending unitary Whole, the Definite Integral offers itself to us as a bridging device between the physical world that it has helped to shape in modern times and the abstract world of the psycho-logical, wherein we become most aware, perhaps, of our spiritual selves.

The definite integral is a metaphor for bridging the gap between continuity and discontinuity, between the continuous and the discrete, between the unified and the separate, between the one and the many. Is this not the underlying message, for example, in the following words of Paul to the Corinthians?

> To each is given the manifestation of the spirit for the common good. To one is given through the Spirit the utterance of wisdom, and to another the utterance of knowledge according to the same Spirit, to another faith by the same Spirit, to another gifts of

healing by the one Spirit, to another the working of miracles, to another prophecy, to another the ability to distinguish between spirits, to another various kinds of tongues, to another the interpretation of tongues. All these are inspired by one and the same Spirit, who apportions to each one individually as he wills.

For just as the body is one and has many members, and all the members of the body, though many, are one body, so it is with Christ. For by one Spirit we were all baptized into one body—Jews or Greeks, slaves or free—and all were made to drink of one Spirit.[27]

The one Spirit is God. God is the Absolute to which all members of the body, though many, are one. In this sense, God may, indeed, be thought of as a Definite Integral. I would argue that Paul unknowingly but beautifully applied this model of the definite integral to the situation of Christianity.

Christianity is a way that works in making sense of our metaphysical realm. It works. It has worked for centuries. It will continue to work for those who so choose. But limiting the application of this model to Christianity is a little like insisting that it be used in straight mathematics only to compute areas. For those who want to fly to the metaphysical moon, so to speak, we must lift out the abstract idea, plant it in our hearts, and help it develop.

The one is the many. The many are one. We find different ways to realize this. Some are better than others. I, myself, am partial to the Unitarian Universalist way, with its emphasis on a unity that does not diminish an underlying diversity—that web of interconnectedness that is only there because of the separateness of individuals. Yet I recognize Unitarian Universalism as only one way among many, and I, like so many others today, struggle not to discount the different ways embraced by others. This is not an easy struggle, for on the one hand, it leads to a relativity that affirms nothing and, on the other, it winds up as a dogma of idolatry and intolerance. The metaphor of the definite integral, while acknowledging that many ways work, nonetheless ensures that, at least in practice, some ways work better than others. This leads us to an important consideration of the nature of judgement.

TOWARDS A STRUCTURE OF JUDGEMENT

There is an old Zen Buddhist story about the master who held a bat over his student's head saying, "If you say this is a stick, I will hit you with it. If you say this is not a stick, I will hit you with it. Speak. Is it a stick or is it not a stick?"

The Western mind often has difficulty with the kind of predicament that this story sets up. There seems to be no positive solution, and we who have grown up with a Western mentality may find ourselves scratching our heads in puzzlement or frustration. When it comes to defining the criteria for judgement, the situation that confronts Western society today in general, and Western religion in particular, provides us with a parallel situation. "Here is a list of X, X, X, and X, a religious canon, so to speak. If you say these are the criteria for making religious judgements, I will show you why you're wrong and we will fight. If you say these are not the criteria, I will show you why you are wrong and we will fight. Speak. Is this list a canon or not?"

While this is a deliberate exaggeration, nonetheless it points to a very real and immediate problem confronted by the contemporary liberal religious community and particularly by Unitarian Universalism. Being consciously noncreedal, Unitarian Universalists celebrate diversity and honor a multiplicity of views and values. In the last century, this tolerance has led us to become "Welcoming Congregations" to much more than just the gay and lesbian community for which the phrase is specifically directed. Our collective attempts to *include* the distanced voice, the "other," have contributed much to our strength as a liberal religious voice. Such attempts have also raised legitimate concerns often framed simply as "Well, what *do* we stand for?"

What, in other words, is the limit of differences? How do we find the normative? How do we find that delicate balance between tolerance and censorship, between being open and having no substance? How do we decide what we will *exclude* as well as what we will *include?* A number of efforts have been made to tackle this problem of canon making for liberal religions.[28] Underlying all of these attempts to proscribe a basis for judgement within the liberal religious community is a growing awareness that we can and must choose a view from among many views without losing sight that our choice is just one among many. As Wayne Booth puts it, "We find ourselves dwelling in a newly created, animated *uni*-verse of possibilities, in which each particular obtains its full life by virtue of being *in* the whole."[29]

David Tracy similarly suggests that different truths only appear to be in opposition to each other, that the various traditions are, rather, particular disclosures of a truth we can only know symbolically. As with the model of the definite integral, we must transcend particularity, working always toward a mutual understanding. For Tracy, this mutual understanding will come about only with dialogue. Through the interchange of conversation we will "come to understand each other's experience by means of analogy with our own experiences,"[30]—hence Tracy's call for an *analogical* imagination.

To Tracy, the *process* of understanding is an interactive one where the text of the classic "interprets" the reader/receiver even as the receiver interprets the classic. The key point here is in the sharing of an experience (i.e., a process) that simultaneously intensifies one and distances one from reality. When that experience is focused on "the self-manifestation of an undeniable power not one's own articulated . . . in . . . the language of scandal and mystery," then the experience, says Tracy, is fundamentally religious in nature.

Morton Smith has warned against resorting to any arbitrary and ad hoc divine intervention in exercising judgement calls. "For good observation," he says, "it is of course necessary to study with sympathy. But for good judgement it is necessary to regain objectivity."[31] In so speaking he offers something of a countervoice to both Tracy and Booth. Booth argues that we "come to the act of judging" through a comparative, communal process of "coduction." "Such a process," he notes "is obviously about as different as possible from what logicians claim to do before offering to share a universally valid proof. Coduction can never be 'demonstrative,' apodeictic: it will not persuade those who lack the experience required to perform a similar coduction."[32] Tracy, with his ultimate appropriation of Christianity as the worldview of his choice, implies a reliance on precisely that divine intervention that Morton so summarily dismisses.

These voices are representative of the two distinct, seemingly antithetical positions that have so often troubled human religious endeavor: authority as centered in the real world versus authority centered in a transcendent divinity. Do we judge a set of criteria to be a canon because it serves such functions as upholding, representing, reflecting, and encouraging a Truth that transcends, a truth that is God's Word or the Way of Brahma? Or are these criteria definitive simply because we (whoever we are) have gotten together and collectively (and sometimes not so collectively) decided they form a canon?

I offer the model of the definite integral from mathematics as a metaphor for bridging the "gap" between these two poles. I borrow here from the language of Korzybski to help reveal this bridging aspect of the definite integral. In one passage, for instance, he describes the summation process involved in integration as one that can carry us "from metaphysical action at a distance to a physical action by contact.[33]

> We can easily see that in terms of *action* a continuous series gives us *action by contact,* since consecutive elements are indefinitely near each other. As the differential and integral calculus were built on the structural assumption of *continuity,* the use of the calculus brings us in touch not only with our x but also with its indefinitely close neighbor $x + dx$. We see that the calculus introduces a most important structural and semantic innovation; namely, that it is a language for describing *action by contact.*[34]

In another passage he emphasizes that, on a psycho-logical level, the concepts involved in the notion of the definite integral

> will be very useful in any line of endeavor. Here we have already learned how, somehow, to translate discontinuous jumps into 'continuous' smooth entities. Because of the structure of our nervous systems we 'feel' 'continuity', yet we can analyze it into a smaller or larger number of definite jumps, according to our needs. The secret of this process lies in assigning an increasing number of jumps, which as they become vanishingly small, or tend to zero, as we say, cease to be felt as jumps and are felt as 'continuous' motion, or change, or growth or anything of this sort.[35]

Thus, in the realm of our real world (i.e., physical reality), we *act by contact*. We gather together and collectively sum up ever more carefully defined criteria: on this basis we make judgements that approximate as nearly as possible an Absolute judgement or wisdom. We do this to bring order out of the chaos of our physical existence, and we do this with awareness that some ways work better than others. We do this, further, with the conviction that *no* way will ever be quite good enough - always some "gap" will remain.

Yet at the same time, we also "feel" the continuity of these assorted pieces of individual wisdom forming our canon. We have, in effect, the capacity to make a leap of faith: the point at which Achilles catches up with the tortoise, the point at which the limiting process of the definite integral yields an exact prescription, the point at which a divine sacredness blatantly "interferes" (as Smith views it) with physical phenomena. This is the point at which discontinuity (particularity) becomes continuity (universality). Or, to place the situation in a non-Western frame of reference, this is the point where the student turns to his/her guru-master, wrests away the bat, and screams "Nonsense!" In short, both poles are necessary and, indeed, are one.

In contemporary society, the metaphorical possibilities of mathematics have been little appreciated or examined. Yet lifting up this metaphorical aspect invites us to reconsider the structure of our judgement by offering us a symbolic picture of that structure. The definite integral of calculus provides us with a skeletal picture, a picture of a continual, never-ending process that, in many specific versions, approximates a final, absolute judgement. If we embrace this picture metaphorically, putting flesh on its bare bones, we discover that the differences we experience in the exercising of these specific ways ultimately disappear in the very unfolding of the process. We obtain the unobtainable—and we are justified in our confidence that our judgement will lead to ultimate Truth. Yet, paradoxically, we never "get there," for the Truth always remains beyond our comprehension, and we will inevitably always stumble about, seeking out dialogue in an effort to understand and assess how someone else's truth may or may not be just as good as our own.

META-STEPPING

Tracy's *dialogical* model is beautifully articulated in more secular language by Booth. For Booth, we operate in metaphorical worlds. He notes five such basic worlds, the fifth being the world of all metaphors. Each of these "fictions"

> is an "imitation of life" not by virtue of copying any detail from life but by realizing the way in which certain circumstances or settings belong to, or "fit," or even cause, certain conditions of soul—happiness or misery or despair; anger or delight or amusement; reconciliation or revolt. Life—the whole of it—really *is* that (meaning *like* that), because we now know that for some people in some circumstances that is how it really has been.[36]

Booth goes on to note: "The trick is to find those myths that not only *work* but *work better* than other myths, an accomplishment which intuitively has much to do with how well myths of reality hold together and match reality, i.e., with coherence and correspondence.[37] The language Booth uses is generally compatible with that drawn from the realm of mathematics. Indeed, he even draws on a computer metaphor to introduce his five metaphorical worlds. It is not to the mechanistic realm of analogy that I am now inclined, however. It is, rather, to that fifth type of metaphor, the "metaphor of metaphors" that mathematics itself, rather than its computerized offspring, may best "fit." Many historians and scientists, as Booth and others have pointed out, regard the language of mathematics, particularly mathematical equations, as "not just literal but *real:* they exist before their discovery, as a kind of Platonic form waiting to be discovered."[38] Yet, as we noted in chapter 1, Booth also raises up the possibility that even mathematical equations are "just metaphors."

There is a tension here—the same kind of tension that has plagued the whole of religious dialogue for centuries, and that we have encountered over and over even in this short study. What is real? What is symbolic? What is the difference? I have, in this study, fairly consistently been inconsistent. I am a realist, I have said, but also an idealist. I have held that the literal is not the same as the metaphorical, and yet, in practically the same breath, I have contended that no line between the two can be drawn. Fact, I have even said, is a matter of taste. Well, ouch. If that statement is, in fact, true, then it no doubt leaves a pretty sour aftertaste in the mouths of the few objectivists who are even willing to try it out.

Such a concept simply does not "work" from the perspective of someone tuned in strictly to the logical aspects of the physical world. That there are alternative ways of viewing the world has been well illustrated in recent years (thanks in large part to the efforts of the feminist movement) and has been a constant voice in this study. But the alternative view that I have been suggesting seemingly goes one step farther, latching onto the dual play between the rational and the irrational as an important part of the human experience. From this perspective, ours is a world of paradox and our existence in this world allows us to experience this paradox. Ours is a world of good and bad, of love and hate, of male and female, of yin and yang, of the universal and the particular, of one and two.[39] Ours is a world where, as Suares's put it, "the human mind is in a state of total contradiction,"[40] and where our God is the God of Paradox, the God of the Definite Integral. Moreover, just as Suares relied on "the sacred language of letter-numbers" to help unravel this world of contradiction,[41] so, too, can we choose to rely on the picture of the definite integral formed by Leibniz and the strange loops of Hofstadter's metamathematics to help us make sense of this nonsense.

For in what is perhaps the ultimate paradox, it is through mathematics that we who have inherited the legacy of Western science may find our best chance of comprehending the logic of this illogic. It is here, in the world of numbers, that we can observe the interaction of different levels of complexity that lies at the heart of paradox.[42] It is in numbers that a three-dimensional Sphere can communicate, if not with a two-dimensional Flatlander, then at least with the human mind. Consciousness not only toys with such mixed levels, it may actually exist only as a result of some "intrinsically high-level phenomenon," as Hofstadter calls it.

To Hofstadter, for example, Gödel's theorem of incompleteness suggests[43] "that there could be some high-level way of viewing the mind/brain, involving concepts which do not appear on lower levels, and that this level might have explanatory power that does not exist—not even in principle—on lower levels."[44] Such a possibility, for Hofstadter, finds the bearer of this "bold hypothesis" with one foot on the level of illogic and one in the realm of logic. "In particular," he says, "it is vital to recall that G's nontheorem-hood *does* have an explanation—it is not a total mystery! The explanation hinges on understanding not just one level at a time, but the way in which one level mirrors its metalevel, and the consequences of this mirroring."[45] "Level-crossing" is what Hofstadter calls it. Meta-stepping is the term I have used here. It is just such meta-stepping that will take us now towards a consideration of an emerging new religion and towards another new metaphorical use of mathematics.

TOWARDS A CANTORIAN RELIGION

As the information/communication age has exploded throughout the twentieth century, our universe has correspondingly shrunk. Today more people know more about more "other" people than ever before in the history of humankind. In unprecedented ways, our modern world is a global world. In the religious arena, this global vision has made accessible to the ordinary individual an unparalleled diversity of faith traditions. Often, increased access to such religious "information" has facilitated a greater appreciation for the religious tradition of the "other" and a fertile cross-seeding of religious ideas and customs. Inevitably, some of these ideas and practices appear to be "incommensurable" (to adapt the language of theologian Kenneth Surin), and, in such instances, it has often led as well to both intra- and interreligious conflict.

Out of these tensions and opportunities has emerged in recent years a pluralistic theology of religions. Englishman John Hick was one of the first religious scholars to address this religious pluralism and to try to render it a comprehensible and useful insight in a global religious world. His contributions to the growing literature on religious pluralism have been substantial, and his voice is one that the contemporary theological world, while often disagreeing with, nonetheless feels compelled to examine. In this section, we will review Hick's main contributions and some of the criticisms and concerns that have surfaced in the earnest attempt by the theological community to deal with his suggestions.

John Hick was born in Scarborough, Yorkshire in 1922. He grew up attending the Anglican church, and by the time he was eighteen, was an evangelical fundamentalist Christian.[46] In an autobiographical essay,[47] he recounts three transformative events that helped to shape his gradual turn to a more liberal Christianity and, eventually, to a religiously pluralistic outlook. The first of these events was the complaint, by eighteen ministers and elders in the late 1960s, based on his religious views of the virgin birth, against Hick's reception into the Presbyterian Church. The second was his move to Birmingham in 1967 where he encountered for the first time large Muslim, Sikh, Hindu, and Caribbean Pentecostal Christians. The third was the furor with which the traditional religious community greeted his mythological interpretation of the Incarnation, first publically detailed in the 1977 publication *The Myth of God Incarnate*.[48]

Hick, then, experienced the painful effects of religious intolerance both personally and second hand through his active work with religious minorities. In a sense, he was/is the product of an information/communication age that widened his vision as it narrowed the distance between different religious traditions. His is a vision of a global society that welcomes religious pluralism. The potential value to humankind of such a vision is not the total homogenization of religious views, but rather the creation of a freer, more tolerant, more mutually appreciative world community. In his words,

> a mutual mission of the sharing of experiences and insights can proceed through the growing network of inter-faith communities. Such mutual mission does not aim at conversion—although occasionally individual conversions, in all directions, will continue to occur—but at mutual enrichment and at cooperation in face of the urgent problems of human survival in a just and sustainable world society.[49]

Few would dispute this goal of a just and sustainable world culture, although not all are convinced that Hick's approach will produce such a world, nor even that Hick is himself primarily interested in the attainment of such a society in the here and now. Indeed, Hick is indisputably vague as to the nature of the desired outcome of human religious endeavor. He does not locate such an outcome firmly within this world, although he also does not deny the possibility. Rather, what he consistently and unrelentingly suggests is that all religious effort strives to transform human existence from a state of "self-centredness" to a state of "Reality centredness." "The great religious traditions," he says, "are to be regarded as alternate soteriological 'spaces' with which, or 'ways' along which, men and women can find salvation/liberation/ enlightenment/fulfillment."[50] He describes the gradual recognition of this thesis within modern society as a Copernican revolution wherein the center of religious endeavor is Reality; the old Ptolemaic view, on the other hand, centered around a specific religious faith that was accepted as superior.[51]

Hick posits[52] the existence of some ideal realm that various religious traditions interpret either as "a personal God or nonpersonal Absolute, or as the cosmic structure or process or ground of the universe."[53] This transcendent reality (variously, the Ultimate, Ultimate Reality, the Supreme Principle, the Divine, the One, the Eternal, the Eternal One, the Real, etc.) is what Hick terms the Real *an sich*. He distinguishes between this Real in itself and the Real as we perceive it in much the same way that Kant distinguished between the noumenal and phenomenal worlds[54] or Wittgenstein between "seeing" and "seeing-as."[55] The Real *an sich* is religiously ambiguous.[56] Humans do not experience the Real in itself; rather, their experience is filtered by individual perceptions and cultural/historical orientations. Thus the Real *an sich* is understood "by different people, or indeed by the same person at different times, in both religious and natural ways."[57] When it *is* experienced religiously, it is "experienced and thought by different human mentalities, forming and formed by different religious traditions, as the range of gods and absolutes which the phenomenology of religion reports."[58] The various faith traditions, therefore, are based on non-illusory, experientially real manifestations of the Real *an sich*.[59] All of these manifestations share a basic commonality (mentioned above) of structure: "[w]hat is the same . . . is the transformation of human existence from self-centredness to Reality-centredness."[60] At least some of these traditions bear additional distinctive and important "family" resemblances.[61]

One family resemblance that Hick holds common to all faith traditions is a kind of golden-rule ethics principle.[62] The degree to which this moral prerogative is achieved within the various faith traditions serves, according to Hick, as a basic criterion for judging the effectiveness and appropriateness of any one tradition over another. Hick is consistently vague in recounting more explicit criteria, and he thus leaves himself open to a variety of charges regarding the inability of his theory to provide ethical norms.[63] Of more interest here, however, is not this basic ethical family resemblance, but a second identified commonality, that of the infinite nature of the Real *an sich*.

Hick equates infinity with unlimitedness, which he terms a negative concept in that it is a denial of limitation. "That this denial must be made of the Ultimate is a basic assumption of all the great traditions. It is a natural and reasonable assumption: for an ultimate that is limited in some mode would be limited by something other than itself, and this would entail its non-ultimacy."[64] For Hick, there are several logical consequences of the infinity of the Real *an sich*.[65] 1) It may be "apprehended and described in an infinity of ways."[66] 2) Some of these ways may be incompatible sets of theories.[67] 3) All of these ways are inadequate and, therefore, serve essentially as metaphorical pointers to the Real. 4) Metaphorical inadequacy reinforces the concept of *via negativa*, that is, the notion that we can not say what the Ultimate is, only what it is not. 5) There cannot be a plurality of ultimates, hence "we affirm the true ultimacy of the Real by referring to it in the singular."[68]

Hick's pluralistic hypothesis has encountered mixed reception from the religious community. Perhaps he himself best defends his thesis when he suggests the following advantages of a pluralistic religious outlook. First, it preserves the richness of religious diversity. It leaves humankind free to observe and appreciate religious differences without feeling any "pressure to homogenize them or to depict the objects of religious experience - Yahweh, Brahman, Shiva, the Holy Trinity, *sunyata,* the Dharma, and so on—as phenomenologically alike."[69] Second, it self-regulates. It allows us to recognize the degree to which our faith traditions are products of our own projection and, hence, to be alert to the possibility of "perverted forms of religious experience and practice."[70] Third, it enhances authentic religious dialogue and mutual enrichment. "[F]reedom from the assumption that there is one and only one true religion makes possible a genuine appreciation of other responses to the Real. . . . Authentic dialogue of the 'truth-seeking' kind, in which each participant may gain from the experiences and insights of the others, becomes feasible."[71]

Major criticisms have also been offered of Hick's religious pluralism. It tends, at least as Hick presents it, to neglect ecclesiological questions. It reduces evangelism to social service and mutual enrichment. It fails to provide an adequate means to judge what constitutes a valid turning from self-centeredness to Reality-centeredness.[72] It offers only a vague and obscure understanding of God, a kind of transcendentalist agnosticism. It is itself a "confessional" or particular form of exclusivism. It relativizes religious truth. It undermines the importance of particularity in assessing any self-disclosing of God.[73] It unfairly presumes that a "Ptolemaic" view is unable to "tolerate, or contribute to, the existence of other religions."[74] And so on.

These (and other) insights might be broadly gathered into two groups. The first three criticisms noted here are typical of the concerns of an ethical or procedural nature. The remaining ones are indicative of difficulties perceived in its structure or its metaphysics. While both types of critiques are valuable in the shaping and reshaping of a theology of religion, the focus of this study is on the latter classification. With this in mind, we turn now to an analysis of the structure of pluralism itself and of the metaphysical issues that are intrinsic to that structure. We begin with a shift in perspective (a poem I authored), used to introduce yet another shift in perspective.

A STRANGE METAPHOR

Cantor Religion

> The lamps are different,
> but the Light is the same.
> -Jalalu'l-Din Rumi (thirteenth century)

In the room my mind
sit many different lamps.
The lamp of Christianity, an old oil
lantern, recently wired for electricity,
all the latest scientific gadgets;
when I approach,
it springs on automatically.
I trust this lamp:
it was the light in the hallway
when I was small
and afraid of the dark.
I use this lamp even now, oh,
not all the time . . . but
when I have moments free,
in fancy Gothic cathedrals
or tiny country chapels
smelling of warm waxed wood.

The Eastern lamp is hand-crafted copper,
gondola-shaped, wick lit
Aladdin's lamp, it charms
with ancient promise
of untold treasure, I must
but rub it and attend, oh
there, can you see?
the earnest, handsome Buddhist
from Sri Lanka
who resides in the basement of my house,
who laments that the young women
in this country don't care much
for the color of his skin. Me?
I'm old. I love the rich
blue-black glow which lives
in the light of this lamp.

The Jewish lamp, really seven candles
welded together. The one
in the room my mind
is highly stylized. Contemporary.
Unorthodox. You can't make out much
in its soft flame, mostly abstract
markings, maybe it makes a difference
if you read Hebrew. Still, I love
to search the shadows it forms
for things familiar and strange,
as order out of nothing
in only seven days
and bushes that burn
with the Sabbath light
now and forever Amen.

In this land where I was born
are Native lamps; mine
a gray clay
artifact, discovered lying
by a tattooed Erie Indian
whose body was dug from a pit
and whose spirit finds me yet today
when I dig my bare toes
deep into the earth
and listen to the breath
of the wind.

All these and more are the lamps
which rest in the room
my mind, yet the one
I cherish most is the chalice
that ignites my heart,
for I see in its light
the room my mind
with all its magnificent lamps,
among them the chalice
that ignites my heart
which shows the room my mind
with all its magnificent lamps,
Dear God of many iterations,
may all their light shine on
and on and on, like a Cantor set
transcending.

CANTORING

In the thirteenth century, the Sufi mystic Jalalu'l-Din Rumi expressed his sense of the Divine via the many-lamps-one-light comment that grounds the poem above. Indeed, "lamps" form an overt metaphor in this poem, representing collectively the different religions of our pluralistic culture. However, another metaphor is at work here that may be less obvious. This is the mathematical metaphor of the Cantor set.

The Cantor set is a mathematical concept attributed to Georg Cantor, a mathematician who lived in the last half of the nineteenth and the beginning of the twentieth centuries. A deeply religious man, he was particularly interested in medieval theology and its arguments on the nature of the continuous and the infinite. His father was a Christian convert from Judaism and his mother a Catholic. Because of his own interest in religion, the younger Cantor pursued a career in philosophy, physics, and mathematics rather than the more practically inclined field of engineering urged upon him by his father. His Danish parents moved to Frankfurt, Germany, when Cantor was nine years old, and he spent virtually all of his life in Germany. He studied in Zurich, Göttingen, and Berlin and spent a long, although checkered, teaching career at the University of Halle.

In 1883 he published an essay called "On Linear Aggregates" which dealt with the "actually infinite" as a definite mathematical being, capable even of definition by number.[75] Although Galileo had preceded him more than two hundred years earlier in setting the stage for considering the infinite as "actual," this view was so contrary to universal understanding of the infinite as unbounded growth that Georg Cantor became a mathematical heretic. His mathematical peers accused him of encroaching on the realm of the philosophers and of violating the principles of religion. His worst enemy turned out to be his own former professor, Leopold Kronecker, who led a vicious and relentless attack on Cantor. Regarding his theory of *trans*finite numbers in much the same way as the ancient Pythagoreans had regarded the discovery of *ir*rational numbers, Cantor's contemporaries withheld recognition of his work and blocked every possible advancement of his career. Cantor, being high-strung by nature, suffered a nervous breakdown in 1884, the first of a series of mental bouts that were to plague him for the rest of his life. He died in a mental hospital in Halle in 1918.

It must have taken Cantor a great deal of courage to set forth his ideas, for even he had trouble accepting them. As he wrote in his 1883 essay:

> I conceive the infinite in the definite form of something consummated, something capable not only of mathematical formulations, but of definition by number. This conception of the infinite is opposed to traditions which have grown dear to me, and it is much against my own will that I have been forced to accept this view. But many years of scientific speculation and trial point to these conclusions as to a logical necessity, and for this reason I am confident that no valid objections will be raised which I shall not be in the position to meet."[76]

His confidence was overoptimistic as great paradoxes ultimately arose out of his work. For many people even today, these "antinomies" (as Bertrand Russell calls them) have yet to be adequately addressed. While it would be impossible to do adequate justice to Cantor's theory of sets in the limited space of this chapter, we can lift up and explore a few of his provocative ideas. In particular, we can examine them for the richness they might lend to our understanding of a religiously pluralistic world.

Most of us are comfortable with the notion of sets of things, whether or not we define this notion formally. There are, for example, a certain number of people in this room. We can count the number of people in this room and, accordingly, assign a cardinal number to this set, as when we count 10 (or 30 or 150) people in a room. Because we have a system of ordering such cardinal numbers, namely by counting 1, 2, 3, 4, 5, and so on, we also have a means of doing something humans seem perpetually inclined to do—*comparing* various sets. Thus we say one set is greater than, less than, or equal to another. We make such comparisons all the time, either explicitly or implicitly. One city is bigger than another, one item costs less than another, one room has more people in it than another, and so on. What we are really doing in all such instances is comparing the measures of plurality that we assign to each collection. When we try to extend this concept from a finite set (such as we have been talking about) to an infinite set, our intuition rebels and we tend to say it does not make any sense to measure the plurality of an infinite collection. Yet this is precisely what Cantor did with his theory of aggregates.

Consider, for example, the set of all counting numbers. That is the set containing 1, 2, 3, 4, 5, 6, 7 and so on indefinitely. Then, consider a "smaller" set of numbers that we take from this larger set of all counting numbers, for example, the set of all even numbers: 2, 4, 6, 8, 10, 12, 14 and so on. By pairing up numbers from each of these two sets, rather as a kindergarten teacher might have boys and girls pair up to go to the drinking fountain, it becomes apparent that there are just as many of one kind as of the other. That is, the pairs come out evenly—no left-overs.

$$1 \quad 2 \quad 3 \quad 4 \quad 5 \quad 6 \quad 7 \ldots$$
$$2 \quad 4 \quad 6 \quad 8 \quad 10 \quad 12 \quad 14 \ldots$$

Our imaginations easily accept this pairing-up principle, even though this process of pairing-up continues indefinitely. Formal mathematics would say we are demonstrating a one-to-one correspondence. In a very practical sense, there are just as many even numbers as there are counting numbers. Put that in a little different language and we see that a part of a collection is not necessarily less than the whole: it may be equivalent to it. *The part may have the power of the whole.*

Cantor assigned a "cardinal" number to the size of this set of infinite counting numbers. The symbol looked different from our usual cardinal number symbols (10, 30, 150, etc.): call it "*a*." Soon he discovered other infinite sets that were "bigger" (i.e., had a higher "power") than "*a*." There was a continuous type with power "*c*" and a functional type with power "*f*." There were others, too.[77] None of these new infinite sets could be paired up with the counting numbers. Furthermore, he discovered that "*a*" was the smallest of all such cardinal or *trans*finite numbers, as they came to be called. Cantor realized that these transfinite numbers were related to each other in mathematically describable ways (e.g., $2_a = a$). He also realized that the set of transfinite numbers *a, c, f,* and so forth, could be ordered but never completed. There was a smallest, but no biggest transfinite. On the other hand, what was the number of all such transfinite numbers, that is, the aggregate of all aggregates, the cardinal number of the set that contains all sets? Now *this* cardinal surely would be the last transfinite, the "truly ultra-ultimate step in the evolution of the abstraction we call number."[78] The problem was it had already been shown that there was no such last transfinite. Contrary to the laws of logic, this antimony points to a realm in which *the infinite both is and is not infinite.*

Another feature of Cantor's theory involves a further extension of the subdivision process noted earlier. We could, for instance, find a subset of the set of all even numbers, which was also "equivalent" to the set of counting numbers. For example, every second number could be "removed" from the set of even numbers, and the following pairing could be obtained:

$$2 \quad 4 \quad 6 \quad 8 \quad 10 \quad 12 \quad 14 \ldots$$
$$4 \quad 6 \quad 10 \quad 14 \quad 18 \quad 22 \quad 26 \ldots$$

Like the original example, this process of "thinning out" could be repeated indefinitely.

Recently, James Gleick presented a pictorial variation on this theme. The idea here is to begin with a solid line and thin it out by removing the middle third; then remove the middle third of each remaining segment, and the middle third of what is left from that thinning out, and so on. The Cantor set is the dust of points that remain (see figure 4.2[79]). Their total length is zero, yet they are infinitely many. Thus, a Cantor set represents *an actuality that is infinitely many yet infinitely sparse.* All Cantor sets that are cre-

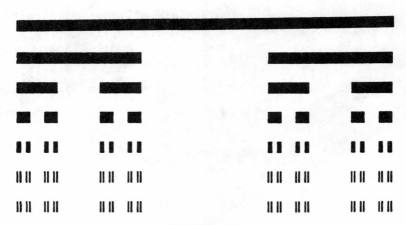

FIGURE 4.2
The Cantor Dust

ated in this manner of thinning out or breaking up a line are said to have a dimension somewhat more than a point, but less than that of our two-dimensional world. In mathematics, the dimension is represented by a real number somewhere between 0 and 1. This dimension is fractional and belongs to the new geometry known as fractal geometry. Analogous examples of constructing Cantor sets by this thinning out process are possible in other dimensions. The "Swiss cheese" dust in figure 4.3[80], for instance, represents an

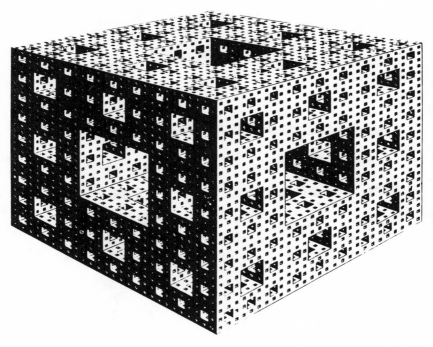

FIGURE 4.3
Constructing with Holes

entity that is more than a two-dimensional line, but less than three-dimensional space.

Cantor dusts are examples of discontinuities that are remarkably applicable to our physical world. Benoit Mandelbrot, the founder of fractal geometry, has created Cantorian mathematical distributions for stars in a galaxy and for galaxies in the universe. While his creation is merely a mathematical model, it bears an uncanny resemblance to the actual (and hitherto inexplicable) stellar distributions charted by astronomers. As mathematician Ivars Peterson puts it:

> Astrophysicists have now confirmed that as the model predicts, mass within the universe is distributed throughout space like a three-dimensional Cantor set, with large regions of space left empty. Cantor-set fractals describe not only the way matter clusters in space but also the way it clusters in time. Cantor sets seem to describe cars on a crowded highway, cotton price fluctuations since the nineteenth century, and the rising and falling of the River Nile over more than 2000 years.[81]

We find here an intriguing connection between the abstract, esoteric world of the infinite and the physical world as we know it. To echo Georg Cantor, *infinity becomes "actual" rather than merely "potential."* Gleick said it more graphically when he observed that "In the mind's eye, a fractal is a way of seeing infinity,"[82] and then offered a picture of a computerized "sea-coast" as a way of envisioning this infinity (see figure 4.4[83]). Fractal geome-

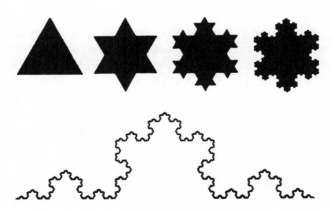

FIGURE 4.4
The Koch Snowflake: "A Rough but Vigorous Model of a Coastline"

try, the child of Cantor set theory, thus offers us a way to transverse that strange gap between the material world of the physical and the immaterial, speculative realm of the metaphysical. Traditionally, such a connecting bridge has been religion, but here it might be equally well described by the term "mathematics."

As we have seen, mathematics, and particularly the mathematical legacy of Georg Cantor, leads us to conclusions that are disturbingly paradoxical: the part may have the power of the whole; the infinite both is and is not infinite; something exists that is both infinitely many and infinitely sparse; infinity becomes actual rather than potential. Attempts in the twentieth century to deal with such paradoxes have been many and varied and are too complex to more than mention here.[84] However, one result of this endeavor may have particular relevance to a theology of religious pluralism, namely, Kurt Gödel's proof in the 1930s regarding the Axiom of Choice. Loosely stated, Gödel showed that in certain logical systems one must choose between either completeness or consistency.[85] That is, if the system is known to be consistent, it is impossible to be assured of completeness, and vice versa. The implication of this unsettling discovery is that in certain structural systems (including the structure set up by Cantor's set theory) there will always be at least one question that cannot be answered within the framework of the system itself. *Incompleteness is intrinsic to the structure of the system.*

RELIGION OF ALL RELIGIONS

It is my contention that the structure of the religious pluralism put forth by John Hick is essentially Cantorian. The poem introduced earlier as a strange metaphor is one attempt to illustrate this structure, for it is really a descriptive listing of the elements in the set of all religions. Not all religions are named/described, of course. Christianity is the first, followed by Buddhism, Judaism, Native American religion (this last lumped, admittedly erroneously, as one single tradition). Next is the ellipses—"all these and more." Here is reference to the fact that the list goes on and on. However, one additional religion is described and this is the "Cantor" religion, the aggregate of all aggregates, the religion that is composed of all religions.

Assuming some simple notation and abbreviation (let X =

Christianity, B = Buddhism, J = Judaism, N = Native American) then, in mathematics, R, the set of all religions, could be "defined" quite simply as $R = \{X, B, J, N \ldots\}$. The hypothesis put forth here is that R is itself a religion, and, hence, can be listed as an element in this set $R = \{X, B, J, N, \ldots R, \ldots\}$.

One deficiency of this study is that this hypothesis remains just an hypothesis, the only supporting "evidence" for its validity being purely speculative. In fact, it is probable that even John Hick, who identifies himself clearly as a Christian, would resist losing his Christian identity for an "R" identity. Perhaps the religion that today most closely and overtly *acts* as an "R" religion is Unitarian Universalism. *UU*ism, incidentally, has suffered in recent years from most, if not all, of the criticisms leveled at Hick's theology of religious pluralism. Of late, the accusing finger has even condemned *UU*ism (which dates its religious heritage solidly back to the fifteenth century) as not a "real" religion. It would not be unexpected, therefore, to find resistance to the general hypothesis set forth here that R, the set of all religions, is itself a religion. Yet, those who *would* grant this possibility and those who suggest that humankind is even now moving in the direction of a global religion may be pleasantly surprised (or sadly dismayed) at the implications that the Cantorian-like structure of R may call forth.

It is interesting to observe that John Hick, in his explication of religious pluralism, occasionally employs (perhaps unknowingly) Cantorian language metaphors. When he addresses the nature of ethical, aesthetic, and religious meanings, for instance, he uses set-like language: " 'Situation' is a relational notion. A situation, for X, consists of a set of objects which are unified in X's attention and which have as a whole a practical dispositional meaning for X which is more than the sum of the meaning of its constituent objects."[86] His whole discussion of "family-resemblance" concepts has its analogue in group theory, and at least once he explicitly suggests that there "may be a 'Gödel's principle' in metaphysics."[87] Beyond these direct metaphors, however, lies a whole realm of discourse that might be seen to implicitly evoke Cantorian mathematics.

In his discussion of the divine ineffability that he applies to the Real *an sich*, for instance, he concludes that "it is obviously impossible to refer to something that does not even have the property of 'being able to be referred to'. Further, the property of 'being such that our concepts do not apply to it' cannot, without self-contradiction, include itself."[88] The structure of this argument is precisely the structure that arose from Cantor's "aggregate of all aggregates" legacy and the conclusion that the infinite both is and is not infinite. Drawing the parallel in religious pluralism, we are left with the suggestion that the Real *an sich* (God, the Ultimate, etc.) both is and is not infinite.

Hick seems to accept this antinomy at some level, but he frames it as a feature of our human capacity (or, rather, incapacity) to perceive the infinite dimensions of an infinite reality. Thus, when he concludes that "God is not apprehended as infinite, or as limitlessly this or that, but is apprehended under concrete images which vary in magnitude from the definitely limited to the indefinitely great,"[89] we can hear the echo of Cantor's dilemma in the face of his conception that the infinite is "in the definite form of something consummated." Cantor, however, equated the infinite with the quasi finite and made the potential "actual," a step Hick was unwilling to take. If, however, the structure of Hick's religious pluralism is essentially that of Cantor's theory of transfinite numbers, then the suggestion arises naturally that the Real *an sich* is similarly finite.

A full recognition and acceptance of the Cantorian-like structure of religious pluralism would similarly challenge or suggest revision of other Hick conclusions. For example, Hick has contended that "as finite observers we could never directly experience, observe, verify, the infinite dimensions of an infinite reality."[90] Yet the fractal "visualization" research currently being investigated in modern chaos theory at the very least casts doubt on this restriction.[91] More provocatively, it lends impetus to the suggestion that the Real *an sich* is infinite but bounded, an idea that seems to be directly contrary to Hick's exegesis.[92] Likewise, when Hick insists that "there cannot be a plurality of ultimates" and that, therefore, we affirm the true ultimacy of the Real by referring to it in the singular,"[93] we suspect that Hick would have difficulty accepting Cantor's logic. Cantor not only accepts a plurality of ultimates; he orders and ranks them.

Considerations of the previous sort do little to counter suggestions that religious pluralism offers only "a vague and obscure" understanding of the Ultimate. Aside from the dubious presumption that any *other* religion offers a less vague and obscure understanding, it might be argued that a fully developed "Cantorian" religion would confront this issue head-on. Such a religion would recognize the obscurity inherent in the structure of religious endeavor, and it would work perhaps more self-consciously than any other religion to obtain clarity of understanding in spite of this intrinsic ambiguity.

In addition to its implications regarding the nature of the Real *an sich*, a "Cantorian" religion calls forth a reexamination of the relationship of one religion to another and to the realm of religious endeavor taken as a whole. Religious pluralism, when considered as a religion among religions, must fit right alongside the other elements in the set that contains all religions. In this regard it can be as exclusivist (or inclusivist) as any other religion, a fact lending credence to the critique that Hick's pluralistic hypothesis is itself confessional and, hence, exclusivist in nature. This possibility is mitigated, however, by the fact that "R contains R." Religious pluralism, as conceived here, is the religious tradition that is open to and thus composed of all religious traditions. While it takes its place right alongside other religious traditions, its content is substantially different from others. Its content is explicitly pluralistic, not exclusivistic. Its content is global, not parochial.

It is useful at this point to reconsider some questions of structure. Schematically, as we have seen, this *global or Cantorian religion* may be represented by the set notation $R = \{X, B, J, A, \ldots R, \ldots\}$. It is conceivable, however, that the collection of all the various and assorted religious endeavors common to our world is not itself a religion. To distinguish this possibility from the case above, I introduce the notation R', where $R' = \{X, B, J, A, \ldots\}$. R' is identical with R in all ways except that R' does not contain R', whereas R does contain R. Within this collection of religions, R', we could prioritize one over another. That is, while remaining conscious of the whole of R', we could choose to work entirely from within one framework, say that of Christianity or Buddhism, or any other *one religion among many*. Schematically, I designate this possibility by highlighting the symbol for that one dominating religion, as in $R' = \{X, \boldsymbol{B}, J, A \ldots\}$. Such a structure (coupled with a fluid highlighting pattern) is consistent with what is known in current theological circles as a comparative philosophy of religions. Unlike either the global theologian or the comparativist, an *exclusivist* would say that the set of all (true) religions $R' = \{X\}$ (*or*

{*B*} *or* {*J*}). For the exclusivist, the set of all religions would include only one member. *An inclusivist,* on the other hand, would adhere *to a framework* where $R' = \{X, B, J, A, \ldots\}$ but where (for instance) X contains as sub-elements B, J, A and so on. More precisely, $X = B^\wedge$ (or $X = J^\wedge$ or $X = A^\wedge$) where $B^\wedge$ stands for a "not yet realized" or a *perfected B.* In the inclusivist view, all other religions are really just subtracks of a primary overriding one.

This schema points to possible distinctions among the major trends in contemporary theological scholarship. In this view, a globalist recognizes the existence of a plurality of religions but focuses religious endeavor on the collective entity. A comparatist likewise recognizes the existence of the larger set and chooses as the primary religious orientation any member of the set, but not the collective set itself. An exclusivist disregards the collective entity, selects one and only one member of the set as the religious orientation, and effectively denies the existence of the rest of the set by adding a qualifying value judgement. An inclusivist disregards the collective entity, selects one and only one member of the set as the religious orientation, and effectively treats it as a collective entity.

Such a skeletal rendering of the various approaches to religious endeavor must bear the criticism of oversimplification. It strips the bones of the flesh, so to speak. Simultaneously, however, it has the advantage of allowing us a sort of X-ray perception. From the lens of this tool, we see that *all* of these approaches focus on one particular religious framework over another. In the case of religious pluralism, the focus is R, the collective entity, the plurality of religions. Accordingly, charges against religious pluralism that it undermines the importance of particularity, that it relativizes truth, that it assumes Ptolemic narrowness, and so forth, are, on the basis of structure alone, as legitimate or illegitimate as they are for the comparative, exclusivist, and inclusivist approaches. What is different and distinctive of religious pluralism is the nature of the specificity.

Herein, beneath all this X-ray scanning, lies the heart of the matter. A religion that is composed of all religions is, like Pythagorean irrationals or Cantorian transfinites, something new, or, at least, something newly perceived. The hue and cry against John Hick and the work that he has stimulated has been understandably reactionary, sometimes vicious. Yet, like that of his Cantorian counterpart of a century ago, it can be repressed but not eliminated by a mere lambasting. A more productive approach, and fortunately one that many scholars are following, is to build on this work, to define its limitations and to allow the seeds it has dropped to fully bloom.

METAPHOR MUDDLES

In these last few sections I have suggested that Hick's work describes a new religion, a religion of pluralism. Further, I have argued that the structure of this new global religion parallels the structure of Cantorian set theory and, therefore, lends itself to a metaphorical interpretation that is fundamentally mathematical. There are obvious difficulties with my argument, and I turn now to an elucidation of some of these metaphor "muddles."

One area left conspicuously undeveloped in this essay is the whole realm of the ethical implications of religious pluralism. Hick's efforts in this arena have been inadequate and clearly invite further research. Another area of concern that requires further thought lies in resolving differences that appear (sometimes even in murderous ways) between people from different religious communities (different sets of the Cantorian covering set) who believe, quite passionately, that theirs is the one true religion. My personal opinion is that resolution of this problem lies in the adoption of a Cantorian view: however, I recognize that even in so saying I am contributing to the dilemma of those who *believe their* way is *the* way. Clearly this problem needs to be addressed at some point.

Objections, too, may be raised regarding the general tenor of my argument. For one thing, it relies on a method of parallelism[94] for its logical persuasiveness. Secondly, it freely (and perhaps questionably) applies language and concepts from one field of investigation to those of another. Both of these challenges (and there may be others that I have overlooked) warrant consideration.

But while these are legitimate concerns, they are secondary issues and they belong, in my view, to a separate or additional study. Of more immediate import are concerns relating to the fundamental nature of religion. Indeed, I have not really addressed the issue of what qualifies as a religion, let alone substantiated that a Cantorian-like system would qualify. Instead, I have more or less lifted up Hick's work and said—quite probably to Hick's eventual dismay[95]—"Look, here is a new religion." Yet, even if I have done an injustice to Hick's intent, the possibility of such a religion is still significant and invites further exploration.

A number of legitimate questions necessarily arise out of such an exploration. Does not my assumption of a religion composed of all religions presuppose certain commonalities between extremely diverse religions? If so, what are they? On the other hand, incorporation of such diverse systems into one whole must surely be fraught with incommensurability. How is such incomensurability resolved? Similarly, do I not just gloss over some very serious antinomies, ignoring them rather than really attending to them? Finally, how do I justify a movement to a new religion when religions are considered, at the very least, things with histories, practices, commercial location, and the like? Surely a religion of all religions possesses none of these properties.

All of these more primary questions suggest valid reservations to the argument I have presented in the last portions of this chapter. However, since they also relate to the value of this study as a whole, I will take them up, together with a brief overview of the total work, in the following concluding chapter.

SUMMATION

It seems appropriate that a work drawing so heavily on mathematical metaphors would end, not with a last chapter or a conclusion or even a summary, but with another mathematical metaphor. Hence, I write this *summation,* an adding up of all the disjointed pieces that fill these pages in order to make them into a whole. There have been some surprises for me in carrying out this study. I have gained some insights and I have lost some expectations along the way. For one thing, I did not realize that so much of what I would wind up with would be in the nature of a metaphysics. No one could have been more surprised than I was when, a couple of chapters into the book, a good friend of mine, a philosopher, said to me, "Sarah, what you are trying to do is very, very hard. You are writing a metaphysics."

If I had been less far into the work right then, his comment and his caution might have stopped me totally. Somehow, I had not known I was writing a metaphysics. Had I known, I would not have started the writing, for I felt (and feel) ill qualified to tackle such a lofty task. Writing a little bit *about* metaphysics, which is what I thought I was doing, is not at all the same thing as creating one. I still carry a strong cultural conditioning within me, believing in the KISS routine: Keep It Simple, Stupid. Of one thing I am now certain—this work has not followed that routine.

As I reread the preceding pages, therefore, I fluctuate between feeling excited and dismayed. I am excited because I recognize the potential value of the assorted data I have gathered together. I am dismayed because there are times when my ideas are not fully drawn out and clarified or when they are poorly connected to each other—the sort of thing that leaves one open to criticism, ridicule, and/or disdain. I am challenged by the first, but fearful of the others. Thus, one of the things I lost when completing this work was the expectation that I would produce something so tightly structured that it would leave both my ideas and my credibility invulnerable to premature dismissal. Yet even with the gaps in my presentation —sometimes even glaring dark holes—I am excited enough by the total sum of the accumulated "evidence" to try to highlight some of the potential value this "whole" has for the future of both liberal religion and society.

First, I briefly reframe the main thrust of my perspective to accommodate contemporary wisdom. Ours is a world steeped in contradiction and paradox. Our minds, that is, our cognitive processes, appear to rely heavily on metaphor (with its "is and is not" character) and are likewise made of the fiber of contradiction and inconsistency. Mathematics, by offering us a meta-structure within which we can place both the universe and our minds, promises us the hope of reaching a kind of understanding and acceptance of our place in the universe. Fundamental to this epistemy is the notion that there is not just one epistemy, but that there are epistemies— many ways of knowing. Again, mathematics provides us with a pattern so that we might collect all of these different (often contradictory, paradoxical) ways of knowing into an integrated whole, a whole that, paradoxically, we can only partially know.

An assumption underpins this perspective: on the level of the physical realm, our attempts to grapple with the meaning and nature of our existence, that is, to define our metaphysics, are filtered by such factors as our sensory perceptions, cultural experiences, and language limitations. However, throughout the study I imply (if I do not directly state it) that these physical filters are themselves part of a larger *meta*physical kaleidoscope that filters different spiritual worlds. We ourselves might think of ourselves as existing not only on a physical level, but simultaneously on a meta-level (which we can only partially grasp) in which we represent a particular kaleidoscopic "setting"—one spiritual world among many. Summed together in an infinite process, these separate spiritual worlds (which might be thought of as roughly equivalent to Leibniz's monads) form an Ultimate spiritual world. We are fractal reflections or holographic mirrors of a larger transcendant "Holygraph." We are, in effect, metaphors for the Spirit.

The language and imagery that I have used to illustrate this perspective is both metaphorical and mathematical. I have tried to illustrate that throughout the ages humankind has fused metaphor and mathematics (using whatever math world[1] was common to the time) into ways of knowing and describing metaphysics. The value of this union of mathematics and metaphor as a method for help-

ing our predecessors understand their spiritual existence has been demonstrated in chapter 3. That it may be as valuable a method for helping contemporary society come to understand its spiritual existence is the heart of this thesis and the reason for my continued excitement as I reexamine the preceding pages of this document.

Thus, contemporary religion might well deal with a metaphysics that has been illuminated by mathematical metaphors. Here, perhaps, I need to sharpen the relationship between religion, theology, and metaphysics that I laid out in the Foreword of this work. In that Foreword, I suggested that metaphysics was an umbrella term encompassing religion, which was itself an umbrella term encompassing theology. That this relationship exists is certainly not universally accepted. Schleiermacher, for instance, suggests almost the opposite relationship when he separates metaphysics and morals from religion and suggests that the former "invade" the latter.[2] Yet, for Schleiermacher, metaphysics is the explaining of the universe and religion is the "intuition of the universe."[3] In his view: "to accept everything individual as a part of the whole and everything limited as a representation of the infinite is religion. But whatever would go beyond that and penetrate deeper into the nature and substance of the whole is no longer religion, and will, if it still wants to be regarded as such, inevitably sink back into empty mythology."[4] This is not so different from the perspective I outlined in the Foreword, although it suggests perhaps a different graphic display. At heart, the difference for Schleiermacher between religion and metaphysics or theology is precisely the heart, that is, the emotions and the intuition as separated from the reasoning and the intellect.

Perhaps Schleiermacher (1767–1834), writing in a day and age when reason could be seen as a threat to religion, was just looking at the connection between these realms from a different angle than I do. When I look at it, I do not see the same polarization. Hence, I imbed religion, with its emphasis on the emotive and intuitive *and also* with its desire to explain and understand, within a larger frame of human endeavor that seeks to understand *and* intuit the nature of all existence. With this in mind, a definition of religion more congenial to the general tenor of this work is that offered by Clifford Geertz: "Religion is a system of symbols which acts to establish powerful, pervasive and long lasting moods and motivations in people by formulating conceptions of a general order of existence and clothing these conceptions with such an aura of factuality that the moods and motivations seem uniquely realistic."[5] Religion, to Geertz, involves *both* the emotive (long lasting moods and motivations) *and* the intellect (formulating conceptions).

Yet even this definition does not distinguish between metaphysics and religion, and as is clear from my schematic depiction in the Foreword, I do make a distinction. This distinction lies in the notion that there are explanations of the nature of being, knowledge, and reality that do not center on a specific system of belief and worship built around God (or the Ultimate, the Divine, the Real, etc.) To be more explicit, religion, in my view, involves the acceptance of a transcendent Ultimate, the God of the Definite Integral, something that goes beyond human existence. Whether this transcendent Ultimate resides wholly in the physical world (as secular humanists would have it) or involves some heavenly center (as early emanation theories held) or anything else seems to me to be a product of the dominant metaphor at work in society. Theology, correspondingly, becomes the study of these dominant metaphors and how they interpret this transcendent. But let me paint this notion with thicker brush strokes.

We humans are incredibly curious creatures. We want, to borrow from the oracle at Delphi, to "know ourselves." We want, actually, to know more than that. We wrestle with all sorts of questions about the world around us and about our relationship to it. We question the meaning of our existence—and of our death. This struggle for understanding takes us on many different paths and through many different dominant metaphors: Christianity, Hinduism, Taoism, Judaism, Islam—paths we loosely gather together under the nomenclature *religion*.

We are also self-reflective creatures. We study *ourselves*. We look at ourselves even though, by our very physical compositions, the attempt is doomed to partial success. Still, we try. Sometimes, the best we can do is to examine our surroundings, hoping that in the process we will catch a glimpse of our own reflection. When we examine closely those particular religious paths that we seem to follow so naturally, when we haul out microscopes and tape measures and cameras (or divining rods, astrological charts, Tarot cards) in order that we might better come to *know* these paths (ways, Taos), we engage in *theological inquiry.*

We are, however, limited creatures. Something always is incomplete in our knowledge, or at least in our ability to relate it to one another and to ourselves. We can never quite see where the path leads, or what it is like, or even if it continues past the current hill. While we seem to recognize this limitedness without difficulty, we nonetheless often feel compelled to justify it. Considered from a purely intuitive realm, we call this recognition of our limitedness, of the mystery in life, *faith*. On the rational level, it turns into something that varies from path to path and from person to person, but that inevitably relies for its expression on *metaphor*. As Whitehead noted, the "history of philosophy and theology is the history of changing interpretations of metaphors and replacement of one metaphor by another metaphor."[6]

However, we must recall Korzybski's caution that the map is not the territory. Metaphors leave lacunae. When we name our metaphors, we run into the possibility of miscommunication, of gaps we cannot bridge. Korzybski, more than any other twentieth-century writer, drew our attention to the "unsane" calamities that often accompany our naming of things. No matter how hard we try, we can never capture with our language the nature of the territory we experience. The early biblical writers used YHWH, and that only hesitatingly, to avoid naming the unnameable. We, too, are caught by the need for a practical mechanism of communication. Like those ancient prophets, we rely on partial resemblances, on maps, on metaphors, to communicate our experiences.

It is via metaphor that we share our experience of both the profane and the sacred. It is the *re*presentation rather than the *pre*sentation, that we find in our books on religion, theology, and metaphysics. And it is because somebody's choice of representation does not match or is not understood by somebody else or is interpreted as a presentation, rather than representation, that we so often find ourselves imbedded in "unsane" calamities such as religious self-righteousness and persecution. Does the Ultimate *present* itself as the light in the cathedral window, as the bread at the last supper, as the statue of Buddha? Or are these but symbols, metaphors of something only partially conceived?

The issue is not lightly dismissed. When I was pregnant with my first child, I remember besieging my obstetrician with the age-old question, "What do you think, Doc, is it a boy or a girl?" He smiled—one of those smiles that said he had been here before.

"Yes," he replied. "That's right. Boy or girl." So, too, is the issue of metaphor versus reality, of map versus territory. Historically, this issue has been at the root of many tensions, the Unitarian Universalist heritage being illustrative of but one of them. Like boy or girl, it seems to me that the question of distinction lies only in the birthing.

Right now, contemporary society needs a new birthing. Our old metaphors, our old languages are not working—not just for Unitarian Universalists, but for religion in general. The liberal religious voice is declining. The threat of religious invasion into the political world is skyrocketing and brings with it the potential for religious war. As Gary Wills puts it: "Already the makings of a 'cultural war' are present in the religious attacks on pornography, homosexuality, abortion, and the eroticism of rock music and television. We hear again the old myth that the Roman Empire was sluiced to ruin in a slither of lubricity."[7] The religious paths we follow have worn down and we need to revitalize them, or build new ones altogether.

A few years ago, I had the opportunity to hear Arthur Peacocke lecture at the Chicago Center for Religion and Science on the "Challenge of Science to Theology and the Church." He spoke of the need in our churches for evolving a new language usage that would reach the multitudes. I could not have concurred more wholeheartedly. Yet when I listened carefully, I heard him phrase his positions only in old language, in traditional Christian patterns. When I questioned him, he had no new symbols to offer, and his hesitancy here seems to indicate to me that we have much work to do in this arena. We have new roadways to design and build, and new bridges to create.

This study has been, in part, an attempt to create one of those new bridges. By suggesting that we bring mathematical metaphors into the realm of religion, I am endorsing a new language usage— novel, at least, for contemporary society. Mathematics, while not always understood, is at some level respected by both the secular and religious domains in our culture, and by both the fundamentalist and the liberal. My hope is that it will command enough neutrality and commonality to allow even highly polarized segments of our society to dialogue with one another. It is by the vehicle of dialogue that we may avoid the "cultural wars" that Wills forecast. True dialogue is society's best shot at not merely suppressing such war, but of promoting genuine tolerance and of effecting mutual and voluntary change. Anything that will bring forth such dialogue is worth trying out. It is the contention of this study that mathematics is a good place to begin fashioning those new symbols that will reach "the multitudes."

The two mathematical metaphors that I offered in Chapter 4, (God as the definite integral, and a Cantorian religion), are only two of many potential such metaphors. However, they illustrate the potential impact of *contemporary* mathematical ideas on *contemporary* society. A Cantorian religion, for instance, identifies what might be a here-to-fore unrecognized phenomenon in our culture: the birth of a religion-composed-of-religions that does not supersede other religions, but merely takes its place alongside them as a viable alternative. Such an alternative, nonetheless, is highly appropriate and appealing in a world that the information age has in many ways unified.

It can be argued, as we noted earlier, that such a global religion is not really a religion because it has no history, no specific location, no communal customs. That it has no history is not really a valid criticism, because, in a sense, anything newly born has no history. Religions *are* born. Christianity, for one, has a clear and decisive birth date that we honor and celebrate yearly. Religions die, too. No doubt Peacocke's comments about the need for creating new religious symbols reflected, in part, a larger societal concern about the potential death of traditional religion.

Similarly, the reservation that a Cantorian religion has no specific or commercial location may be dismissed on the grounds that it is too young to have developed such locations. Rather, like the house churches of early Christianity, a global religion may be springing up within the well-established "houses" of traditional religions—for example, in Unitarian Universalist churches. A poll of one such church community, for instance, noted that 38% of the respondees viewed Unitarian Universalism as "an emerging, universal religion," second only to the 62% who saw it as "a distinctive, humanistic religion."[8]

The issue of communal customs might be addressed in the same manner, but a note of caution needs to be sounded lest this critique be prematurely discounted. Common practices and customs imply a certain commonality of interests, that is, shared properties of the religion. A religion composed of all religions is fraught with incommensurabilities. So, too, I would point out in partial response, do our "normal" religious traditions have internal inconsistencies and contradictions. Indeed the history of religion is filled with the (sometimes bloody) attempts of humankind to deal with such disparities.

Still, it is fair to argue that a religion, any religion, must have certain properties that, by and large, all members of the religion accept. There should be certain commonalities among the extremely diverse religions that compose a global religion. I can, of course, only speculate as to what these commonalities might be. One possible candidate, as Hick points out,[9] is a sort of Golden Rule expectation. Another common property might be a commitment to a spiritual life that is intensely experiential, active and practical. A third characteristic that diverse religions might be expected to share could include a commitment to fostering a spiritual insight that would supersede and perhaps even eliminate all personal desire for knowledge, happiness, virtue, occult power, and so forth. Paradoxically, however, these very same things might be seen as acceptable and even necessary ways to acquire that spiritual insight. Other candidates for common properties of a Cantorian religion are that it be centered on love, that it involve a feeling of union with a transcendent Ultimate, that it not be self-seeking.

But some new common properties are emerging beyond such preexisting commonalities of the diverse religions that compose the set of all religions, properties that are peculiar to the religion itself and that distinguish it from other religions. Here is where the benefit of a contemporary mathematical metaphor may aid our intuition, may actually help us realize "something new," as modern theories of metaphor hold. To cite but one example, a religious tradition composed of other religious traditions directly substantiates the claim that *the part may have the power of the whole.* Rather than relativizing specific religious truth, it provides a platform from which more than one truth may be affirmed as THE truth. In other words, the outstanding new characteristic of a Cantorian religion is an unequivocal openness to diversity. There is evidence that such a view is actually developing in modern society. Robert Gottlieb, for instance, seemed to be addressing this notion when he wrote in his introduction to a select collection of America's contemporary spiritual voices that the "first shared premise [among these voices] is a wide-ranging respect for the spiritual traditions of others."[10]

Of course, these "truths" need not "look" much like one another, at least not on a superficial level. Nor, I hasten to point out, does this imply that virtually anything qualifies as truth. Just as in Cantorian logic only certain "parts" can be equated to certain infinite sets, analogously we might infer that only certain religious truths may be equivalent to each other. Furthermore, just as in set theory there is no final transfinite number, so, too, among religious truths there may be no "greatest" truth. Our quest for ontological (existential, epistemological, etc.) certainty may be found, as Gödel's work would suggest, only at the cost of consistency. Indeed, a religion based on a plurality of religions may leave us forever struggling with an Axiom of Religious Choice.

Religious pluralism is not a new idea. Rumi, for instance, wrote his "many lamps, one light" idea in the thirteenth century. In our increasingly global society, however, the concept is accessible to a wider variety of people than ever before. As a new critical mass of opinion (to employ yet one more mathematical metaphor) is approached, it is more than conceivable that something new is also emerging in the religious arena. The liberal religious voice must be ready to meet this challenge of the new. Indeed, the liberal religious voice, if it is to persevere, must meet the challenge of all that is new.

Three constant, interrelated subthemes of this study point to the tremendous endeavor that meeting "all that is new" will entail. First is the theme of the filtering mind, the human who selectively "knows," and, on a meta-level, a universe that is selectively "real." Second is the theme of contradiction, with its promise of resolution on a meta-level that, paradoxically, we can never quite attain. Third is the theme of the existence of a level of reality that transcends our normal space/time reality, but to which we nonetheless have access in some sort of consciousness. From time to time in this study, I have raised various questions associated with these subthemes—questions dealing with the nature of the paranormal, with the evolving capacity of our minds, with the impact of the computer on our future, with the revision of our scientific criteria of consistency and coherence, with our ability to understand and control our capacity to filter and select from a "primordial chaos" that, quite frankly, I never even attempt to define.

These questions are important for they are questions, as the works I summarized in chapter 1 tend to show, with which our society as a whole is struggling today. These are metaphysical questions, dealing with issues such as who we are, what our existence is all about, how we arrive at understanding and meaning. These are the issues to which the bridge-which-is-this-work leads. This bridge is built with question marks—with straw more than brick, with allusions, many of them mathematical, rather than fact. Yet the question marks, the straw, the allusions are girded with the stuff of life—the footnoted data, the bricks of the scholars who pave our way, the very mathematics that builds "simulated" realities out of computer hardware. Perhaps, given both the bridge and the girders, we will eventually traverse this bridge and find the answers to those questions. Perhaps we will even discover, with time, the answer to everything.

And perhaps, just perhaps, it will turn out to be, as Douglas Adams put it in *The Hitchhiker's Guide to the Galaxy,* only "42."[11]

AFTERWORD

Some readers may question the relevance of raising certain extraneous themes and ideas in this thesis, particularly ones that seem to be only minimally connected to the main thesis of the work. Why, for instance, should we entertain a subtheme dealing with the possible existence of a realm of unconsciousness that might be accessed paranormally when we are primarily investigating the relationship of metaphor, metaphysics, and metamathematics? Topics such as the paranormal are highly speculative and open up a dimension of thought often associated with "pseudoscientific theories, crackpot ideas, and scientific hypotheses based more on wishful thinking than empirical observation," as Richard Morris puts it in his discussion of ideas that are on the *fringes* of science.[1] I contend that these ideas are cropping up with increased frequency in many recent scientific expositions, including mathematical exposes. Most often, such fringe ideas are treated unsympathetically.[2]

I believe we have been too hasty in such treatment and that the scientific world is in danger of fulfilling Paul Feyerabend's prophesy: "Leading intellectuals with their zeal for objectivity . . . are criminals, not the liberators of mankind."[3] Beneath this provocation, according to a profile of Feyerabend that appeared in a recent issue of *Scientific American* "lies a serious message: the human compulsion to find absolute truths, however noble, too often culminates in tyranny of the mind, or worse. Only an extreme skepticism toward science—and open-mindedness toward other modes of knowledge and ways of life, however alien—can help us avoid this danger."[4]

Richard Morris appears to sense this same need for openness when he differentiates between the *fringes* of science alluded to above and the *edges* of science, which he sees as a fruitful and necessary area for speculation. While the fringe areas lead to pseudoscience, the edges of science hold ideas that "can, in some sense be called truly scientific." According to Morris, there are two basic kinds of thought that lie on these "edges" of science. "On one hand, there are kinds of speculation, engaged in by scientists, that are more philosophical than scientific in nature. On the other hand, there is speculation that has no solid theoretical or experimental justification."[5] Both categories are necessary, says Morris, to promote the advancement of science. "Exploring the edges of science is an attempt to discover what physical reality might possibly be like, not an attempt to work out the details of what it is. We could say that mainstream and frontier science seek to map out the known world, while edge science tries to understand what kinds of worlds might be possible."[6]

The three subthemes that I identified in the Foreword of this work fall, I believe, into this realm of the edges of science. For that matter, my main thesis (that mathematics is and has been used throughout history as a metaphorical connecting device between metaphysics, theology, and religion) may fall into this realm as well, although I hope that chapter 3 has done much to dispel this possibility. In Gödel's incompleteness theorem we find mathematical (hence, scientific) precedent for one of my subthemes, that the scientific criteria of consistency needs to be reexamined. The other two identified subthemes have less overt scientific backing. Even here, though, we may note that ideas from the mathematician Leibniz foreshadow the existence of a paranormally accessible realm of consciousness, and the kaleidoscopic imagery found in my filter theme of consciousness has analogues in the mathematical field of complexity. Still, differentiating between "edges" and "fringes" or even the "frontiers" of science seems tricky at best. Hindsight often has much to do with the distinction. Popular bias also affects what is labeled "fringe" and what is labeled "edges." While we can do little to affect the influence of hindsight beyond waiting for it, we can, and I believe we must, "be willing to discard ingrained outlooks and prejudices; [we] must ask, not what the limits of the universe seem to be, but what they could be. [We] must ask what kinds of bizarre phenomena the laws of physics might allow, and think about the seemingly impossible in order to find out what reality is."[7] Morris's passage here actually refers to physicists. I have generalized his reference to these physicists by replacing the word "they" with the word "we." I take such liberties with his writing because I believe his admonitions are far too important to limit them to a narrowly restricted segment of the scientific population. I believe they are too important to restrict to the scientific population at all. In particular, those of us who are involved in religion, theology, and ministry need to harken his message.

The line that separated science and religion was deeply etched into our collective consciousness following the scientific revolution of the eighteenth and nineteenth centuries. Today, this line is changing. As Morris notes, "the boundaries between physics and metaphysics have become blurred.[8] If this present work has been at all successful, then we must allow that the boundaries between mathematics and metaphysics have become similarly blurred. Or perhaps they have always been blurred, and we are only just now beginning to recognize the blur for the metaphorical bridge it is. What we look for, what we allow into our filtering minds is important. We need to be careful not to prematurely omit bizarre ideas simply because they are unpopular, for to do so may deprive us of a wonderful picture. As Holmes Rolston put it in his critical survey *Science and Religion,* "We never catch black holes, DNA molecules, neuro-transmitters, or tectonic plates unless there is, preceding the catch, a mental state that goes looking for them. We catch patterns with a frame of mind."[9] The speculative subthemes included in *What Number Is God? Metaphors, Metaphysics, Metamathematics and the Nature of Things,* and, indeed, the larger focus of the work itself, are, I hope, effective attempts to alter that frame.

Today's liberal religious minister, in my view, is an ideal candidate to promote such exploration. I would enlarge that statement. In a tradition that has historically championed freedom of religious inquiry, it is the *responsibility* of the liberal religious leader to promote such exploration. It is my hope and expectation that the ideas that I have raised in the preceding chapters will not be buried in the forgotten corner of some scholarly library. Better that they be shared and discussed within our liberal religious communities and within the wider community of educated society as well.

As a first step towards making the ideas more accessible to a wider audience, I would like to see these mathematical metaphors (and all their attendant implications) addressed from the liberal religious pulpit. One year, I myself offered to the church I was serving five sermons based on different mathematical metaphors. General response to these expressions from the pulpit was very favorable and led to some excellent dialogue, at least between preacher and congregant.[10] Another year, I expanded this dialogue through an adult education workshop, which provided greater opportunity for group discussion and feedback. I am currently planning a similar seminar designed to reach the non-Unitarian Universalist community.

Our liberal religious, and, indeed, our wider societal community stands now at the edge of a new way of thinking, of a paradigm shift, of a shift in the kaleidoscopic setting. We are, I believe, a society in flux. We are uncomfortable in this chaos. There is uncertainty in it. The old may depart from the scene as the new comes into focus. The liberal religious leader who is conscious of this shift, who understands at least some of the dynamics behind it, who is willing to approach it openly and non-anxiously, and who welcomes the opportunity that inevitably accompanies such chaos is the prophet of our time. May this exploratory work on mathematical metaphors be a partial witness to the current situation and need of humankind.

APPENDIX A
UNDERSTANDINGS OF SIGN, SYMBOL, METAPHOR, AND MODEL IN RELIGION AND MATHEMATICS (SUMMARY OF AN EMPIRICAL STUDY)

A RIDDLE

She is as ancient as humankind but as new as the greatest minds that pursue her. Schoolchildren (and some adults) often shudder at the mere mention of her, yet scientists adore her and nearly everyone acknowledges her importance in our modern technological society. Almost no one sees a place for her in church. Who is she?

INTRODUCTION TO STUDY

This illusive "lady"[1] is mathematics. Loosely (metaphorically) speaking, the question lying at the heart of this investigation is "Why isn't she in church?" She used to be, of course. Great minds from the ancient Hindus to the proponents of the new nonrelativistic physics have found in mathematics a mediation between the natural world and the spiritual realm.[2] Mathematics has even been called the divine language. Yet today the "divine" connection is hidden and remote at best. In most of our religious houses, it is nonexistent.

This study presupposed that a renewal of this divine aspect of mathematics will contribute to the overall spiritual health of our contemporary religious institutions. Granting this admittedly debatable assumption, how, then, might such a renewal unfold? This study hypothesized that the root of renewal lies in our willingness to embrace mathematics as a metaphorical language. More explicitly, it explored (or began to explore) the degree to which we humans currently view mathematics as a metaphorical language; the differences, if any, in our willingness to ascribe to mathematics notions such as sign, symbol, metaphor, and model; our emotional attitudes toward mathematics; and current assumptions about the strength of connection between mathematics and religion.

STUDY DESIGN AND EXECUTION

Because this was a *beginning* exploration conducted with limited resources and a tight time frame, two practical considerations greatly influenced the design of this study. First, it needed to be manageable in scope, and second, it needed to address those who would be most likely to have given thought to or to have had some experience with the issues involved.

A sample of seventy-four different names was selected at random from a master roster compiled of all faculty members of the various sciences and mathematics departments at the University of Chicago, the University of Chicago School of Divinity, and the Association of Chicago Theological Schools (ACTS) connected with the university. A survey was tested and refined[3] and then distributed to these seventy-four professionals in the fields of mathematics, science, and religion. Seven of these faculty members responded in some manner so as to be self-excluded from the study (for example, being "philosophically opposed" to surveys or feeling "unqualified" to address the issues), and another forty-four did not respond at all. Thus, all results and interpretations have been made on the basis of responses from roughly one-third of the original sample.

Two limitations of the study are immediately clear. First, the study in no way ascertained the views of today's *general* population. It unabashedly addressed a highly educated and specialized group: all conclusions necessarily need to be tempered by awareness of this restriction. Then, too, the disappointingly low response rate raises additional questions regarding the reliability of the study.

A third limitation is less readily apparent, namely, that gender-related patterns of response were not discernible. The inclusion of question 10 in the survey indicates the original intent of the study design to address this issue. Furthermore, the sample population contained a substantial number of (apparently) female names. Unfortunately, only four females actually chose to respond to the survey. Such a small percentage return provided an insufficient method of identifying significant gender-oriented trends. Other demographic information gathered included the respondees' general level of familiarity with mathematics and their major area of occupation.

The survey itself consisted of eight short-answer "substance" questions dealing with the topics hypothesized, three demographic questions, and two open-ended substance questions, as reproduced below.

1. How much connection do you see between mathematics and religion?

1	2	3	4	5
Virtually				A Great
None				Deal

2. How much connection do you see between mathematics and science?

1	2	3	4	5
Virtually				A Great
None				Deal

3. Which of the following comes closest to describing your view of mathematics?

1 A set of *signs* which are manipulated in a logical manner and which help reveal the fundamental laws of nature.
2 A *symbolic* language which helps to articulate the intelligibility we find in the universe.
3 A language filled with *metaphors* for the way in which the world works.
4 A medium for *modeling* reality.
5 All of the above

4. Which *best* describes your interpretation of "2":

1 sign
2 symbol
3 metaphor
4 model
5 meaningless
6 other (please specify)

5. Which *best* describes your interpretation of "$_a\int^b f(x)\, dx$":

    1 sign
    2 symbol
    3 metaphor
    4 model
    5 meaningless
    6 other (please specify)

6. "$E = mc^2$" is an example of (check as many as applicable)

    1 the abstraction of a naural law
    2 a model
    3 a relation between symbols
    4 the inviolate truth
    5 God's design
    6 a uniquely human mental exercise
    7 other (please specify)

7. Mathematics is (check as many as are applicable)

a. rigid	g. flexible	m. emotive
b. exact	h. open	n. bland
c. objective	i. rational	o. animating
d. subjective	j. irrational	p. dull
e. precise	k. sterile	q. exciting
f. beautiful	l. useful	r. demonic

8. The existence of mathematics validates the claim that all is not metaphor.

1	2	3	4	5
Strongly Disagree				Strongly Agree

9. Are you primarily involved in the area of

    1 mathematics   2 science   3 religion   4 philosophy   5 other

10. Please note your sex:

    a. Male   b. Female

11. Please note your highest level of study in mathematics:

    a. General mathematics (arithmetic, geometry, and/or high school albegra)
    b. College alegbra and/or trigonometry and/or beginning statistics

c. Calculus

d. Advanced mathematical studies

12. Can you elaborate on your understanding of the meaning of the following terms: signs, symbols, metaphors, and models?

13. Do you feel there is a difference in significance and use between religious and mathematical signs, symbols, and models, etc., and, if so, please help identify that difference.

RESULTS AND INTERPRETATIONS

Five different categories of response are associated with this study: overall or *total* results, responses of those indicating *less* familiarity with *math*ematics (question 11, parts a and b), responses of those indicating *high* familiarity with *math*ematics (question 11, parts c and d), responses of those indicating primary involvement in the area of *religion* or philosophy, and responses of those indicating primary involvement in the areas of *science* and *math*ematics (question 9).

The slight overlap should be noted between the categories of "High Math" and "Religion" and also between "High Math" and "Science/math." In other words, those who indicated less familiarity with mathematics were uniformly involved in religion, while those who indicated high familiarity with mathematics were most likely, but not uniformly, involved in areas of science or mathematics. One person (a woman) indicated dual involvement in both science and religion.

Questions 3 and 8 provided basic feedback on the degree to which we humans (more accurately, a select subset thereof) currently view mathematics as a metaphorical language. What stands out clearest in regard to question 3 is that respondees tended to regard mathematics as a symbolic language (39%) or as a set of manipulable signs (26%). More than a quarter (26%) of all respondents indicated a preference for all four terms (signs, symbols, metaphors, and models). A few respondees could not choose between the terms and so marked more than one response. Only one respondee indicated a view of mathematics that was primarily metaphorical in nature.

Those who most frequently favored the view of mathematics as "a symbolic language which helps to articulate the intelligibility we find in the universe" were those currently involved in religion. Respondees from the area of science and mathematics were most likely to see mathematics as "a medium for modeling reality." Those who had least familiarity with mathematics (all of whom were also involved in religion) were most likely to view mathematics as "all of the above," that is, as a combination of descriptions involving signs, symbols, metaphors, and models. High mathematics awareness and/or professional involvement in mathematics/ science seems to be correlated with *no* conception of mathematics as a language filled with metaphors.

Question 8 addressed the issue of metaphor in mathematics from a slightly different perspective. Two major voices in the current theological world are those of the critical realist and the deconstructionist, both of whom rely heavily on the importance of metaphor in our religious understandings. To the deconstructionist, the world is known only through metaphors. That is, all is metaphor: nothing exists except through the medium of metaphorical language. The critical realist, on the other hand, assumes that much is metaphor, but not everything. Sallie McFague, a representative of the critical realist position, contends that the way in which we approximate our experience, whether it be poetic, religious, scientific, or otherwise, is always metaphorical, and that healthy metaphors are at the heart of creativity. Yet McFague has a curious habit, not well acknowledged, of alluding to mathematics whenever she attempts to assure her readers that *all* is not metaphor.[4] Question 8 sought to challenge or to support the contention that mathematics in some way offers a universal absolute that is nonmetaphorical.

Responses to question 8 suggest that those involved with religion and, particularly, those less familiar with mathematics are somewhat more prone to support McFague's apparent supposition than are those more familiar or involved with mathematics and the sciences. However, the relatively large percentage of NRs (no responses) in all categories coupled with a few penciled in comments (for example, "I don't understand the question.") suggests that this question may have been too specialized for many respondents to fully grasp, at least in its present phrasing and context.

Questions 4, 5, and 6, address differences in perception of the use of terms such as sign, symbol, metaphor, and model within mathematics, that is, internally. The two open-ended questions at the end of the survey (questions 12 and 13) elicit differences perceived externally, that is, between the terms as applied to mathematics and as applied to religion.

Questions 4, 5, and 6, containing examples of the Hindu-Arabic numeral for the concept of two, the notation for the definite integral of calculus, and Einstein's famed equation $E = mc^2$, respectively, explore the respondees' conceptions of these four terms at assorted levels of complexity. Those with less math familiarity tended to identify "2" as a sign slightly more frequently than as a symbol, whereas all other groups most often called it a symbol. Those with high knowledge of mathematics and also those coming from the fields of science/mathematics most often identified the definite integral as a symbol; those with less math familiarity not unsurprisingly most often labeled the notation "meaningless." As a total group, responses to question 5 were well dispersed throughout the set of possibilities. Tabulations of question 6 responses indicate that Einstein's equation was most often described as a law by respondees in "high math," "religion," and "science/mathematics" categories and was described about equally as law, model, or symbol by those with less math familiarity and by the group as a whole. Notably, no one at all identified "2" as a metaphor and no one at all identified Einstein's equation as "the inviolate truth." It is also curious that, while scientists and mathematicians were generally willing to see mathematics as a medium for modeling reality (question 3), they were much less willing to describe the specific examples found in questions 4, 5, and 6 as models.

The first open-ended question (question 12) sought to ascertain the understandings those surveyed held of the terms sign, symbol, metaphor, and model. The second open-ended question examined differences perceived between, on the one hand, the significance and use of these terms in mathematics and, on the other, their significance and use in religion. Overall, the responses tended 1) to confirm the assumption of ambiguity in the meanings respondees ascribed to the terms and 2) to suggest that respondees view the use of the terms within the two fields as fundamentally different from each other. A trend seems to be emerging, however, that mitigates these differences, which, not incidentally, are identified only vaguely.

That ambiguity exists was not immediately apparent. Indeed,

individual surveys presented comparisons and distinctions between the terms in fairly cohesive, consistent manners. Yet when the comments were regrouped according to genre, for example, all comments about signs, all about symbols, mixed and even contradictory reactions became more obvious. Consider, for example, the following statements taken from the completed surveys:

> Sign and symbol are very similar in meaning.
> I don't have a clear distinction between signs and symbols.
> [A] symbol is metaphor.
> Signs . . . can have a metaphorical sense.
> I don't see any real distinction between sign and symbol, except that symbol seems to be the more common term.
> A symbol . . . portrays some reality, but does not participate in it.
> Symbols participate in the reality.
> A sign not only points to some reality, it is involved in it.
> Symbols . . . indicate meaning by participating in the reality **sign**ified. (emphasis added)
> Metaphor is a symbol.
> A metaphor is a species of symbol.
> A model is a complex of metaphors and symbols.

While the boundaries between sign, symbol, metaphor, and model were poorly delineated, the language with which they were most frequently described nonetheless suggested characteristic ideas associated with each term. Signs tend to *point to* something, to be *arbitrary* and to be *concrete, physical* or *visual*. Symbols (generally) seem to *participate* in the reality or context which they invoke and to have more to do with value, imagination, and the *psychic*. Metaphor suggests a *comparison* between *realities*, one of which is usually simpler or more familiar than the other. Models have more to do with *behavior*: for example, they *show how* something *operates*, they *reflect ways* of doing this or that, they are constructions, they form *structures* or *frameworks* for *operations*, they are *constructed, useful* cases.

Demographic analysis of the responses to question 12 provide an additional insight, namely that those surveyees not involved in religion responded less frequently and more briefly than those involved in religion. This apparent disinterest on the part of the mathematics/scientific community became even more pronounced in the responses to question 13. One such person responded cryptically, "Never really thought about it." End of comment.

The remaining five respondees from the area of mathematics/science seemed[5] to note differences in the use of the terms in mathematics and in religion. Differences cited, however, were difficult to categorize. One person, for instance, noted a difference between formal meanings found in mathematics and informal ones found in religion. Another discussed the role of mathematics (as opposed to religion) in drawing inferences about how systems behave. A third sensed a difference in that mathematics has no necessary connection to anything outside of itself, while religion is concerned with something external to its own terms and logic. This latter comment draws on the only echo of commonality in responses of mathematicians/scientists—namely, that mathematics is in some sense self-contained, not needing to draw on external sources for its validity.

The remaining responses, all from the field of religion, ran the continuum from "no difference" to "not much difference" to "maybe" or "it depends" to "some difference" to "yes." There was slightly more response on the "yes" end than on the "no" end. The more common themes centered on the measurability, mechanism, and rationality of mathematical signs, symbols, metaphors, and models as opposed to the greater fullness, less precision, and larger truth of their religious counterparts. One respondee was perhaps particularly attuned to the underlying presuppositions of this study when he noted that "The focus or slant (between mathematical and religious signs, symbols, etc.) is different, but they are merging, as math and physics begin to ask more and more fundamental questions—how old is the cosmos? where is the edge of space?"

Question 7 assessed the emotional response of the surveyees to mathematics. All five categories almost unanimously (95%, 91%, 100%, 94%, 100%, respectively) agreed that mathematics is useful. Other descriptive terms frequently associated with mathematics include rational, precise, exact, beautiful, and objective. There appears to be a correlation between high math familiarity/involvement and willingness to describe mathematics as beautiful. Two groups (high math and science/math) also identified mathematics as being flexible, exciting, and rigid noticeably more frequently than did those with less math familiarity or those involved primarily in the area of religion. Curiously, those involved in science/math identified mathematics as being flexible and being rigid with equal frequency. Terms less likely to be attached to mathematics included, across the board, irrational, sterile, emotive, dull, and demonic. No one at all described mathematics as bland.

Question 1 evaluated the degree of connection (undefined) that respondees believe exists between mathematics and religion. Those involved in science/math and those more familiar with mathematics saw the least connection. Other groups were more evenly dispersed in their assessments, perhaps suggesting some uncertainty in their choices. On the other hand (question 2), all respondees unequivocally felt that a high degree of connection exists between mathematics and science.

CONCLUSIONS

As a whole, the study suggests that mathematics is not valued in our culture as a metaphorical language nor is it seen as contributing much to religion. These contentions seem to be most strongly supported by those with high awareness of mathematics and least professional involvement in religion. All groups surveyed agreed on the usefulness of mathematics, but apparently that usefulness does not extend to examination of religious issues. However, much ambiguity exists, even among the religious community, regarding the meanings and nature of the terms sign, symbol, metaphor, and model; and there is evidence that all groups (to varying degrees and with varying intents) recognize at least some relevance of sign, symbol, and model to both mathematics and religion.

Whether or not today's society views mathematics as an indicator of the existence of absolute certainty or as an alternative to the notion that all is metaphor remains an open question.[6] Those most sympathetic to future exploration of this and other issues raised in the study are most likely to be those who combine some degree of familiarity with mathematics with an explicit interest in religion. Thus, if the illusive lady of mathematics is to reappear in contemporary churches, it will most likely be at the invitation of those open to rethinking established patterns of thought. One such person probably stands behind the following commentary made regarding both the content of this study and the study itself:

Both religion and mathematics make use of signs and models. Initially I supposed that symbols and metaphors were more apt to be found in religion than mathematics. Perhaps, though, "$E = mc^2$" might be thought of as either/both symbol and metaphor? Perhaps also as a model. E/m/c I would understand as signs. This is fascinating.

NOTES

FOREWORD

1. *Webster's New Twentieth Century Dictionary* is one such source..

2. See, for example, John Hick, *An Interpretation of Religion: Human Responses to the Transcendent* (New Haven: Yale University Press, 1989), 10.

3. They have, of course, been preceded by such mathematician/ philosophers as Leibniz, Newton, and Descartes, all of whom were religiously motivated to undertake their studies. Nor have I mentioned twentieth-century philosophers such as Bertrand Russell and W. V. Quine whose works, while strongly mathematical, have had a less direct connection to religion and theology.

4. For further reading on Wittgenstein, see S. G. Shanker, *Wittgenstein and the Turning-Point in the Philosophy of Mathematics* (London: Croom Helm, 1987). Brief essays on all five can be found in the *Handbook of Metaphysics and Ontology,* ed. Hans Burkhardt and Barry Smith, 2 vols. (Munich: Philosophia Verlag, 1991).

5. One concise source for further reading on the role of metaphor in religion is Arthur Peacock, *Intimations of Reality: Critical Realism in Science and Religion,* The Mendenhall Lectures, 1983 (Notre Dame, Indiana: University of Notre Dame Press, 1984).

1. META-VIEW

1. Paul Davies. *The Mind of God* (New York: Simon and Schuster, 1992), 140.

2. Philip J. Davis and Reuben Hersh. *The Mathematical Experience* (Boston: Houghton Mifflin Co., 1981), 335–36.

3. Davis and Hersh, *Mathematical Experience,* 336, Quoting from D. Hilbert, "On the Infinite," in *Philosophy of Mathematics* (Benacerraf and Putnam).

4. John M. Carpenter. "Shifting Structure of Mathematical Paradigms," in *The Metaphors of Consciousness,* ed. Ronald S. Valle and Rolf Eckartsberg (New York: Plenum Press, 1981), 470.

5. Mathematicians tend to see the effect of Gödel's theorem in dif-

ferent ways. Paul Davies, for instance, notes that Gödel's theorem "put paid to this [Hilbert's] strictly formalist position. Nevertheless, many mathematicians retain the belief that mathematics is only an invention of the human mind, having no meaning beyond that attributed to it by mathematicians." On the other hand, he observes that most scientists today still hold dear an article of faith regarding the truth of mathematics: "The belief that the underlying order of the world can be expressed in mathematical form lies at the very heart of science, and is rarely questioned" (Davies, *The Mind of God*, 140–41).

One important arena in which this belief is currently being explored is through the work of Alan Turing, who expanded upon Gödel's ideas with the publication in 1950 of a now-famous article on "Computer Machinery and Intelligence." In this article we find the first exposition of what has become known as a "Turing machine." A Turing machine is not really a machine at all, but rather, a procedure or *algorithm* such as those detailed sets of operational procedures that may be programmed and run on a computer. The concept of a Turing machine is of central importance for contemporary work in mathematics, computer science, physics, and other disciplines. Artificial intelligence investigators often suggest that an algorithm might exist that would match the workings of the human brain. In this view, all mental qualities (thinking, feeling, intelligence, understanding, consciousness) are features of an *algorithm* being carried out by the brain. If such an algorithm can be found, then any computer that runs it would, in effect, become a mind. An excellent (although critical) source for further study of this fascinating idea that even mind can be expressed in mathematical form is Roger Penrose's *The Emperor's New Mind* (New York: Oxford University Press, 1989).

6. Carpenter, "Shifting Structure," 470.

7. Not all dictionaries list the word. The *English Oxford Dictionary* defines "metamathematics" as "the philosophy of mathematics."

8. Carpenter, "Shifting Structure," 468.

9. See, for instance, Korzybski or Bois for a general semantics view on this issue. Also, in view of the general thesis of my study, the following passage, taken from Carpenter's article on the "Shifting Structure" is of interest: "Self-reference speaks directly to the issue of human consciousness. When human beings explore the external world, the world of objects, events and their interrelationships, the system of logic and scientific reasoning being used is not self-referent and, therefore, Gödel's theorem is irrelevant. However, whenever we have attempted to explore the nature of our own thought processes and consciousness (that is, the nature of ourselves), we act in a self-referent manner. At this point, Gödel's theorem takes on *metaphorical* relevance. It suggests that when the human individual attempts to understand him- or herself, truth must have a definition apart from logical provability" (471).

10. Says Douglas Hofstadter: "If one uses Gödel's Theorem as a metaphor, as a source of inspiration, rather than trying to translate it literally into the language of psychology or of any other discipline, then perhaps it can suggest new truths in psychology or other areas. But it is quite unjustifiable to translate it directly into a statement of another discipline and take that as equally valid" (Gödel, Escher, and Bach: An Eternal Golden Braid [New York: Vintage Books, 1979], 696).

11. Hofstadter, *Gödel, Escher, and Bach*, 26–27.

12. Ian G. Barbour, *Religion in an Age of Science*, vol. 1, *The Gifford Lectures, 1989–91* (San Francisco: Harper, 1990), 28.

13. Frank B. Dilley. *Metaphysics and Religious Language* (New York: Columbia University Press, 1964), 2.

14. Davies, *The Mind of God*, 33.

15. Paul K. Moser, ed., *Reality in Focus* (Englewood Cliffs, N.J.: Prentice Hall, 1990), 3.

16. Nicholas Lobkowicz. "Metaphysics: History and Terminology," vol. 2 of *Handbook of Metaphysics and Ontology*, ed. Hans Burkhardt and Barry Smith (Munich: Philosophia Verlag, 1991), 528–29.

17. Lobkowicz, "Metaphysics," 528.

18. Ibid., 530.

19. Ibid. Lobkowicz cites Hegel as one such philosopher.

20. J. Samuel Bois, *The Art of Awareness*, 3d ed. (Dubuque, Iowa: Wm. C. Brown Co., 1978), 8.

21. Ibid., 4.

22. Ibid., 9.

23. Ibid., 10.

24. Ibid., 20–21.

25. Ibid., 106.

26. H. H. Price, "Paranormal Cognition and Symbolism," in *Metaphor and Symbol: Proceedings of the Twelfth Symposium of the Colston Research Society*, University of Bristol, March 28–31, 1960, Edited by L. C. Knight and Basil Cottle (London: Butterworths Scientific Publications, 1960), 78.

27. Ibid., 79.

28. Ibid., 81.

29. Ibid.

30. The capitalization is Price's.

31. Price, 89.

32. See, for example, Bois's preface to the first edition of *The Art of Awareness*.

33. Lawrence Leshan and Henry Margenau, *Einstein's Space and Van Gogh's Sky: Physical Reality and Beyond* (New York: Macmillan Publishing Co., 1982), 20–21.

34. Ibid., 28.

35. Ibid., 33.

36. The scientific domain operates, according to the authors, on a geometric-like model that relates primary experience to conceptual construction through a correspondence theory that allows for mathematical quantification. The model then transfers the conceptual construction back into the area of primary experience as a prediction. Ibid., 72–91.

37. Ibid., 123–24.

38. The sensory state of consciousness I take to be primarily our ordinary empirical scientific realm; the clairvoyant is a reality where "all things flow into one another and are part of a larger whole that makes up the entire cosmos"; the transpsychic is where "the individual is perceived as an entity in its own right, but is also a part of the total One of the cosmos, so that no definite line of separation is possible"; and the mythic reality is where "anything can be identical with anything else once they have been connected with each other spatially, temporally, or conceptually. Ibid., 165–66.

39. Ibid., 164.

40. Ibid., 160.

41. Ibid., 161.

42. Ibid.

43. Ibid., cf. 161 and 205.

44. Robert Ornstein and Paul Ehrlich, *New World New Mind* (New York: Simon and Schuster, 1990), 29.

45. Ibid., 19.

46. Ibid., 30.

47. Ibid., 74.

48. Ibid., 72.

49. Ibid., 74.

50. Ibid., 90.

51. Ibid., 92. Examples given of this phenomena include the way a personal insult dominates attention; the fact that viewers of violent movies believe that there is more violence in the world than do nonviewers of violent films; increased incidence of health examination upon the news release that the wife of President Ford had breast cancer, etc.

52. Bois, *Art of Awareness*, 309.

53. Ornstein and Ehrlich, *New World New Mind*, 196.

54. Bois, *Art of Awareness*, 299.

55. Ornstein and Ehrlich, *New World New Mind*, 120.

56. Ibid., 148.

57. "To us," say Ornstein and Ehrlich, "most religions and spiritual groups have, at their core, a vital message: that all human beings are

connected to one another, affecting one another's fate and that of the world, and that people must find within themselves a moral compass for orienting both people and environments" (ibid., 145).

58. Hofstadter, *Gödel, Escher, and Bach*, 337. Hofstadter himself is generally unsympathetic to such fringe areas of science as the paranormal. (See Douglas Hofstadter, "World Views in Collision: The Skeptical Inquirer versus the National Enquirer," *Metamagical Themas: Questing for the Essence of Mind and Pattern* (New York: Basic Books, 1985], 91–114). His theory, nonetheless, can be interpreted in ways that are more open to these possibilities.

59. Hofstadter, *Gödel, Escher, and Bach*, 371.

60. Ibid., 370.

61. Ibid., 375.

62. Ibid., 386. "Chunked" is a term meaning a high-level perception of complex arrays. It originated in the realization that chess masters perceived the distribution of chess pieces in chunks. The master's "mode of perceiving the board is like a filter; he literally *does not see bad moves* when he looks at a chess situation—no more than amateurs see *illegal moves.* . . . Anyone who has played even a little chess has organized his perception so that diagonal rook moves, forward captures by pawns, and so forth, are never brought to mind" (idem., 286).

63. Ibid., 291–93

64. Ibid., 302.

65. Ibid., 478.

66. Ibid., 387.

67. Ibid., cf. 327–28.

68. Ibid., see 251–60 and 479.

69. Ibid., 478.

70. Ibid., 407.

71. Ibid., 377.

72. Ibid., 263.

73. Ibid., 406.

74. Ibid., 28.

75. Davies, *The Mind of God*, 79.

76. Sallie McFague, *Metaphorical Theology: Models of God in Religious Language* (Philadelphia: Fortress Press, 1982), 15.

77. Janet Soskice, *Metaphor and Religious Language* (Oxford: Clarendon Press, 1985), 15.

78. Ibid., 50.

79. Colin Turbayne, *The Myth of Metaphor*, rev. ed. (Columbia, South Carolina: University of South Carolina Press, 1970), 12.

80. W. H. Leatherdale, *The Role of Analogy, Model and Metaphor in Science* (Amsterdam: North-Holland Pub. Co., 1974), 64.

81.   Robert D. Romanyshyn, *Psychological Life from Science to Metaphor* (Austin: University of Texas Press, 1982), 34.

82.   Ibid., 153.

83.   Ibid., 34.

84.   Robert D. Romanyshyn, "Science and Reality: Metaphors of Experience and Experience as Metaphorical," in *The Metaphors of Consciousness*, ed. Ronald S. Valle and Rolf von Eckartsberg (New York: Plenum Press, 1981), 12–13.

85.   One notable exception, according to Romanyshyn, may be seen in the arena of quantum theory, particularly as interpreted by Niels Bohr whose work "implies a radical recovery of the metaphorical character of reality" (*Metaphors of Consciousness*, 14).

86.   Ibid., 15.

87.   Ibid., 15.

88.   Soskice is unambiguous about her position: "The introduction of misleading psychological terminology into definitions of metaphor arises from a failure to distinguish two tasks: that of providing a nominal definition that allows us to identify metaphor, and that of providing a functional account that tells us how the metaphor works" (*Metaphor and Religious Language*, 16). She is not altogether unsympathetic to the spirit of the psychologizing, however, as evidenced a page later when she states that "the tendency to speak of metaphor as though it were a special kind of mental act is by no means without significance in our study. It is an important feature of metaphor that, if the metaphor is a good one, in appreciating it one goes well beyond the bare formulation of the utterance."

89.   In this I am following the precedent of Mark Knapp, R. L. Birdwhistell and others. Knapp, for instance, notes that "Verbal and nonverbal communication should be treated as a total and inseparable unit" (Mark L. Knapp, *Nonverbal Communication in Human Interaction*, 2d ed. [New York: Holt, Rinehart, and Winston, 1978], 20.)

90.   There appears to be no one definitive classification of the theories of metaphor. Soskice, for example, categorizes the various accounts as falling into three basic groups: those that portray metaphor as decorative *substitutions* for some literal description (or a comparison), those that are *emotive* in that they produce a unique affective impact, and those that are *incremental* in that they add or bring something cognitively new to the situation. (*Metaphor and Religious Language*, Chapter 3.) Ricouer, on the other hand, groups them broadly as either tension or substitution theories, the latter having five basic suppositions that the former calls into question (See Paul Ricoeur, *Interpretation Theory: Discourse and the Surplus of Meaning* [Fort Worth: Texas Christian University Press, 1976], 49).

91.   See, for example, Soskice, *Metaphor and Religious Language*,

3–10. Soskice traces the source of the substitution theory, not to Aristotle, but to "those philosophers of the seventeenth century who chose as their model the arguments of mathematics and the new sciences" (idem., 12).

92. Sallie McFague, *Models of God: Theology for an Ecological, Nuclear Age* (Philadelphia: Fortress Press, 1987), 33.

93. Cf. Max Black, *Models and Metaphors* (Ithaca, New York: Cornell University Press, 1962), 39–42.

94. Cf. Frank B. Dilley, *Metaphysics and Religious Language*, 79.

95. Cf. Ricouer, *Interpretation Theory*, 46–53.

96. Cf. McFague's *Models of God*, 33; or Barbour's *Religion in an Age of Science*, 47.

97. In chapter 21 of the *Poetics*, Aristotle writes that a " 'metaphorical term' involves the transferred use of a term that properly belongs to something else; the transference can be from genus to species, from species to genus, from species to species, or analogical" (See Soskice, *Metaphor and Religions Language*, 4).

98. Soskice, *Metaphor and Religious Language*, 49.

99. Hofstadter, *Gödel, Escher, and Bach*, 614.

100. Ralph Ross, *Symbols and Civilization: Science, Morals, Religion, Art* (New York: Harcourt, Brace, and World, 1962), 23–24.

101. Thomas Hobbes, *Leviathan* (1651; reprint London: Penguin Classics, 1985), 115.

102. Ibid., 261.

103. Ross, 23.

104. McFague, *Metaphorical Theology*, 34.

105. James Gleick, *Chaos: Making a New Science* (New York: Viking, 1987), 77.

106. Wayne C. Booth, *The Company We Keep: An Ethics of Fiction* (Berkeley: University of California Press, 1988), 356.

107. Barbour, *Religion in an Age of Science*, 99.

108. Timothy L. S. Sprigge, "Idealism / Realism," vol. 2 of *Handbook of Metaphysics and Ontology*, ed. Burkhardt and Smith, 377.

109. Davis and Hersh, *Mathematical Experience*, 321.

110. M. Mitchell Waldrop, *Complexity: The Emerging Science at the Edge of Order and Chaos* (New York: Simon and Schuster, 1992), 334.

111. Ibid., 31–32.

112. Ibid., 330.

113. Ibid., 185.

114. Ibid., 235.

115. Will Hively, "Life Beyond Boiling," *Discover* 14, no. 5 (May 1993): 87–91.

116. See, for example, Alan Lightman, *Great Ideas in Physics* (New York: McGraw Hill, 1992), 189.

117.   Lewis Thomas, *The Fragile Species* (New York: Macmillan, 1992), 171.

118.   Barbour, *Religion in an Age of Science,* 34.

119.   Hofstadter, *Gödel, Escher, and Bach,* 10.

120.   Ibid., 383.

121.   Richard Morris, *The Edges of Science* (New York: Simon and Schuster, 1990), 209.

122.   Ibid., see also p. 64.

123.   There is some precedence for holding this contradictory position, at least if I read Burkhardt and Smith correctly. They say, for instance, that Alfred North Whitehead "aimed to synthesize realism and idealism" (Burkhardt and Smith, *Handbook of Metaphysics,* 378). Furthermore, "Some faint analogy exists between the traditional contrast between realism and idealism and that of realism and anti-realism as currently specified by Michael Dummet (born 1925). The anti-realist about a class of objects thinks that the principle of bivalence (that a proposition must either be true or false) does nor apply to statements about them. Many idealists are realists, in this sense, about the physical" (idem, 379).

124.   To understand this topological concept, cut a long narrow strip of paper, give it a single twist, and paste the ends together. The "figure 8" which results is one-sided, not two-sided. The Boston Museum of Science has developed a "soapsuds" version of the strip which truly gives it a continuous (as opposed to a pieced together) smooth surface. For another metaphorical use of this mathematical idea, see Sarah Voss, "Depolarizing Mathematics and Religion," *Philosophia Mathematica* (Virginia Beach: Grunwald Publishers, vol. 5, series 2, no. 1/2, June 1990): 129–41.

125.   Photo courtesy of Dan M. Sullivan, University of Nebraska at Omaha.

2. IMAGE-INATION IN MATHEMATICS AND RELIGION

1.   Some reservations or restrictions on the idea that metaphor has something to do with images can be found in Leatherdale, *The Role of Analogy,* 116–18.

2.   From *Webster's New World Dictionary* of the American Language, College edition, 2d College Ed., ed. David B. Guralnik, (New York: The Word Publishing Co.), 1972.

3.   I am persistent, as this study shows.

4.   Clifford Geertz, for instance, defined religion as "(1) a system of symbols which acts to (2) establish powerful, pervasive and long-lasting moods and motivations in people by (3) formulating conceptions of a

general order of existence and (4) clothing these conceptions with such an aura of factuality that (5) the moods and motivations seem uniquely realistic." (*The Interpretation of Culture* [New York: Basic Books, 1973], 90–91.)

5. See Appendix A for a summary of this study.

6. This treatment is highly linear and analytical. In our modern Western culture, with its current scientific/technological emphasis, variations on this approach have appeared even within the religious realm. For example, Ralph Burhoe, an early and strong proponent of *scientific* theology, has defined religion in terms of values ranked along a pyramidal continuum.

> "it is possible for man to arrange his concepts of what is valuable in the form of a logical pyramid where the numerous concrete and mundane values are represented in the large area of the base of the pyramid, and the single word or abstract concept that represents man's supreme value is at the highest peak of the pyramid." The several layers of words or ideas near the peak of the pyramid would be the region representing my definition of religion, where we would find words representing comprehensive systems of positive values such as 'life.' ("Potentials for Religion from the Sciences," *Zygon* 5 no. 2 [June 1970]: 115.)

Any pyramidal vision contains a tendency toward hierarchical thinking, and Burhoe embraces this aspect wholeheartedly. When it comes to making value judgements, hierarchical thinking is a valuable and perhaps even essential mode of thought. However, while I recognize it as one valid "way of seeing," I (somewhat hierarchically) think there are often "better" ways of seeing, at least for our present-day religious climate. In this regard, I am drawn to the *metaphorical* theology that Sallie McFague envisions and that consistently promotes a multitude of perspectives, all of which act to enliven and revitalize each other. McFague rests her theology on the belief that metaphors and models reflect human thought and mediate reality to us, albeit partially and approximately. According to McFague, metaphors and models govern and shape our religious life. Metaphorical theology is decidedly nonhierarchical. "[T]here is no suggestion," she insists, "of a hierarchy among metaphors, models, and concepts" (McFague, *Metaphorical Theology,* 26).

7. McFague, *Metaphorical Theology,* 26.

8. Ibid., 37.

9. It could arguably be called a continuum of symbolic language or a continuum of signs, or even of modelling. The choice is largely a matter of preference. I lean towards metaphorical language because of its connotation as "ways of seeing."

10. Cf. Tillich's chapter on "Symbols of Faith," in *Dynamics of*

Faith (New York: Harper and Brothers, 1957), or McFague's chapter on "Metaphor, Parable, and Scripture" in *Metaphorical Theology*.

11. This problem, as we will see, is pervasive in the study of metaphorical language. Ultimately it points to the general failure of this work to clarify the meaning of the four terms: sign, symbol, metaphor, and model. Thus, while I opened this chapter with the hope that I would "bring some clarity to the meanings of these terms, or, at the least, to make the confusion more understandable," it will become increasingly clear that, in actuality, I have only heightened our awareness of the endemic confusion surrounding our collective usage of the terms.

12. The difference between the "process of abstraction" and the "use of metaphorical language" (in the broad sense in which I have used it here) may *be* largely one of semantics. We will revisit this topic later in the chapter.

13. Walter Diethelm calls this a "metaphorically applied sign" (*Signet, Signal, Symbol,* [Zurich: ABC Verlag, 1976], 220.

14. Diethelm, *Signet, Signal, Symbol,* 221.

15. For further reading, see Black's chapter on "Models and Archetypes" (*Models and Metaphors*); Barbour's chapter on "Models and Paradigms" (*Religion in an Age of Science*); or chapter 2 in Leatherdale's *Role of Analogy.* Leatherdale maintains that the commonality among all different types of models is that they are species of analogue (42). Like Black, he also distinguishes between mathematical and theoretical models (50). For a different treatment based on the structural thinking of economist-philosopher Kenneth Boulding, see Bois's section on "Mental Models and Their Use" in *Art of Awareness*.

16. McFague, *Metaphorical Theology,* 9.

17. Interestingly, in early interpretation of scriptural numbers there appears to be a connection between the cross and the number three. According to Hopper, one commentary on Barnabas noted, for example, that "because the cross was to express the grace [of our redemption] by the letter T, he says also '300.'" Says Hopper, "T, or 300, is thereby made *the symbol of the cross*" (emphasis added) (Vincent Foster Hopper, *Medieval Number Symbolism: It's Sources, Meaning, and Influence on Thought and Expression.* [1938. Rpt. Norwood, Pa.: Norwood Editions, 1977], 75–76)

18. Cf. Barfield's "secondary" meanings. Owen Barfield, "The Meaning of the Word 'Literal,'" *Metaphor and Symbol: Proceedings of the Twelfth Symposium of the Colston Research Society,* University of Bristol, March 28–31, 1960, ed. L. C. Knights and Basil Cottle (London: Butterworths Scientific Publications, 1960), 48.

19. My thanks for this metaphorical comparison to Tom Gilbert, who "borrowed" the analogy from Phil Hefner, who "borrowed" it from Gene d'Aquili.

20. Soskice, *Metaphor and Religious Language*, 75.

21. Barfield, "Meaning of the Word," 53.

22. Examples include abstract terms such as *"progress, tendency, culture, democracy, liberality, inhibition, motivation, responsibility—*there was a time when each one of them, either itself or its progenitor in another tongue, was a vehicle referring to the concrete world of sensuous experience with a tenor of some sort peeping, or breathing or bursting through. But now they are just 'literal' words—the sort of words we have to use, when we are admonished *not* to speak in metaphors" (Barfield, "Meaning of the Word," 53).

23. Barfield, "Meaning of the Word," 55.

24. Ibid.

25. F. W. Dillistone, *The Power of Symbols in Religion and Culture* (New York: Crossroad, 1986), 27.

26. Ibid., 28.

27. An interesting variation on this theme that has wider implications for our concrete, physical world may be found in one of the exhibits at the Boston Museum of Science. In this exhibit, you are asked to look at a turning object by positioning yourself so that first one eye and then the other confronts a darkened filter, rather like wearing half a pair of sunglasses. Switching this filter from eye to eye has the astonishing effect of apparently *reversing* the direction of the object's spin.

28. According to my own thesis, my metaphor here is a strongly literal one: the human being *is* a filtering device. In spite of my aversion for idolatry (which is how McFague interprets such identification between a metaphor and its reference), and in spite of the general character of this work that (I hope) strongly purports a "one way among many" perspective, I still find myself unwilling to put forth the less definitive rendering "the human being *acts as* a filtering device." I am not sure I can defend this inconsistency.

29. Sal Restivo, *The Social Relations of Physics, Mysticism, and Mathematics* (Dordrecht: D. Reidel Publishing Co., 1983), 35. Although it is not crucial to my point here, Restivo (for whom the social is pervasive) gives an interesting account of the state of the art of epistemology as it applies to current theories of parallelism between mysticism and physics. While Restivo disagrees with many of the conclusions that are drawn from these theories, he values them as adaptive strategies developing in a society that is searching for alternatives to a scientific (rational) strategy. His account of Siu's theory, I should emphasize, is a small part of a whole chapter on "The Pitfalls of Parallelism" (i.e., parallelism of mysticism and science, especially physics). Restivo here merely reports Siu's "radical" view without endorsing it. Nonetheless, in a personal communication, he acknowledged that he sees Siu's radical view as an important part of a

larger social effort to reconceptualize the nature of objectivity. For more on Siu, see R. G. H. Siu, *The Tao of Science* (Cambridge: Technology Press, 1958).

30.   Dillistone, *Power of Symbols*, 24. Leatherdale, on the other hand, argues that "although the dividing line between literal and metaphorical cannot be too confidently or dogmatically drawn, there is a genuine distinction to be made" (*Role of Analogy*, 120). He allows, however, that "its elucidation is not immediately obvious" and involves vague criteria such as "'ostensivity,' 'meaning,' 'fulness,' 'truth,' 'appropriateness,' 'ambiguity,' and 'normal usage'" (121).

31.   See also the reference to Morris's *Edges of Science* in chapter 1, p. 39. Morris cites, for example, the new inflationary theories of creation (which predict "that our universe should be very close to the borderline between an open and a closed universe") as being theories that may be untestable. Says Morris, "inflationary universe theories have a characteristic encountered with increasing frequency in contemporary physics and cosmology. In recent years, theoretical speculation has had a tendency to outpace experiment. To an increasing extent, new theoretical ideas have had a tendency to gain wide acceptance long before there is any hope of testing them experimentally. In some cases, the members of the scientific community have shown a willingness to accept ideas that cannot be tested at all" (New York: Simon and Schuster, 1990), 65.

32.   Restivo, *Social Relations*, 36.

33.   Ibid., 37.

34.   While the previous quotation is taken from a section in which Restivo is simply reporting radical ideas, I believe it is consistent with his general perspective that truth is just one more of the cultural resources that humans use to further social interests. In a later work on the social construction of mathematics, for instance, he notes that

> There are indeed limits to the explanatory power of externalities in the analysis of mathematical and scientific knowledge. But there is more beyond those limits than pure thought. Not only is the inside social structure of a science a determinant of the form and substance of knowledge in that science; the scientist is also a social structure. . . . The idea that mathematical knowledge is a social construct does not necessarily lead to some sort of naive or radical relativism. But the avoidance of these forms of relativism depends on developing a complex and dynamic notion of *objectivity as a social fact* rather than a simple matter of coordinating "things in the world" and "terms that refer." (Emphasis added; Sal Restivo, *The Sociological Worldview* (Cambridge: Basil Blackwell, 1991), 164.   •

It might be noted that Restivo here also outlines an argument that the search for mathematical truth has been linked historically with various kinds of theological quests: "The connection between mathematics and religion is thus closer and deeper than most people, used to thinking about the warfare between science and religion, imagine," he concludes (ibid., 165).

35. A similar viewpoint may be found in the field of cognitive psychology, which questions empiricism in favor of contextualistic alternatives. Such alternatives question the notion that meaning is generated by the external environment and that knowledge is established by the object of sensory experience. Contextualism holds, among other things, that meaning changes as situations and contexts shift over time. See, for instance, Diane Gillespie. *The Mind's We: Contextualism in Cognitive Psychology* (Carbondale & Edwardsville: Southern Illinois University Press, 1992), chapter 2.

36. Ibid., 43.

37. Soskice, *Metaphor and Religious Language*, 42.

38. See the section on "Cantoring" in chapter 4 for a clearer understanding of "bounded but infinite."

39. For a justification of exploring such speculative subthemes in a work that is purportedly about the relationship between metaphors, metaphysics, and metamathematics, please see the "Afterword."

40. Karl J. Smith, *The Nature of Mathematics*, 4th ed. (Monterey, California: Brooks/Cole Publishing Co., 1984), 171.

41. Lynn E. Gerner, *Calculus and Analytic Geometry* (San Francisco: Dellen, 1988), 39.

42. M. A. Munem and D. J. Foulis, *Algebra and Trigonometry with Applications*, 2d ed. (New York: Worth Publishers, 1986), 301.

43. McFague, *Metaphorical Theology*, 28, 84, 87, 89.

44. Black, *Models and Metaphors*, 225.

45. Bois, *Art of Awareness*, 211.

46. Soskice, *Metaphor and Religious Language*, 63.

47. Leatherdale, *Role of Analogy*, 1.

48. Ibid., 27–32.

49. Booth, *Company We Keep*, 302f.

50. Turbayne, *The Myth of Metaphor*, 219–33.

51. Black, *Models and Metaphors*, 232.

52. Ross, *Symbols and Civilization*, 165.

53. Lewis Thomas takes this one step further when he develops a four-category taxonomy of language (which, he notes, always relies heavily on metaphor). Small talk and proper, meaningful language form the first two categories in his taxonomy, and poetry forms the last. The third class, which he describes as "an entirely new form of communication" and "the only genuinely universal human language," is mathematics. "If you want to explain to someone else how the universe operates at

its deepest-known levels, all the way from occurrences in the distant cosmos to events within the nucleus of an atom, you cannot do so with any clarity or even any real meaning using any language but mathematics" (*Fragile Species,* 171). Thomas's statement underscores a metaphysical problem that I have alluded to in several places in this work but have not yet made explicit. The metaphysical issue, which is too complex to address in any great detail, is a question of how we traverse the gap between the assorted internal worlds of our individual minds (which allow us to comprehend or attempt to comprehend "how the universe operates at its deepest-known levels") and the external world or worlds of whatever we believe to be not a part of ourselves. It is my contention that mathematics is a bridge by which we can make this transition. Thomas seems to confirm my own experience of mathematics as a language that includes signs, symbols, metaphors, and models, and that utilizes this metaphorical aspect in order to provide that bridge.

54.   Philip J. Davis and Reuben Hersh, *Descartes' Dream: The World According to Mathematics* (San Diego: Harcourt Brace Jovanovich, 1986), 304.

55.   Ibid., 252.

56.   Ibid., 287.

57.   Tobias Dantzig, *Number: The Language of Science* (New York: MacMillan, 1930), 97–98.

58.   Lewis Thomas has generalized this notion to predict that mathematics will be *the* main language of the future ("Why We'll All Speak Math," *World Monitor* 3, no. 12 [December 1990]: 17–20).

59.   Dantzig, *Number,* 99.

60.   Ibid., 87.

61.   Ibid.

62.   Ibid., 88.

63.   Cf. McFague, *Metaphorical Theology,* 107.

64.   Dantzig, *Number,* 245–46.

65.   That this emotional investment is of a religious nature is supported by Hopper's work. See *Medieval Number Symbolism,* 130.

66.   Dantzig, *Number,* 248.

3. HOLY MATHEMATICS

1.   Black, *Models and Metaphors,* 242.

2.   Quoted in Davis and Hersh, *Mathematical Experience,* 54. An interesting (and disturbing) footnote to this footnote is the recent and unprecedented request on the part of influential members of the U.S. National Academy of Science to revoke Shafarevitch's membership in the

organization because of his alleged anti-Semitic writings (*Cedar Rapids Gazette* [Iowa] 29 July 1992, 7A).

3. See E. T. Bell, *Numerology* (Westport, Conn.: Hyperion Press, 1933), vol. 3; and Hopper, *Medieval Number Symbolism*, ix.

4. Dirk J. Struik, "Stone Age Mathematics," *Scientific American* (December 1948): 48.

5. Bell, *Numerology*, 40–41.

6. Hopper, *Medieval Number Symbolism*, 6.

7. See, for instance, chapters 1 and 8 of Bell and the Preface of Hopper. It is of particular interest to note that Hopper treats the works by both Bell and Dantzig (whose quotations surfaced in the end of my chapter 2) as "very recent considerations of the ancient and modern variations of Pythagoreanism" (Ibid., xi).

8. Bell, *Numerology,* 4.

9. Mathematics, according to Bell, is "better off without" the numerology of Plato (34); those who dabble in numerology are "very queer fish indeed" (33); the woman who "caught" the "elusive nuptial number of Plato" was so able to make "strict mathematical sense of everything in [Plato's] obscure passage" that "even a philosopher may have to take his hat off to a woman" (30–31). Consider also his comments about the recurring "nightmare" of James Thompson's numerological equation *LXX/333 = .210*: "If the nonsense of it is not obvious without explanation nothing that anyone can say will make it so. You either have a clear head or you have not" (39).

10. In his preface, for instance, Hopper notes that medieval number philosophy "often appears as sheer nonsense or at best as the product of extraordinarily confused thinking" (Hopper, *Medieval Number Symbolism*, ix).

11. Although his study manages to cover a wide time frame, Hopper's primary emphasis, as the title of his work would suggest, is on medieval number symbolism.

12. Hopper, *Medieval Number Symbolism*, vii.

13. Ibid., 3.

14. Ibid., 11.

15. Ibid., 14.

16. Ibid., 8.

17. Ibid., 35.

18. Ibid., 28.

19. Ibid., 47–48.

20. Ibid., 57.

21. Ibid., 84.

22. Ibid., 113.

23. Ibid., 117.

24. Ibid., 45.

25. Ibid., 93.

26. Ibid., 103. Hopper here applies this idea specifically to the medieval writer, but it is just as applicable to the view of number symbolism held in other eras.

27. Quoted in Hopper, *Medieval Number Symbolism*, 12.

28. Quoted in Hopper, *Medieval Number Symbolism*, 34.

29. Quoted in Hopper, *Medieval Number Symbolism*, 46.

30. Ibid., 48.

31. Ibid., 78.

32. Quoted in Hopper, *Medieval Number Symbolism*, 208.

33. Ibid., 108.

34. Bell, *Numerology*, 61.

35. Irrational numbers are those that can*not* be expressed as the ratio of two *whole* numbers. The exact source of my information regarding the drowning of the Pythagorean brother who discovered the existence of irrational numbers has been lost to me. But a variation of the legend is referred to in Karl Smith, *Nature of Mathematics*, 224. Almost any good mathematical history (e.g., David M. Burton, *The History of Mathematics* (Boston: Allyn and Bacon, 1985) or Howard Eves, *An Introduction to the History of Mathematics,* 6th ed. (Philadelphia: Saunders College Publishing, 1990) will provide further reading on the Pythagorean number philosophy. Much of this, to the modern reader, is curiously entertaining, if nothing more. To the Pythagoreans, for example, a number was either perfect, deficient, or abundant, depending on whether the sum of its proper divisors equals, is less than, or exceeds the number itself. Six, being the sum of $1 + 2 + 3$, therefore, is a perfect number. Thus, God created the world in six days.

36. Carlos Suares, *The Cipher of Genesis: The Original Code of the Quabala as Applied to the Scriptures,* (Berkeley: Shambhala Publications, 1970), 62.

37. A similar situation occurs within the Arabic alphabet. Annemarie Schimmel, for example, writes that "Among mystically minded Muslims, the possibility of interchange between letters and numbers has led to highly sophisticated operations in the realms of quranic exegesis, prognostication, and frequently poetry, especially in the clever use of chronograms" ([*The Mystery of Numbers*, New York: Oxford University Press, 1993], 18). Western culture has, in general, undervalued Arab and various other non-European contributions to mathematics, a fact that is unfortunately reflected by the subtle bias of omission in this present work. This absence, however, suggests a fertile area for further investigation.

38. Ibid., 61–63.

39. Ibid., 73.

40. Ibid.

41. Bell, 138.

42. Ibid., 135.

43. Ibid., 145.

44. Ibid., 140.

45. Hopper, *Medieval Number Symbolism*, vii.

46. Ibid.

47. Ibid., viii.

48. Ibid., 134.

49. Ibid., 69.

50. Ibid.

51. Quoted in Hopper, *Medieval Number Symbolism*, 81.

52. Quoted in Hopper, *Medieval Number Symbolism*, 47.

53. Hick, *An Interpretation of Religion Human Responses to the Transcendent* (New Haven: Yale University Press, 1989), 104–105.

54. Richard Preston, "Profiles: Mountains of Pi," *New Yorker* 2 (March 1992): 37.

55. Eves, *An Introduction*, 119.

56. Karl Smith, *Nature of Mathematics*, 232.

57. Preston, "Profiles," 48.

58. The Chudnovskys clearly fall into the "pi in the sky" category which John Barrow depicts as one of four alternative philosophies of mathematics. These are formalism, inventionism, Platonism, and constructivism. The Platonist maintains that "pi is really in the sky—and mathematicians simply discover it" (John D. Barrow, *Theories of Everything: The Quest for Ultimate Explanation* [Oxford: Clarendon Press, 1991], 183). Not all scholars use precisely these same four categories. Davis and Hersh, for instance, note only three: Platonism, formalism, and constructivism (Davis and Hersh, *Mathematical Experience,* 318–20). Cf. chapter 1 above. Perhaps the important point to glean from such differences, as Barrow says, is, "that the notion of what is 'true' about the Universe appears to depend upon our philosophy of mathematics" (187).

59. Preston, "Profiles," 53.

60. The brothers actually liken the computer not to a kaleidoscope, but to a web—a web of connections made by an intricate network of cables and analogous, in their opinion, to the human brain. "Your brain is the same way. It is mostly made of connections. If I may say so, your brain is a liquid-cooled parallel supercomputer. [Your nose] is the fan" (Ibid., 45). We will revisit this metaphor in the section on computer and chaos theory.

61. Ibid., 64.

62. Preston, "Profiles," 39.

63. David Osborn, "Mathematics and the Spiritual Dimension," *The Clarion Call* 2, no. 4 (Fall 1989): 36.

64. Ibid., 37. At this time, I am unable to date this particular sutra precisely. According to a telephone conversation (August 1992) with David Bainum, assistant editor of the now defunct *Clarion Call,* it may be traced back at least as far as the Middle Ages, and perhaps much further. However, the idea that it embodies, i.e., the dual spiritual/secular role of Vedic mathematics, is ancient (3d century, B.C.).

65. Ibid., 35.

66. Takashi Yoshikawa, *The Ki* (New York: St. Martin's Press, 1986), 2.

67. Karl Smith, *Nature of Mathematics,* 12.

68. Ibid., 3.

69. See Yoshikawa, *Ki,* 7; and Karl Smith, *Nature of Mathematics,* 12.

70. Struik, "Stone Age Mathematics," 49.

71. Burton, *History of Mathematics,* 102.

72. Ibid., 102–103.

73. Christopher Butler, *Number Symbolism* (New York: Barnes and Noble, 1970), 3.

74. Ibid., 18.

75. Ibid., 5.

76. Ibid., 11.

77. Ibid.

78. Ibid., 13.

79. Rachel Fletcher, "Proportion and the Living World," *Parabola* 13: no. 1 (Feb. 1988), quoting from van der Waerden (*Science Awakening* [1961]: 93), 40.

80. Fletcher, "Proportion," 44. Fletcher gives here a nice summary of the proportions as they appear in the human body, the nautilus shell, and in plant forms such as daisies, sunflowers, pinecones, apple blossoms, and the snow iris.

81. Butler, *Number Symbolism,* 18.

82. Ibid., 19.

83. Burton, *History of Mathematics,* 425.

84. Ibid., 105.

85. David E. Mungello, *Leibniz and Confucianism: The Search for Accord* (Honolulu: University Press of Hawaii, 1977), 122.

86. Butler, *Number Symbolism,* 165–66.

87. Ibid., 167–68.

88. Ibid., 3.

89. Fletcher, "Proportion," 42. Ian Stewart and Martin Golubitsky say much the same thing in *Fearful Symmetry* ([Oxford: Blackwell, 1992], 245) regarding Plato's notion that "God ever geometrizes": "Our

central argument has been that Plato's assertion is justified—not as a statement about a personal deity, but as a metaphorical way of expressing the existence of many of the regular patterns in the world around us. . . . From a sufficiently deep and general viewpoint, geometry and symmetry are synonymous. According to Felix Klein, each type of geometry is the study of the invariants of a group of transformations; that is, the symmetries of some chosen space. Symmetries, in turn are captured by a group theory. So, if Plato and Klein are correct, then God must be a group-theorist."

90.   Butler, *Number Symbolism*, 6.

91.   Burton notes that "Descartes' career marks the turning point between medieval and modern mathematics" (*History of Mathematics*, 342).

92.   Ivars Peterson, *The Mathematical Tourist* (New York: W. H. Freeman, 1988), 84.

93.   Ibid., 84.

94.   Ibid.

95.   Turbayne, *Myth of Metaphor*, 66.

96.   Burton, *History of Mathematics*, 344.

97.   Ibid., 345. Such dissonance is hardly unique. Leibniz, for instance, was strongly motivated in his work by his ecumenical thinking and by his desire to integrate diverse religious perspectives into one philosophical system. Nonetheless, because of "his infrequent church attendance and rare communion, the general consensus was, ironically, that he was an unbeliever and consequently no clergyman would preside at the funeral. Only his secretary, Eckhart, attended him at the grave" (Mungello, *Leibniz and Confucianism*, 5).

98.   Turbayne, *Myth of Metaphor*, 66.

99.   Ibid., 68.

100.   Ibid., 66–67.

101.   Bell, *Numerology*, 141.

102.   Philip J. Davis and Reuben Hersh, *Descartes' Dream*, 207.

103.   Hobbes, *Leviathan*, 104.

104.   Hobbes considered metaphor one of the four abuses of language and speech, for he thought that when people "use words metaphorically," they "thereby deceive others" (*Leviathan*, 102). See also chapter 2 of this study.

105.   Davis and Hersh, *Descartes' Dream*, 207.

106.   Davis and Hersh, following Purcell, sum up scientific naturalism in four points: "that absolute rational principles do not explain the universe, that there are no *a priori* truths, that metaphysics is a cover up for ignorance, and that only concrete scientific experimentation and investigation yields true knowledge" (ibid., 208).

107.   See, for example, Barrow, *Theories of Everything*, 1.

108. Fletcher, "Proportion," 38.

109. See chapter 2. Leatherdale summarizes Aristotle's connection between analogy and metaphor by noting that the analogy $A/B = C/D$ was "immensely widened" in scope by considering it as a similarity between two relationships, namely the relationship $A:B$ and the relationship $C:D$. It was, according to Leatherdale, "just such a broadening of the concept of analogy which enabled Aristotle to interpret some forms of metaphor as essentially analogical and to regard such metaphors as the particular hallmark of creative genius in poetry" (*Role of Analogy*, 31). Robert Lawlor, in an article in *Parabola*, points out that an analogy of the restricted form $A:B :: B:(A+B)$ is a unique geometric proportion of three terms made of two which has been called the "Golden Proportion" and which he likens to "the first mystery of the Holy Trinity: the Three that are Two." Calling it suprarational or transcendent, he holds that the golden proportion is "the most intimate relationship . . . that the universe can have with Unity, the primal or first division of One. For this reason the ancients called it 'golden,' the perfect division, and the Christians have related this proportional symbol to the Son of God" (Robert Lawlor, "The Measure of Difference," *Parabola* 15, no. 4 [November 1991]: 12).

110. Fletcher, "Proportion," 38.

111. Stewart and Golubitsky, *Fearful Symmetry*, 266.

112. Fletcher, "Proportion," 38.

113. Ibid., 38.

114. Stewart and Golubitsky, *Fearful Symmetry*, 28.

115. Quoted in Stewart and Golubitsky, *Fearful Symmetry*, 44.

116. Ibid., 44.

117. Ibid., 5.

118. Barrow, *Theories of Everything* 123. See also Stewart and Golubitsky, *Fearful Symmetry* 266–67.

119. James P. Crutchfield, et. al., "Chaos," *Scientific American* (December 1986): 46.

120. Stewart and Golubitsky, *Fearful Symmetry*, xix.

121. Ibid., 269.

122. Barbour, *Religion in an Age of Science*, 29.

123. Ibid.

124. Stephen Hawking, *A Brief History of Time: from the Big Bang to Black Holes* (New York: Bantam, 1988), 175.

125. See, for example, Stewart and Golubitsky, *Fearful Symmetry*, 262–56.

126. The Mandelbrot set has since become, according to James Gleick, a "public emblem for chaos" (*Chaos*, 22).

127. We will reencounter this topic in chapter 4.

128. Carl Zimmer, "Shell Game" *Discover* 13, no. 5 (May 1992): 40.

129. Gleick, *Chaos*, 239.

130. Gleick, *Chaos*, 183.

131. Ibid., 186.

132. Ibid., 186.

133. Ibid., 107.

134. Barrow, 207. Barrow notes, however, that just as there exist mathematical operations which are non-computable, the world is not totally algorithmically compressible. What our brains seem to do is to "effect an algorithmic compression upon the Universe whether or not it were intrinsically so compressible" (201). Barrow contends that this is done by a process of truncation, of cutting off our information input at some point. What he is talking about is essentially what I have described earlier in this work as the filtering process.

135. Davis and Hersh, *Descartes' Dream*, 255.

136. Ibid., 253. "The computer thinks, the computer knows, the computer remembers, the computer learns. The computer says. We load it (as we load a horse or a wagon). We instruct it (as would a patient teacher). We command it (as a sergeant commands a private). The computer fouls up. If we put garbage in, the computer gives garbage out. The computer is to blame" (253).

137. See, for example, Ivars Peterson, "Recipes for Artificial Realities," *Science News* 138 (24 November 1990) 338, or Michael Rogers, "Now, 'Artificial Reality,'" *Newsweek* (9 February 1987): 56–57.

138. Malcolm W. Browne, "Lively Computer Creation Blurs Definition of Life," *New York Times*, 27 August 1991, B8.

139. Ibid.

140. See chapter 1 above.

141. Waldrop, *Complexity*, 280.

142. Quoted in Waldrop, *Complexity*, 327.

143. Ibid., 329.

144. Barrow, *Theories of Everything*, 203.

145. See Chapter 5, Stephen C. Pepper, *World Hypotheses* (Berkeley: University of California Press), 1942.

146. Davis and Hersh, *Descartes' Dream*, 260.

147. Hofstadter, *Gödel, Escher, and Bach*, 408–9. Quoting from J. M. Jauch, *Are Quanta Real?* (Bloomington: Indiana University Press, 1973), 63–65.

148. For another strange metaphor that has much the same message, consider Hofstadter's "Ant Fugue" (*Gödel, Escher, and Bach*, 310–33).

149. See Fritjof Capra, *The Tao of Physics* 3d ed., Boston: Sham

bhala, chapter 10 and Afterword; Marilyn Ferguson, *The Aquarian Conspiracy* (Boston: J. P. Tarcher, 1980); F. David Peat, *Synchronicity* (New York: Bantam, 1987), chapter 6; Michael Talbot, *The Holographic Universe* (New York: Harper Collins, 1991); Stanislav Grof with Hal Zina Bennett, *Holotropic Mind* (San Francisco: Harper, 1990).

150. Jeff Hecht and Dick Teresi, *Laser: Supertool of the 80's* (New Haven and New York: Ticknor and Fields, 1982), 211.

151. Nick Herbert, *Quantum Reality: Beyond the New Physics* (Garden City, N.Y.: Anchor Press/Doubleday, 1985), 79.

152. Grof, *Holotropic Mind*, 8–9.

153. Ferguson, *Aquarian Conspiracy*, 179.

154. See chapter 1, *Metaphysics*.

155. Dantzig, *Number*, 245.

156. Ferguson, *Aquarian Conspiracy*, 180.

157. Capra, *Tao of Physics*, 320.

158. Ibid.

159. Grof, *Holotropic Mind*, 10.

160. Physicist Paul Davies writes, for instance, that "other writers, such as Fritjof Capra in *The Tao of Physics* and Gary Zukav in *The Dancing Wu Li Masters,* have emphasized the close parallels between quantum physics and oriental mysticism, with its emphasis on the unity of existence and the subtle relationships between the whole and its parts" (*Superforce* [New York: Simon and Schuster, 1984], 220).

161. A relevant discussion of the term "maya" as it is used here may also be found in Capra, *Tao of Physics*, 88. Maya, he points out, "does not mean that the world is an illusion, as is often wrongly stated. The illusion merely lies in our point of view, if we think that the shapes and structures, things and events, around us are realities of our measuring and categorizing minds. Maya is the illusion of taking these concepts for reality, of confusing the map with the territory."

162. Ferguson, *Aquarian Conspiracy*, 180.

163. Ibid., 181.

164. Ibid., 186.

165. Ibid.

166. Ibid., 185.

4. GOD THE DEFINITE INTEGRAL AND CANTORIAN RELIGION

1. Davies, *Superforce*, 221.

2. See Talbot, *Holographic Universe*, 27–29, 291 and Ferguson, *Aquarian Conspiracy*, 182. Note also Price's argument ("Paranormal cognition," 21–26).

3. Munqello, *Leibnez and Confucianism*, 85. Quoting from Leibnez, *Monadology*, no. 62.

4. Mungello, *Leibnez and Confucianism*, 85–86.

5. Ibid., 82–83.

6. See chapter 3. Hopper notes succinctly that "The observable efforts of Greek philosophy were generally directed toward the resolution of multiplicity into unity" (*Medieval Number Symbolism*, 38–39).

7. The number symbolism involved in divination traditions such as those set forth in the *Book of Changes* are, unfortunately, among the intriguing omissions that time considerations forced me to "filter out" in my treatment of the subject in the first section of chapter 3. However, the interested reader may refer to Michael Loewe's study on "China" (*Divinations and Oracles,* ed. Michael Loewe and Carmen Blacker [London: George Allen and Unwin, 1981]) for an excellent summary of the various divination methods among the Chinese.

8. Mungello, *Leibniz and Confucianism*, 15, and 116 for a more detailed listing.

9. Ibid., 84.

10. Ibid.

11. Quoted in Mungello, *Leibniz and Confucianism,* 85.

12. Ibid., 85.

13. Ibid., 128.

14. Ibid., 130.

15. Ibid., 125.

16. Ibid., 126.

17. Ibid.

18. Of the Cartesians, Leibniz' wrote "And I have demonstrated to them by means of mathematics that they themselves do not at all have the true laws of nature . . ." (Mungello, *Leibniz and Confucianism,* 81) Mungello also refers to Leibniz' position that "philosophical disputation could be replaced by a smooth exchange between two computers. In this context, discussing philosophy would be akin to sitting down with one's abacus and calling to a friend, 'Let us calculate.' " (61) Perhaps, given recent developments in artificial intelligence, Leibniz was simply ahead of his time.

19. Cf. chapter 3, "Metaphysics."

20. Mungello, *Leibniz and Confucianism*, 61.

21. Burton, *History of Mathematics*, 389.

22. McFague, *Metaphorical Theology,* 128.

23. Capra, *Tao of Physics*, 116–17.

24. I. Douglas Faires and Barbara T. Faires. *Calculus*, 2d ed. (New York: Random House, 1988), 250–51.

25. A concise, readable exploration of Greek thought regarding the constitution of objects as aggregates of atomistic units versus the essential

oneness and changelessness of the world may be found in Carl B. Boyer, *The History of the Calculus and Its Conceptual Development* (New York: Dover, 1949), chapter 2.

26.   Alfred Korzybski, *Science and Sanity: An Introduction to Non-Aristotelian Systems and General Semantics,* 3d ed., (Garden City, N.Y.: Country Life Press Corporation, 1933), 752. Interestingly, Korzybski relies heavily on this same model of the definite integral as a fundamental inspiration for his work in general semantics. "It is true," he says, "that in the beginning we did not suspect that the semantics of the calculus are indispensable in education for *sanity.* It is the *only* structural method which can reconcile the as yet irreconcilable high and lower order abstractions" (575). The crux of Korzybski's logic might be summed up in one of his own passages.

> We know . . . that there is a fundamental difference between different orders of abstractions. Physical abstractions have always characteristics which are left out, and our higher order abstractions are further removed from life, but they have all the characteristics included. The problem of sanity being a problem of adjustment, we must somehow correlate these abstractions in which characteristics are *left out* with those which include all characteristics, and so *must* proceed by *approximations.* Mathematical methods, particularly those of the differential and integral calculus, have evolved the best technique of *approximation* in existence today, which, as we have seen, is strictly connected with *linearity or additivity.* (613)

Korzybski's extension of the use of the integral calculus as a metaphor for processes that are psychological rather than physical sets some precedent for my own extension of it to the realm of the spiritual.

27.   I Corinthians 12:8–14.

28.   Some of these (Badger, Knapp) rely heavily on lists drawn from their own considerable experience, a method, incidentally, rather reminiscent of the earliest sense of canon as being "listmaking." Others emphasize what has been (Christ) or should be (Godbey) excluded. Altieri notes the need to avoid reducing the decision to one of social interest; David Tracy suggests a reception theory that examines the effect a candidate for such criteria would have on the reader/receiver; Wayne Booth stresses a process of coduction wherein we become "friends" with the text. The Reverend Duncan Howlett says—only partially metaphorically—that we could use a loose-leaf Bible.

29.   Booth, *Company We Keep,* 336.

30.   John H. Weston, "David Tracy's the Analogical Imagination: a Precis and Commentary" Unpublished pamphlet, 1989, 3.

31.   Morton Smith, "Historical Method in the Study of Religion," *On Method in the History of Religion,* ed. James S. Helfer (Middletown, Conn.: Wesleyan University Press, 1968), 15.

32. Booth, *Company We Keep*, 73.

33. Korzybski, *Science and Sanity*, 642.

34. Ibid., 640–41.

35. Ibid., 578.

36. Booth, *Company We Keep*, 345–46.

37. Ibid., 352.

38. Ibid., 303f.

39. For more on the role of paradox in human communication, see Paul Watzlawick, *Pragmatics of Human Communication*, New York: W. W. Norton, 1967.

40. Suares, *Cipher of Genesis*, 73.

41. Ibid.

42. For further reading, see Anatol Rapoport and Albert M. Chammah, *Prisoner's Dilemma: A Study in Conflict and Cooperation* (Ann Arbor: University of Michigan Press, 1965).

43. Suggests, he emphasizes, "though by no means does it prove!" (*Gödel, Escher, and Bach*, 708).

44. Ibid.

45. Ibid., 709.

46. Gavin D'Costa, *John Hick's Theology of Religions: A Critical Evaluation* (Lanham, Maryland: University Press of America, 1987), 6.

47. John Hick, "Three Controversies," a paper presented to the Pacific Coast Theological Society at Berkeley, California, 1983. Subsequently published in Hick's *Problems of Religious Pluralism* (New York: St. Martin's Press, 1985), 1–15.

48. *The Myth of God Incarnate* is a volume of seven essays edited by Hick (London: SCM Press, 1977).

49. Hick, *Problems*, 44.

50. Ibid., 37.

51. Ibid., 52–53.

52. Hick, *Interpretation*, 243.

53. Hick considers the cosmic structure of the universe a nonpersonal interpretation of the Real. He suggests that these two ways of experiencing the Real (personal and nonpersonal) are analogous to the wave/particle theory of light known to present-day physicists (Hick, *Interpretation*, 245; *Problems*, 98–99).

54. Hick, *Interpretation*, 241.

55. Hick, *Problems*, 17–19.

56. Hick, *Interpretation*, 24.

57. Hick, *Problems*, 25.

58. Hick, *Interpretation*, 242.

59. Ibid.

60. Hick, *Problems*, 92.

61. Hick, *Interpretation*, 3.

62. Ibid., 311–13.

63. Surin, for instance, lambastes Hick's program as a "vulgar historicism" which "shamelessly reinforces the reification and privatization of life in advanced capitalist society" (Kenneth Surin, "Towards a 'Materialist' Critique of 'Religious Pluralism,'" in *Religious Pluralism and Unbelief: Studies Critical and Comparative*, ed. Ian Hamnett (New York: Routledge, 1990), 114–19.

64. Hick, *Interpretation*, 237.

65. See Hick, *Interpretation*, chapter 14 for Hick's explication of these points.

66. But not, according to Hick, in just any way.

67. Incommensurability does not, for Hick, preclude the possibility that all these ways "constitute intellectual frameworks within which the process of salvation/liberation can proceed." (Hick, *Problems*, 94)

68. Hick, *Interpretation*, 249.

69. Hick, *Problems*, 107.

70. Ibid.

71. Ibid., 108.

72. D'Costa, *John Hick's Theology*, 180.

73. Ibid., 142.

74. Ibid., 147.

75. For an excellent discussion of the concept of infinity, see Rudy Rucker's *Infinity and the Mind: The Science and Philosophy of the Infinite* (Boston: Birhauser, 1992).

76. Dantzig, *Number*, 211.

77. See Burton, *History of Mathematics*, chapter 12 for a careful elaboration or Dantzig, *Number*, chapter 11, for a more readable explanation of Cantor's transfinite numbers.

78. Dantzig, *Number*, 226.

79. Gleick, *Chaos*, 93.

80. Ibid., 101.

81. Peterson, *Mathematical Tourist*, 122.

82. Gleick, *Chaos*, 98.

83. Ibid., 99.

84. A slightly technical but still very readable resource on the various attempts to deal with these paradoxes and on Gödel's theorem of incompleteness can be found in chapters 7 and 5, respectively, of Davis and Hersh's *The Mathematical Experience*. A more detailed resource is Burton, *History of Mathematics*, 611–35.

85. See, also, chapter 1.

86. Hick, *Problems*, 20.

87. Hick, *Interpretation*, 354.

88. Ibid., 239.

89. Ibid., 259.
90. Ibid.
91. Gleick, *Chaos*, 95.
92. See, for example, Hick, *Interpretation*, 259.
93. Ibid., 249.
94. An interesting analysis of the technique of parallelism may be found in Restivo, *Social Relations*, 22–42.
95. Hick, himself, would deny that he is suggesting a new religion.

SUMMATION

1. Restivo makes a good case for the existence of different math worlds at different historical periods operating under different social conditions. See Restivo, "The Social Construction of Mathematics" in *The Sociological Worldview*, 161–73.
2. Friedrich Schleiermacher, *On Religion*, intro. and trans. Richard Crouter (Cambridge: Cambridge University Press, 1988), 96–105.
3. Ibid., 104.
4. Ibid., 105.
5. Geertz, *Interpretation of Culture*, 91.
6. Alfred North Whitehead, as quoted in "Congregational Polity and Covenant," *A Transcript (unrevised) of Three Lectures* (talk by James Luther Adams, Meadville/Lombard Winter Institute, Chicago), 38.
7. Gary Wills, *Under God: Religion and American Politics* (New York: Simon and Schuster, 1990), 24.
8. *The Peoples Voice*, (Newsletter, Peoples Church Unitarian Universalist, Cedar Rapids, Iowa) 1 July 1992.
9. Hick, *Interpretation*, 195.
10. Robert S. Gottlieb, *A New Creation: America's Contemporary Spiritual Voices* (New York: Crossroad, 1990), 13.
11. Douglas Adams, *The Hitchhikers Guide to the Galaxy* (New York: Pocket Books, 1989), 180.

AFTERWORD

1. Morris, *Edges of Science*, 197.
2. See, for instance John Allen Paulos's chapter on "Pseudoscience" in *Numeracy: Mathematical Illiteracy and Its Consequences* (New York: Hill and Wang, 1988) or the *Skeptical Inquirer* collection edited by Kendrick Frazier, *The Hundredth Monkey and Other Paradigms of the Paranormal* (Buffalo, New York: Prometheus Books, 1991) for scathing analyses typical of the scientific elite.

3.   John Horgan, "Profile: Paul Karl Feyerabend," *Scientific American* (May 1993): 36.

4.   Ibid.

5.   Morris, *Edges of Science,* 198.

6.   Ibid., 200.

7.   Ibid., 201.

8.   Ibid., 221.

9.   Rolston Holmes, III, *Science and Religion:* A *Critical Survey* (New York: Random House, 1987), 10.

10.   Sermon titles were "Towards a Cantorian Religion," "Gödel On Evil," "Dare To Be Average," "Visions of Easter," and "Approaching the Limit: The Importance of Seeking the Unreachable." Of these, the first two were explicitly preannounced as based on mathematical metaphors. I discovered that math anxiety kept some people away from the second one, so I slipped the third mathematical metaphor in unannounced as a canvass sermon ("Dare To Be Average"). "Visions of Easter" I had originally intended to title "The Isomorphism of Jesus and Christ," but decided a less overt introduction of this theme would be more suitable to the intergenerational needs of the day. The fifth sermon was a "purchased" title. During a church-wide fundraiser, a member of the congregation "bought" the right to title one of my sermons, then surprised me by coming up with one that almost cried out for a mathematical interpretation.

Subsequently, I was approached about sharing one of these sermons with a non-*UU* church group, had a ten-year-old boy grapple (successfully) with the essentially mathematical image promoted in the Easter service, was told by a self-described "nonmathematical" poet that she always came for my "math" sermons, and was assured that the purchaser of the silent auction title "got far more than his money's worth." But then, of course, he only paid $20 for it. The purchaser, incidentally, gave his own brief introduction to my sermon, telling the congregation why he had chosen this particular title. I was slightly, but happily, astounded to observe that he, too, used a mathematical metaphor to draw out a spiritual and moral implication. Surely, this interchange was indicative of precisely the kind of relational pulpit that many liberal religious ministers, myself included, are now intentionally endeavoring to shape.

APPENDIX A. UNDERSTANDINGS OF SIGN, SYMBOL, METAPHOR, AND MODEL IN RELIGION AND MATHEMATICS

1.   The gender emphasis is intentional. In languages where words

are genderized, "mathematician" is masculine and "mathematics" is feminine.

2.   For more exploration on this topic see, e.g., Davis and Hersh's *Descartes' Dream* or *Mathematical Experience;* Voss's "Depolarizing Mathematics and Religion"; and Osborn's "Mathematics and the Spiritual Dimension." Two other related resources are Hofstadter's *Gödel, Escher, and Bach* and LeShan and Margenau's *Einstein's Space.*

3.   My thanks especially to Langdon Gilkey, Ian Evison, Tom Gilbert, Tom Burdett for their input into the survey content and format.

4.   See, for instance, McFague's *Metaphorical Theology,* 28, 84, 87, 89.

5.   Some of these comments spoke only of mathematics: any connection they bore to Question 13 was indirect at best.

6.   Besides issues already raised with regard to McFague, this topic lends itself to additional investigation of concerns raised by Kant and Hume.

REFERENCE LIST

Adams, Douglas. *The Hitchhikers Guide to the Galaxy.* New York: Pocket Books, 1989.

Barbour, Ian G. *Religion in an Age of Science.* Vol. 1 of *The Gifford Lectures, 1989–1991.* San Francisco: Harper, 1990.

Barfield, Owen. "The Meaning of the Word 'Literal.' " In *Metaphor and Symbol: Proceedings of the Twelfth Symposium of the Colston Research Society,* University of Bristol, 28–31 March 1960, edited by L. C. Knights and Basil Cottle, 48–63. London: Butterworths Scientific Publications, 1960.

Barrow, John D. *Theories of Everything: The Quest for Ultimate Explanation.* Oxford: Clarendon Press, 1991.

Bell, E. T. *Numerology.* Vol. 3. Westport, Conn.: Hyperion Press, 1933.

Black, Max. *Models and Metaphors.* Ithaca, New York: Cornell University Press, 1962.

Bois, J. Samuel. *The Art of Awareness,* 3d ed. Dubuque, Iowa: Wm. C. Brown Co., 1978.

Booth, Wayne C. *The Company We Keep: An Ethics of Fiction.* Berkeley, University of California Press, 1988.

Boyer, Carl B. *The History of the Calculus and Its Conceptual Development.* New York: Dover, 1949.

Browne, Malcolm W. "Lively Computer Creation Blurs Definition of Life." *New York Times,* 27 August 1991, B8.

Burhoe, Ralph. "Potentials for Religion from the Sciences." *Zygon 5,* no. 2 (June 1970): 110–29.

Burkhardt, Hans and Barry Smith. *Handbook of Metaphysics and Ontology,* 2 volumes. Munich: Philosophia Verlag, 1991.

Burton, David M. *The History of Mathematics: An Introduction.* Boston: Allyn and Bacon, 1985.

Butler, Christopher. *Number Symbolism.* New York: Barnes and Noble, 1970.

Capra, Fritjof. *The Tao of Physics.* 3d ed. Boston: Shambhala, 1991.

Carpenter, John M. "Shifting Structure of Mathematical Paradigms." In *The Metaphors of Consciousness,* edited by Ronald S. Valle and Rolf Eckartsberg, 461–72. New York: Plenum Press, 1981.

Crutchfield, James P., et. al. "Chaos." *Scientific American* (December 1986): 46–68.

Dantzig, Tobias. *Number: the Language of Science.* New York: Mac-Millan, 1930.

Davies, Paul. *The Mind of God.* New York: Simon and Schuster, 1992.

———. *Superforce.* New York: Simon and Schuster, 1984.

Davis, Philip J. and Reuben Hersh. *Descartes' Dream: The World According to Mathematics.* San Diego: Harcourt Brace Jovanovich, 1986.

———. *The Mathematical Experience.* Boston: Houghton Mifflin Co., 1981.

D'Costa, Gavin. *John Hick's Theology of Religions: A Critical Evaluation.* Lanham, Maryland: University Press of America, 1987.

Diethelm, Walter. *Signet, Signal, Symbol.* Zurich: ABC Verlag, 1976.

Dilley, Frank B. *Metaphysics and Religious Language.* New York: Columbia University Press, 1964.

Dillistone, F. W. "The Function of Symbols in Religious Experience." In *Metaphor and Symbol: Proceedings of the 12th Symposium of the Colston Research Society,* University of Bristol 28–31 March 1960, edited by L. C. Knight and Basil Cottle, 104–119. London: Butterworths Scientific Publications. 1960.

———. *The Power of Symbols in Religion and Culture.* New York: Crossroad, 1986.

Eves, Howard. *An Introduction to the History of Mathematics.* 6th ed. Philadelphia: Saunders College Publishing, 1990.

Faires, I. Douglas and Barbara T. Faires. *Calculus.* 2d ed. New York: Random House, 1988.

Ferguson, Marilyn. *The Aquarian Conspiracy.* Boston: J. P. Tarcher, 1980.

Fletcher, Rachel. "Proportion and the Living World." *Parabola* 13 no. 1 (Feb. 1988): 36–51.

Frazier, Kendrick. *The Hundredth Monkey and Other Paradigms of the Paranormal.* Buffalo: Prometheus Books, 1991.

Geertz, Clifford. *The Interpretation of Culture.* New York: Basic Books, 1973.

Gerner, Lynn E. *Calculus and Analytic Geometry.* San Francisco: Dellen, 1988.

Gillespie, Diane. *The Mind's We: Contextualism in Cognitive Psychology.* Carbondale & Edwardsville Southern Illinois University Press, 1992.

Gleick, James. *Chaos: Making a New Science.* New York: Viking, 1987.

Gottlieb, Robert S. *A New Creation: America's Contemporary Spiritual Voices.* New York: Crossroad, 1990.

Grof, Stanislav and Hal Zina Bennett. *The Holotropic Mind.* San Franciso: Harper, 1990.

Hawking, Stephen. *A Brief History of Time: From the Big Bang to Black Holes*. New York: Bantam, 1988.

Hecht, Jeff and Teresi, Dick. *Laser: Supertool of the 80's*. New Haven: Ticknor and Fields, 1982.

Herbert, Nick. *Quantum Reality: Beyond the New Physics*. Garden City, N.Y.: Anchor Press/Doubleday, 1985.

Hick, John. *An Interpretation of Religion: Human Responses to the Transcendent*. New Haven: Yale University Press, 1989.

————. *Problems of Religious Pluralism*. New York: St. Martin's Press, 1985.

Hilbert, D. "On the Infinite." In *Philosophy of Mathematics*. edited by P. Benacerraf and H. Putnam. Englewood Cliffs: Prentice Hall, 1964.

Hively, Will. "Life Beyond Boiling." *Discover* 14, no. 5 (1993): 87–91.

Hobbes, Thomas. *Leviathan*. 1651. Rpt. Ed. and Introduction by C. B. Macpherson. London: Penguin Classics, 1985.

Hofstadter, Douglas. *Gödel, Escher, and Bach: An Eternal Golden Braid*. New York: Vintage Books, 1979.

Holmes, Rolston III, *Science and Religion: A Critical Survey*, New York: Random House, 1987.

Hopper, Vincent Foster. *Medieval Number Symbolism: Its Sources, Meaning, and Influence on Thought and Expression*. 1938. Rpt. Norwood, Pa.: Norwood Editions, 1977.

Horgan, John. "Profile: Paul Karl Feyerabend." *Scientific American* (May 1993): 36–7.

Jauch, J. M. *Are Quanta Real?* Bloomington: Indiana University Press, 1973.

Knapp, Mark L. *Nonverbal Communication in Human Interaction*. 2d ed. New York: Holt, Rinehart, and Winston, 1978.

Korzybski, Alfred. *Science and Sanity: An Introduction to Non-Aristotelian Systems and General Semantics*. 3d ed. Garden City, N.Y.: Country Life Press Corporation, 1933.

Lawlor, Robert. "The Measure of Difference." *Parabola* 16, no. 4 (November 1991): 11–15.

Leatherdale, W. H. *The Role of Analogy, Model and Metaphor in Science*. Amsterdam: North Holand Publishing Co., 1974.

Leibniz, Gottfried W. *The Monadology*. Buffalo: Prometheus Books, 1992.

LeShan, Lawrence and Henry Margenau. *Einstein's Space and Van Gogh's Sky: Physical Reality and Beyond*. New York: Macmillan Publishing Co., 1982.

Lightman, Alan. *Great Ideas in Physics*. New York: McGraw Hill, 1992.

Lobkowicz, Nicholas. "Metaphysics: History and Terminology." Vol 2 of

Handbook of Metaphysics and Ontology, edited by Hans Burkhardt and Barry Smith, 528–29. Munich: Philosophia Verlag, 1991.

Loewe, Michael. "China." In *Divinations and Oracles,* edited by Michael Loewe and Carmen Blacker. London: George Allen and Unwin, 1981.

McFague, Sallie. *Metaphorical Theology: Models of God in Religious Language.* Philadelphia: Fortress Press, 1982.

———. *Models of God: Theology for an Ecological, Nuclear Age.* Philadelphia: Fortress Press, 1987.

Morris, Richard. *The Edges of Science.* New York: Simon and Schuster, 1990.

Moser, Paul K., ed. *Reality in Focus.* Englewood Cliffs, N.J.: Prentice Hall, 1990.

Munem, M. A., and D. J. Foulis. *Algebra and Trigonometry with Applications.* 2d ed. New York: Worth Publishers, 1986.

Mungello, David E. *Leibniz and Confucianism: The Search for Accord.* Honolulu: University Press of Hawaii, 1977.

Ornstein, Robert and Paul Ehrlich. *New World New Mind.* New York: Simon and Schuster, 1990.

Osborn, David. "Mathematics and the Spiritual Dimension." *The Clarion Call* 2, no. 4 (Fall 1989): 32–39.

Paulo, John Allen. *Numeracy: Mathematical Illiteracy and Its Consequences.* New York: Hill and Wang, 1988.

Peacocke, Arthur. *Intimations of Reality: Critical Realism in Science and Religion.* The Mendenhall Lectures, 1983. Notre Dame, Indiana: University of Notre Dame Press, 1984.

Peat, F. David. *Synchronicity.* New York: Bantam, 1987.

Penrose, Roger. *The Emperor's New Mind.* New York: Oxford University Press, 1989.

Pepper, Stephen C. *World Hypotheses.* Berkeley: University of California Press, 1942.

Peterson, Ivars. *The Mathematical Tourist.* New York: W. H. Freeman, 1988.

———. "Recipes for Artificial Realities." *Science News* 138 (November 24 1990): 328–29.

Preston, Richard. "Profiles: Mountains of Pi." *New Yorker* 2 (March 1992): 36–67.

Price, H. H. "Paranormal Cognition and Symbolism." In *Metaphor and Symbol. Proceedings of the Twelfth Symposium of the Colston Research Society,* University of Bristol 28–31 March 1960, edited by L. C. Knight and Basil Cottle. 78–94. London: Butterworths Scientific Publications, 1960.

Rapoport, Anatol and Albert M. Chammah. *Prisoner's Dilemma: A*

Study in Conflict and Cooperation. Ann Arbor: University of Michigan Press, 1965.

Restivo, Sal. *The Social Relations of Physics, Mysticism, and Mathematics.* Dordrecht: D. Reidel Publishing Co., 1983.

———. *The Sociological Worldview.* Cambridge: Basil Blackwell, 1991.

Ricoeur, Paul. *Interpretation Theory: Discourse and the Surplus of Meaning.* Fort Worth: Texas Christian University Press, 1976.

Rogers, Michael. "Now, 'Artificial Reality.'" *Newsweek* (9 February 1987): 56–57.

Romanyshyn, Robert D. *Psychological Life from Science to Metaphor.* Austin: University of Texas Press, 1982.

———. "Science and Reality: Metaphors of Experience and Experience as Metaphorical." In *The Metaphors of Consciousness,* edited by Ronald S. Valle and Rolf von Eckartsberg, 3–19. New York: Plenum Press, 1981.

Ross, Ralph. *Symbols and Civilization: Science, Morals, Religion, Art.* New York: Harcourt, Brace, and World, 1962.

Rucker, Rudy. *Infinity and the Mind: The Science and Philosophy of the Infinite.* Boston: Birkhauser, 1992.

Schimmel, Annemarie. *The Mystery of Numbers.* New York: Oxford University Press, 1993.

Schleiermacher, Friedrich. *On Religion.* Introduction and translation by Richard Crouter. Cambridge: Cambridge University Press, 1988.

Shon, Donald Alan. *Invention and the Evolution of Ideas.* London: Tavistock Publications, 1967.

Sebeok, Thomas A. *A Sign is Just a Sign.* Bloomington: Indiana University Press, 1991.

Shanker, S. G. *Wittgenstein and the Turning-Point in the Philosophy of Mathematics.* London: Croom Helm, 1987.

Siu, R. G. H. *The Tao of Science.* Cambridge: Technology Press, 1958.

Smith, Karl J. *The Nature of Mathematics.* 4th ed. Monterey, California: Brooks/Cole Publishing Co., 1984.

Smith, Morton. "Historical Method in the Study of Religion." In *On Method in the Study of Religion,* ed. by James Helfer. Middletown, Conn.: Wesleyan University Press, 1968.

Soskice, Janet. *Metaphor and Religious Language.* Oxford: Clarendon Press, 1985.

Sprigge, Timothy L. S. "Idealism/Realism." Vol. 2 of *Handbook of Metaphysics and Ontology,* edited by Hans Burkhardt and Barry Smith, 528–29. Munich, Philadelphia, Vienna: Philosophia Verlag, 1991.

Stewart, Ian and Martin Golubitsky. *Fearful Symmetry.* Oxford: Blackwell, 1992.

Struik, Dirk J. "Stone Age Mathematics." *Scientific American* (December 1948): 44–49.

Suares, Carlos. *The Cipher of Genesis: The Original Code of the Quabala as Applied to the Scriptures.* First Berkeley: Shambala Publications, 1970.

Surin, Kenneth. "Towards a 'Materialist' Critique of 'Religious Pluralism,'" In *Religious Pluralism and Unbelief: Studies Critical and Comparative,* edited by Ian Hamnett, 114–19. New York: Routledge, 1990.

Talbot, Michael. *The Holographic Universe.* New York: Harper Collins, 1991.

Thomas, Lewis. *The Fragile Species.* New York: Macmillan, 1992.

———. "Why We'll All Speak Math." *World Monitor* 3, no. 12 (December 1990): 17–20.

Tillich, Paul. *Dynamics of Faith.* New York: Harper and Brothers, 1957.

Turbayne, Colin. *The Myth of Metaphor.* Rev. ed. Columbia, South Carolina: University of South Carolina Press, 1970.

Valle, Ronald S. and Rolf von Eckartsberg, eds. *The Metaphors of Consciousness.* New York: Plenum Press, 1981.

Voss, Sarah. "Depolarizing Mathematics and Religion." *Philosophia Mathematica* Virginia Beach: Grunwald Publishers, vol. 5, series 2 no. 1/2 (June) 1990. 129–41.

Waldrop, M. Mitchell. *Complexity: The Emerging Science at the Edge of Order and Chaos.* New York: Simon and Schuster, 1992.

Watzlawick, Paul. *Pragmatics of Human Communication.* New York: W. W. Norton, 1967.

Weston, John H. "David Tracy's the Analogical Imagination: a Precis and Commentary," Unpublished pamphlet. 1989.

Whitehead, Alfred North. As quoted in "Congregational Polity and Covenant." *A Transcript (unrevised) of Three Lectures.* Talk by James Luther Adams. Chicago: Meadville/Lombard Winter Institute.

Wills, Gary. *Under God: Religion and American Politics.* New York: Simon and Schuster, 1990.

Yoshikawa, Takashi. *The Ki.* New York: St. Martin's Press, 1986.

Zimmer, Carl. "Shell Game." *Discover* 13, no. 5 (May 1992): 38–43.

Zukav, Gary. *The Dancing Wu Li Masters.* New York: Morrow, 1979.

INDEX

Abbot, Edwin, 91
abstraction, 8, 9, 10, 11, 16, 39, 48, 49, 62, 80, 109, 136
Achilles, 25, 119, 124
Adams, Douglas, 156
Adams, James Luther, 151n. 6
antinomies, 3, 135, 142, 146
Aquinas, Thomas, 8
Aristotle, 8–9, 29, 29n. 97, 95n. 109
Arthur, Brian, 34, 36, 101
artificial intelligence, 5n. 5, 6, 6n. 9, 23, 24, 34, 35, 99, 114n. 18
astrology, 19, 73
Augustine, Saint, 75, 76, 81, 82
Axiom of Choice, 140
Axiom of Religious Choice, 155

Bacon, Francis, 9
Barbour, Ian, xiv, 7, 29n. 96, 33, 37, 39, 46, 49n. 15, 62, 97
Barfield, Owen, 51n. 18, 53, 54
Barrow, John, 80, 83n. 58, 94n. 107, 96n. 118, 101, 102
Bell, Eric T., 71, 73, 74, 77, 77n. 34, 79, 80, 93
Beardsley, Monroe, 28
Bible, 68, 93, 122
Black, Max, 28, 46, 49, 58, 59, 62, 63, 71
Bohm, David, 106, 107, 112
Bohr, Niels, 28n. 85
Bois, Samuel, 9–12, 16, 19, 20, 24, 45, 49n. 15, 53, 59, 62, 63, 104
Bolyai, Janos, 94
Booth, Wayne, 32, 63, 122, 123, 125, 126
Boulding, Kenneth, 49n. 15

brain, 5n. 5, 19, 22, 23, 24, 28, 84n. 60, 101, 104–107, 127
Brouwer, L.E.J., 4
Buddhism, 140, 143
Burton, David M., 77n. 35, 87, 89, 136n. 77, 140n. 84
Butler, Christopher, 88–90

Cabala, 89, 114
Cantor, Georg, 3, 37, 132, 134–146
Cantorian set theory, extended to religion, 140–146, 153–155, 160n. 10
Capra, Fritjo, 79, 105, 108n. 161, 115
Carpenter, John, 5
Cartesian coordinate system, 91
Cassirer, Ernst, xi, xii
CBS metaphor, 48, 50, 51
Chudnovsky, Gregory and David, 82–84
Christ, 75, 115, 121, 122n. 28, 160n. 10
Christianity, 35, 81, 93, 115, 121, 123, 128, 132, 140, 143, 150, 153
coherence, 37, 39, 126, 155
computer-life, 101
computers, 5n.5, 6, 21, 23, 24, 34, 35, 63, 64, 73, 82–84, 94, 102, 114n. 18, 126, 137–139, 156; and chaos theory, 37, 94–102; and complexity, 34–36, 158
computer/brain analogy, 24
consciousness, 4, 5, 5n. 5, 6n. 9, 12–24, 18n. 38, 25, 27n. 84, 28n. 86, 33, 53, 54, 56, 74, 107, 127, 155, 158, 159; as the filtering mind,

209

consciousness (*continued*)
155, 159; many ways of knowing,
18, 19, 148; new kind of
perspective, 21; domain theory of,
17, 18, 19; *See also* abstraction,
artificial intelligence, brain,
computer-life, epistemies, filter
theory, filtering, filters, paranormal,
universal certainty
contradiction, 4, 6, 21, 31, 35, 36,
66, 78, 107, 108, 119, 126, 142,
148, 155; as actually infinite, 134;
as old woman/young woman
illusion, 55; *See also* Achilles,
antinomies, Axiom of Choice,
Axiom of Religious Choice,
coherence, inconsistency, infinite
but bounded, infinitely sparse,
monads, one and the many,
paradox, paradoxical, plurality of
ultimates, strange loops, whole and
parts
cosmological harmony, 88
critical realists, 39

Dantzig, Tobias, 65–67, 68, 74n. 7,
107, 136n. 77, 137n. 78
Davies, Paul, 5n. 1, 5n. 5, 7, 7n. 14,
26, 79, 108n. 160, 111
Davis, Philip J., 4, 33n. 109, 64n. 54,
73n. 2, 80, 83, 93n. 102, 94n. 105,
94n. 106, 101, 102, 140n. 84
definite integral, 115, 120, 124
Descartes, Rene, 24, 64n. 54, 80, 91,
92, 94, 101n. 135, 102n. 146
Diethelm, Walter, 44, 48n. 13
Dilley, Frank, 7, 39n. 97
Dillistone, F.W., 45, 53, 55
Dirac, Paul, 109
Dummet, Michael, 39n. 23

edges of science, 39, 56n. 31, 157n.
1, 158n. 6
Ehrlich, Paul, 19–21, 24
Einstein, Albert, 17, 17n. 33, 106

epistemies, 10, 148
Euclid, 93, 95

Feigenbaum, Mitchell, 100
Ferguson, Marilyn, 105, 108, 112n. 2
Ferre, Frederick, 53
Flatland, 91
filter theory, 11, 12, 15, 16, 19, 20,
21, 23n. 62, 24, 25, 33, 55n. 27,
57, 58, 59, 68, 84, 113n. 7, 155,
158
filtering, 20, 48, 55, 58–60, 101n.
134, 104, 107, 155
filters, 15, 29, 36, 57, 60, 104, 148
Fletcher, Rachael, 88n. 79, 90n. 89,
95
Fourier, Joseph, 105, 112
Fuller, Buckminster, 109

Gabor, Dennis, 106
Galileo, Galilei, 61, 92, 104, 108,
134
Geertz, Clifford, 42n. 3, 149, 150n. 5
Geometer God, 96
geometry, Euclidean, 64, 96; fractal,
94, 97, 100, 105; *See also* Abbot,
Cartesian coordinate system,
Flatland, Geometer God, scaling,
symmetry
Gillespie, Diane, 56n. 35
Gleick, James, 32, 98, 100n. 130,
137, 139
God, 2, 5n. 5, 15, 24, 26, 29n. 92,
29n. 96, 34, 46, 50, 51, 71, 72,
74, 76, 77n. 35, 79–85, 88–90,
90n. 89, 93, 95n. 109, 96, 96n.
116, 97, 99, 102, 109, 111, 112n.
4, 114, 115, 117, 120, 121, 123,
127, 128, 129, 131, 133, 142, 150,
152n. 7, 153
Gödel, Kurt, 5–6, 21, 24, 37, 104n.
148, 127, 140, 141, 155
Golubitsky, Martin, 79, 90n. 89, 95,
96, 95n. 111, 96n. 120
Gottlieb, Robert S., 154

Grof, Stanislav, 105–107, 108n. 159, 112
Grosseteste, 75

Hawking, Stephen, 97
Hegel, Georg Wilhelm Friedrich, 8n. 19
Hersh, Reuben, 4, 33, 64, 73n. 2, 80, 83n. 58, 93n. 102, 94n. 105, 94n. 106, 101, 102, 140n. 84
Hick, John, 82, 128–131, 140–142, 144–146, 154
Hilbert, David, 3–5
Hively, Will, 36n. 115
Hobbes, Thomas, 31–32, 93, 94
Hofstadter, Douglas, 5–7, 21, 22, 23–25, 30, 37, 36n. 119, 45, 64, 72, 102–104, 127
Holland, John, 35
holograms, 106–107
holographic, 73, 105–106, 108, 112, 148, 51n. 17, 67n. 65, 80n. 51, 113n. 6
holographs, 102
Hopper, Vincent Foster, 51n. 17, 67n. 65, 73–76, 80, 113n. 6
Husserl, Edmund, xi

idealist, 33, 36, 130, 139, 140
inconsistency, 36, 37, 55n. 28, 107, 148
infinite, 4n. 3, 59n. 38, 91, 114, 130, 134, 137, 139; but bounded, 142
infinite set, 135
infinitely sparse, 137, 140
infinity, 34, 130, 139, 140; becomes actual, 140
irrational numbers, 77, 82, 95, 134
Islam, 150

Jauch, J.M., 102
Jean, Sir James, 2, 109
Joyce, James, 89

Judaism, 134, 140, 150
Jung, Carl Gustav, 89

kaleidoscope, 34, 56, 60, 64, 84, 84n. 60, 108, 148, 158
Kant, Immanuel, 129
Kepler, Johannes, 89
Klein, Felix, 90n. 89, 95
Knapp, Mark, 28n. 89, 122n. 28
Korzybski, Alfred, 6n. 9, 9, 10, 79, 120, 151
Kronecker, Leopold, 71, 134

Leibniz, Gottfried W., 12, 33, 89, 112–114, 127, 148, 158; *See also* monads
Lennon, John, 85
Leshan, Lawrence, 16–19, 24
level of reality, 106, 155
liberal religious leader, 159, 160
liberal religious voice, 122, 152, 155
Lightman, Alan, 36n. 116
Lobachevsky, Nicolai, 94
Lobkowicz, Nicholas, 7, 8
Locke, John, 32
Lufthansa metaphor, 49, 50

Mandelbrot, Benoit, 97, 99, 139
Margenau, Henry, 17, 18, 19, 24
mathematics, 1, 2, 3–7, 8, 10, 16, 24–26, 29n. 91, 30, 31, 32, 33, 36, 37, 39, 41–43, 51, 56n. 34, 60–65, 68, 71–74, 77, 79–80, 81, 82, 83–88, 90, 98, 99, 102, 104, 109–112, 114–117, 119, 120, 126, 127, 134, 136, 138, 140, 141, 148, 152, 156, 158, 159; and metaphor, 32, 61, 72, 148; *See also* definite integral, irrational numbers, number symbolism, pi, transfinite numbers, triangular numbers, turtle shell
Mayerstein, Walter, 26

McFague, Sallie, xiv, 26, 29, 29n. 96, 32, 32n. 104, 44–46, 49–51, 58n. 28, 62, 65, 66, 79, 100, 115
metamathematics, 2–7, 25, 60n. 39, 104, 127, 157, 159
metaphor, 2, 3, 6n. 9, 12n. 26, 18, 25–34, 38, 39, 41n. 1, 42–56, 64, 65, 67, 68, 71–73, 80–81, 84n. 60, 90, 92–95, 98, 100–105, 107, 108, 111, 112, 115, 116, 120, 120n. 26, 121, 124, 126, 132, 134, 140, 145, 147, 148, 149, 150, 151, 152, 154, 155, 157, 159–161; of nature, 97; antithesis of, 64; as bridge, 1–3, 7, 25, 26, 30–32, 36, 39, 56, 64n. 53, 68, 73, 84, 96, 140, 151, 152, 156; as cluster terms, 47, 57, 58; and dialogical model, 125; familiar, 72, 94; filter interpretation of, 58; fused, 72, 81, 90, 148; geometrical, 92; for God, 26, 51, 111, 115, 127; holographic, 105, 112; is and is not nature of, 140, 142, 148; and the literal, 6n. 9, 16, 27, 29n. 90, 31, 33, 47, 51, 53–57, 61, 62, 64, 66, 68, 90, 126; mathematical, 72, 73, 105, 116, 134, 147, 154, 155, 159, 160; as mathematical ratio, 32; of the computer, 102; for the spirit, 148; and sensory picture, 47; strange, 72, 102–104, 132, 140; and structural picture, 48; theoretical, 73; vehicle/tenor theory of, 28; and visual picture, 47; and word picture, 48; See also CBS metaphor, computer/brain analogy, Lufthansa metaphor
metaphysical, 2, 7, 18, 25, 31, 33, 34, 36, 57, 58, 60, 64n. 53, 75, 79, 111–113, 121, 124, 131, 140, 148, 155
metaphysics, 2, 3, 7–12, 18, 25, 26, 29n. 94, 32n. 108, 33, 36, 37, 55, 56, 60n. 39, 61, 89, 90, 94n. 106, 104, 113, 131, 141, 147–151, 157–159

model, 18n. 36, 23, 26, 27, 29n. 91, 39, 41, 42, 43, 44–52, 56, 61, 63, 64, 67, 73, 90, 92, 97, 99, 105–107, 115, 119, 121, 123–125, 139; mathematical, 61–63, 115, 139
monads, 12, 112, 148
Morris, Richard, 39, 56n. 31, 157–159
Moser, Paul, 7
Moses (Biblical), 75, 81
Mungello, David E., 89n. 85, 92n. 97, 111n. 1, 114n. 18
mystic, 114
mystical experience, 89, 108, 114
mysticism, 55n. 29, 73, 77, 108n. 160

Newton, Isaac, 27, 92, 114
Novalis, 71
number symbolism, 51n. 17, 73, 74, 76–78, 80, 81, 83, 86, 88–90, 106, 113n. 7; See also astrology, Bell, Cabala, cosmological harmony, irrational numbers, Pythagorean, Suares, triangular numbers, turtle shell, Vedic verse, whole-number cosmology

objective idealist, 32
one and the many, 39, 73, 111, 113, 115, 120, 121
Ono, Yoko, 85
Ornstein, Robert, 19–21, 24

paradox, 5, 31, 37, 119, 126, 127, 148
paradoxical, 24, 29, 39, 140, 148
parallelism, method of, 145
paranormal, 12–16, 19, 20, 33, 108, 155, 157
Pascal, Blaise, 89
Paul (Biblical), 120
Peacocke, Arthur, xiv, 152, 153

Peat, F. David, 105
Pepper, Stephen, 49, 51, 102n. 145
Peterson, Ivars, 91, 101n. 137, 139n.
  81
Philo, Judeaus, 75, 76, 81, 82, 89
pi, 82–84; *See also* Vedic verse
Plato, 25, 26, 71, 74n. 9, 88–91
Platonic, 21, 64, 83, 126
Plotinus, 76
plurality of ultimates, 131, 142
Preston, Richard, 83n. 57, 84
Price, H.H., 12, 13, 15–16, 19, 59,
  112n. 2
primordial chaos, 12, 15, 32, 33, 55,
  101, 155
process theology, 97
proportion, 88n. 79, 94, 95
Pythagorean, 74–77, 79, 82, 88, 89,
  95, 106, 114, 144
Pythagoreans, 71, 76, 77, 77n. 35,
  79, 87, 89, 90, 134

religion, 2, 7, 21, 29n. 96, 31n. 100,
  32, 33, 37, 39n. 124, 41, 42, 43,
  49n. 15, 54n. 25, 56n. 34, 60, 61,
  64, 65, 68, 71, 73, 82, 84, 88, 94,
  102, 108, 109, 111, 122, 123, 127,
  129–131, 144–146, 148–155;
  Cantorian, 111, 127, 132, 143,
  153, 155; and Chinese thought,
  113; common properties of, 154;
  definition of, 149; Eastern, 108;
  liberal, 111, 148; and mathematics,
  39n. 124, 41–43, 56n. 34, 60, 68,
  73, 85, 86; Native American, 140;
  nature of, 145; *See also* Bible,
  Buddhism, Christ, Christianity,
  Islam, Judaism, liberal religious
  leader, liberal religious voice,
  mystic, mystical experience,
  mysticism, Taoism, Unitarian
  Universalism, Zen
religious pluralism, 82, 128, 130n. 63,
  131, 140–142, 144–145, 155; and
  comparatist, 144; and exclusivist,
  143, 144; as global religion, 141,
  153, 154; and globalist, 144; and
  inclusivist, 143, 144; and pluralistic
  theology, 128; and Real an sich,
  129, 130, 141–143
Restivo, Sal, 55n. 29, 56, 56n. 32,
  56n. 34, 142n. 91, 148n. 1
Richards, I.A., 28, 29, 93, 94
Ricoeur, Paul, 28, 29n. 90
Rolston, Holmes, 159
Romanyshyn, Robert, 27, 28, 30, 32
Ross, Ralph, 31, 32, 45, 63
Rucker, Rudy, 109
Rumi, Jalalu'l-Din, 132, 134, 155
Russell, Bertrand, 3, 135

Santa Fe Institute, 33–35, 101
scaling, 100, 105
Schleiermacher, Friedrich Ernst, 149
Scholz, Christopher, 100
Schon, Donald, 27
Sebeok, Thomas A., 45
Shank, William, 83
signs, 41–49, 56, 61, 64n. 53, 68,
  78, 114
Siu, R.G.H., 55
Smith, Morton, 8n. 16, 33n. 108,
  39n. 123, 56n. 40, 77n. 35, 83n.
  56, 123, 125
Soskice, Janet, 28–30, 53n. 20, 58,
  59, 63, 63n. 46
Sprigge, Timothy L.S., 33n. 108
St. Francis of Assisi, 107
Stewart, Ian, 79, 90n. 89, 95, 95n.
  111, 96, 96n. 120
strange loops, 37, 127
Struik, Dirk J., 73, 87
Suares, Carlos, 77, 78, 80, 126n. 40,
  127
Surin, Kenneth, 128, 130n. 63
Swinburne, Richard, 82
symbols, 4, 5, 10, 11, 21–24, 31n.
  100, 41–49, 54n. 25, 56, 61–62,
  64, 65, 67, 68, 71, 72, 74, 76, 80,
  84, 89, 114, 119, 136, 149, 151–
  153
symmetry, 79, 90, 95–97

Talbot, Michael, 105, 112, 112n. 2
Taoism, 35, 150
theology, 7, 8, 26n. 76, 29n. 92, 32n. 104, 33, 39, 45, 46n. 10, 50n. 16, 62n. 43, 62n. 63, 73, 97, 100, 115n. 22, 128, 131, 134, 140, 141, 149–152, 158, 159
theory of aggregates, 136
Thomas, Lewis, 36, 64n. 53, 65n. 58
Tillich, Paul, 45, 46n. 10, 51, 62n. 43, 66
TOES, 94, 97
Tracy, David, 122, 123, 125
transfinite numbers, 134, 136, 142
triangular numbers, 88
Turbayne, Collin, 27n. 79, 28, 63, 92
Turing, Alan, 5n. 5, 109
turtle shell, 85, 86

Unitarian Universalism, 121, 122, 141, 153
Unitarian Universalist, 121, 122, 153, 160
universal certainty, 4, 5, 94
universality, 100

Valle, Ronald S., 5n. 4, 27n. 84
van Ceulen, Ludolph, 83
van der Waerden, 88
Vedic verse, 84
Vico, G., 53
von Eckartsberg, Rolf, 27n. 84
Voss, Sarah, 39n. 124, 109

Waldrop, M. Mitchell, 34
Wheelwright, Philip, 28
Whitehead, Alfred North, 3, 4, 7, 39n. 123, 151n. 6
whole and parts, 30, 107, 111, 112, 136, 140, 154
whole-number cosmology, 79
Wittgenstein, Ludwig, xi, xii, 129
Wright, Robert, 79

Yeats, William Butler, 89
Yoshikawa, Takashi, 85

Zen, 23, 121